Kindly donated to
ochaber College UHI
y Chris Sangster

Handbook of Office Management

SECOND EDITION

HANDBOOK
OF OFFICE
MANAGEMENT

B. H. Walley

BUSINESS BOOKS
London Melbourne Sydney Auckland Johannesburg

Business Books Ltd

An imprint of the Hutchinson Publishing Group
17 Conway Street, London W1P 6JD

Hutchinson Group (Australia) Pty Ltd
16-22 Church Street, Hawthorn, Melbourne, Victoria 3122

Hutchinson Group (NZ) Ltd
32-34 View Road, PO Box 40-086, Glenfield, Auckland 10

Hutchinson Group (SA) (Pty) Ltd
PO Box 337, Bergvlei 2012, South Africa

First published 1975 under the title
    Office Administration Handbook
Second edition, under present title, 1982
Reprinted 1983 and 1985

Set in Times

Printed and bound in Great Britain by
Anchor Brendon Ltd, Tiptree, Essex

British Library Cataloguing In Publication Data
Walley, B. H.
    Handbook of office management. – 2nd ed.
    1. Office management – Handbooks, manuals, etc.
    I. Title II. Walley, B. H. Office administration
    handbook
    651'3 HF5547

ISBN 0 09 147440 X

Contents

Introduction

This second edition of the *Office Administration Handbook* has been written at a time of unparalled heart searching by office managers about the need to reduce the number of clerical and administrative personnel they control. Quite suddenly it seems many organisations have found the ability to cut their clerical workforce by 25, even 30 per cent. Yet they still carry on most of the same activities and functions as before.

For someone who has for many years preached both the need and the means to reduce administrative costs, these current reductions are saddening. They could have been done much earlier. They could have been spread over a longer period, so causing considerably less pain than emergency actions always ensure. The techniques and methods have been there, but it is obvious that the will, in some instances, has been missing. The two should be inseparable.

There is little that anyone writing a book can do about the forceful push needed to carry out profitable change. In many ways this seems a reflection on social and economic conditions generally, but it reflects above all on the style and competence of the employing organisations. Any author, however, should be able to draw on his experience and management skills to suggest what are likely to be the most effective ways of minimising the cost of office administration. This is the basis of this second edition.

Current heart-searching does not end with the possibilities of reducing the number of administrative people; it is also concerned with the advance of technology in the office.

Office managers are daily bombarded with magazines, pamphlets and visiting representatives, who extol the need to introduce electronic equipment of all kinds. The paperless office, the electronic work station and word processors on a huge scale, are the only way – it is said – to run an administrative function. Scepticism about the electronic miracles which can be leased or bought is out of place.

Yet a more sceptical approach about the introduction of computers might have saved many millions of pounds. Electronic equipment may only increase behavioural problems, worsen working conditions, and cause major organisational and job change, which has to be planned with a care, and perhaps experience, which many companies find extremely difficult to deploy.

All the old problems – motivation, morale, salary policy, grading, organisation structure, simplifying of systems, how to get maximum efficiency from minimum staff – will remain, no matter what equipment is bought. Those who think otherwise will not find this second edition very comforting.

Acknowledgements

I am indebted to the following for permission to reproduce copyright material used in the first edition and again in this edition: Mr H.B. Wright, editor of *Better Offices* (published by the Institute of Directors), for the use of recommended standards for offices. Mr M. Redwood, Managing Editor of John Wiley and Sons Ltd, for permission to publish the 'rule-of-thumb activity sampling observations' from *Work Sampling* by R.M. Barnes. Mr Sid Tasker of the Building Design Partnership for permission to use Figures 5.10 and 5.11.

I am indebted to the following for new material published in this Second Edition: the Editor of the *Financial Times* for permission to quote various rentals of office accomodation; the British Standards Institution for permission to quote various anthropometric measurements and their relationship to office furniture of all kinds; HMSO for permission to reproduce the Crown Copyright material from the Building Research Establishment pamphlets *BRE Digests* Nos 44 and 138 and Paper 38/71; The Humidifier Advisory Service, 21 Napier Road, Kent, for permission to quote details of humidification and associated equipment; Mr Leslie Fairweather, Editor of *The Architects Journal,* for permission to publish details concerning methods of measuring space, from information sheet C1/sfb32; Mr I.P. Palmer of Program Contracts Interiors; D. Meredew Ltd, for permission to use extracts from their catalogue *PU Work Stations*.

I have read the following journals intensively to keep abreast of developments in office administration and equipment. While not quoting verbatim from them, their influence is important: *Management Today; Journal of Systems Management; Financial Times; New Scientist; The Economist; Word and Information Processing; Business Systems and Equipment; Datamation; Management Services; Office Equipment News*.

B.H. WALLEY

Part One

The Office Environment

One

The External Environment

1.1 Introduction

The word 'revolution' is being used more and more frequently in regard to office work and offices generally. The microchip revolution, the paperless office, the age of the word processor and minicomputer are common talking points. Yet it is possible that the technological explosion, important though it is, may need to take second place to the continuing changes in the human factors needed in running an office. Occasionally even these have to be subordinate to the legislation which governments inflict.

It seems right, therefore, to remind the office administration manager of some of the external factors that he will need to consider during the next decade.

1.2 The outside world

The outside world is not like alien space or a hostile planet, but where we all live and hopefully go about our training or jobs. It is then perhaps slightly curious that some managers still behave as if this world is of no concern. Somehow their office can be insulated from the pressures and influences that obviously exist. The fact that the local schools are slack on discipline and allow younsters to try and find jobs with their education far from complete, must be of major concern to anyone who needs to recruit them.

Figure 1.1 shows some of the major influences that an office manager must accept. Technology must seem to predominate, but the importance of the social and economic changes that are occurring must surely give any office manager food for thought.

From experience, only a few office managers attempt to accommodate the external world within their planning or operational procedures, yet technological and social change, national and international economies, change in our institutions, government and trade unions all have a major impact on office activities.

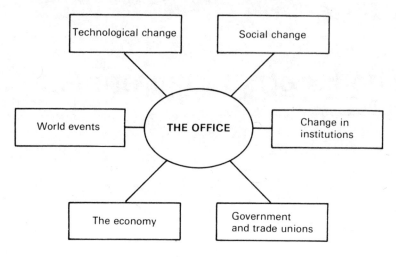

Figure 1.1   *Influences on the office*

1.3   The influences

1.3.1   Technology

A fairly emotive view is usually taken of technological change. 'The collapse of work' will make substantial people unemployed and perhaps unemployable. 'One chip can replace 800 white-collars' is a typical statement. The TUC, even Cambridge academics, have little comfort to offer employees in offices. *Employment and Technology* (TUC, 1979) draws attention to the potential loss of jobs.

The forecasters are certain that computer data processing is no longer the preserve of cloistered computer rooms, but is taking off for each and every office job. Even the commissionaire seems vulnerable. If the computer so far has not been responsible for any major reduction in the office workforce, then that situation is about to change.

The price of all kinds of office equipment is lower now in real terms than it has ever been. The way in which technology is being applied is also fairly well known, though compatibility between different suppliers is a major problem. An even greater problem is the rate of acceptance of such technology and whether normal office people can really use it appropriately.

Perhaps it is important to recognise that it is not word processing, reprographics, electronic mail or electronic correspondence systems that are of major importance, but the interconnection of these technologies into a network. It is the communication of information, not information processing, that is going to change the nature of the work done by all people who work in an office – whether manager, secretary or junior clerk.

While the trade unions might say that the price paid for the destruction of their members' jobs can never be high enough, they will lose everything without pay if they are too destructive. The TUC has introduced training courses for shop stewards and officials on 'technological agreements', to ensure that new technology is only introduced after full and complete negotiations, voluntary redundancy, major redundancy payments and as little general job loss as possible.

A major problem for any office manager is to understand or appreciate the new technology with which he is faced. It is well known that some computer suppliers tend to spread uncertainty in order to increase supplier dependence. A lack of basic knowledge will only enhance this dependence and the amount of hardware bought or leased.

It is very difficult even within a specialist management services department to keep up-to-date. For example, what are the current trends and costs in computer centralisation or decentralisation? Should end-users be actively supported in using timesharing? Should equipment suppliers be changed? Can a software house supply better software than a computer supplier? It may be necessary for consultants to objectively assess current technologies and whether and how the office manager might benefit from them. At £300 per day (1981 levels) the service has to be good.

Training of computer personnel in technology seems essential – even if there is no immediate need for it. Awareness of its existence and potential are vital. Beware, however, that training makes a specialist more marketable.

The office manager may have to go back to first principles and ask why the office exists. Certainly processing and transmitting information come high on the list. Transmission or communication of data is important because normally there will be a human interface in the process.

For an administrative manager, direction, concepts, overall developments may be of more importance than being a computer specialist. Planning becomes very important. Designing and implementing an integrated telecommunications network demands intellectual capacity, but also the ability to ensure that everything dovetails together and users understand what is being done for them and employees adopt the new technology with no industrial relations problems.

Security will need to be upgraded as more and more valuable information is available to anyone with the technical skill to abstract it. However, the same information should also enable a wider spread of control to be undertaken with more subordinates reporting to a manager. It is likely that the organisation can be streamlined too so that the data communication can be more fully used in the business.

1.3.2 Social change

Social change is a constant nagging factor which affects the working lives of most administration personnel. Once, even in the memories of managers still at work and in their prime, there was respect for authority, deference to people in management positions, a strong work ethic, loyalty to the organisation, a refusal to strike for anything save the most extreme and outrageous treatment.

Now there is obvious evidence that in society generally there is more ill-discipline, less regard for others, dissatisfaction with living standards, increased hostility to police and anyone else in authority. This inevitably has spilt over into all working lives. The ill-discipline of pupils at the local school bodes ill for the good work practices needed when work starts. Whether it is educational systems or some other reason, the office manager is faced with growing and serious problems which stream in from the outside world. The methods of motivation that were once adequate, if not of high moral quality, are now redundant. Conflict of all kinds seems on the increase.

It is impossible to put an office in quarantine and hope that the influences of a 'sickly society' will go away. There will inevitably be some of the contagion within the workforce.

A lack of knowledge about company affairs will often lead to suspicions, distrust and worsening relationships between management and staff. Worker education in company affairs is therefore a must and information should be given in as much detail as possible. Knowledge should bring understanding and an appreciation of company difficulties. Whether 'participation' is necessary only local conditions will determine. Defining what is meant by participation could be a problem.

Abdication of leadership by management should not be part of any solution to handle social problems. Leadership may have to change somewhat. 'Follow me' might be preferred to 'you go there'. Disciplinary problems should be high on the list of any 'participation' agreements with unions and shop stewards. A company discipline rule book may have considerable attractions.

First-line supervision may be the most affected by social change and what emerges from it. Its role will need to be thought through very carefully especially the relationship between authority, responsibility and the power of the supervisors to achieve desired results.

1.3.3   Government and trade unions

Lumping the trade unions and government together may seem a little unfair, until it is realised that much recent legislation has been largely inspired by the trade union movement, either directly or indirectly.

The office manager has been faced with a formidable range of Statutes in the last two decades, e.g.

> *Disabled Persons Acts 1944 and 1958*
> *Industrial Training Act 1961*
> *Race Relations Acts 1965 and 1968*
> *Redundancy Payments Act 1965*
> *Equal Pay Act 1970*
> *Contracts of Employment Act 1972*
> *Employment and Training Act 1973*

Social Security Act 1973
Health and Safety At Work etc. Act 1974
Trade Union and Labour Relations Act 1974
Employment Protection Act 1975
Social Security Pensions Act 1975
Sex Discrimination Act 1975
Employment Protection (Consolidation) Act 1978
Employment Act 1980

Compliance is obviously mandatory and it would be an unwise manager who decided to defy legislation or any Statutory Instruments made under any particular legislation. Some Acts have, of course, extended the power and influence of the trade unions and especially local shop stewards. Enforcement of the law is often a key activity in the role of a shop steward. Whether office administrators like it or not, trade union influence does not appear to be slackening a great deal. The Government has stopped large-scale legislation but changes may come with a new administration.

Handling legislation and implementing it effectively is essential. Where necessary it may be wise to use outside specialists to advise on legislation, knowing full well that it must be obeyed. Trade unions will ensure that their own representatives will be fully aware of the legislation and be ready to exploit its provisions as soon as possible.

The problem of handling trade unions generally, and local shop stewards in particular, is bound up with the question of industrial relations. Perhaps a realistic solution might be based on the three 'C's – communication, consultation and commitment. While this might over-simplify the human aspects of the organisation, they do tend to make the problem more manageable than most current industrial relations theory would have managers believe.

1.3.4   Institutions

The final outside influence on an organisation which an administrative manager must consider is that of institutions – everything from schools to the EEC. Rioting in the local comprehensive, abuse of teachers, lack of education in basic subjects, low discipline are not fitting factors for recruiting staff who will be loyal, trainable and disciplined.

The EEC – to take perhaps an extreme case – can exert considerable influence, for example, on participative rules. Professional institutes, to which many managers and specialists belong, will have influence on the organisation through their members – hopefully for good.

Influencing institutions of all kinds may be the best answer to the problems. Whether the particular institution is the Confederation of British Industry (CBI), British Institute of Management (BIM), or the local Polytechnic, 'joining' is always a good option. The dedication of committed Marxists or left-wing socialists in attending trade union branch meetings or ward-party meetings should be an object lesson to any manager who complains that he has no influence on the way 'things are done'. In a pluralist society where groups or institutions obviously have more influence than individuals, it is obviously important that 'groups' express opinions or pressure governments or other policy-makers in a way that is satisfactory to management.

1.3.5   The economy

For the administrative manager the UK economy has two failings – inflation and recession. Cutbacks in staff and inflated salaries have become the recurring nightmare. In times when overheads have rarely been under so much pressure, the nature of the manager's job has changed – but not that much. The problems he faces are the old ones. How to relate the expenses of the functions he controls with the benefits obtained. How to determine salaries that attract and keep good people but do not cause relativity problems either internally or externally.

1.4   Planning and the external environment

The examples given in this chapter suggest that the influences of the external environment are all-pervading. Recognising and accommodating such influences are important – perhaps of paramount importance – in ensuring the efficiency of the administrative function. If any planning of administration is done at all, then the analysis of the external environment and the likely impact it will have should be a starting point.

1.5   Further reading

1   James Morrell, *Britain Through the 1980s,* Volumes 1 and 2, Gower (1980).
2   *Cambridge Economic Reviews,* University of Cambridge (Published annually).
3   R. Filder and D. Wood, *Forecasting and Planning,* Gower (1978).
4   G.R. Cyriax, *World Index of Economic Forecasts,* Gower (Second edition, 1981).
5   A. Toffler, *Future Shock,* Pan (1972).
6   H. Voegl and J.D. Tarrant, *Survival 2001 – scenario for the future,* Van Nostrand Reinhold.
7   *Government Statistics – a brief guide to sources,* Central Statistical Office.
8   J.D. Daniels, E.W. Ogram and L.H. Radeburgh, *International Business Environments and Operations,* Addison-Wesley (1976).
9   A. Evans, *What Next at Work?,* IPM (1979).
10 D.C. Ion, *Availability of World Energy Resources,* Graham and Trotman (1981).

11 A.S. Banks, *et al.*, *Economic Handbook of the World*, McGraw-Hill (1981).
12 M. Whincup, *Modern Employment Law*, Heinemann (Second edition, 1978).
13 K. Mackie, *The Employment Act*, IPM (1980).

Two

The Administration Audit

2.1 Introduction

Efficiency and competence are emotive words. Can administrations have high productivity without work control of a detailed kind? How is it possible to compare the competence of one department or function with another? While it might appear that the manager in charge of accounts has his staff operating at a much higher performance than, say, the supervisor of the general office, how is the difference in competence to be measured?

When an organisation in general is not particularly efficient or profitable, the clerical workforce is often blamed. 'We have too many office people' is the cry. Yet without administrative personnel the technical, production, or scientific activities will just grind to a halt. So, some broad measure of the efficiency of the administrative function is necessary if only to convince non-administrators that it is both useful and efficient. This chapter gives the basis for a broad audit; subsequently others will provide finer detail to determine functional efficiency.

2.2 A broad look at office adminstration

In most organisations providing a service or making a product, added value is an extremely useful measurement of the organisation's efficiency. This will become clearer if added value is defined.

Added value is the difference between the cost of all materials and services purchased from external sources, and the value of the products and services bought by customers. Value is added to the raw materials or power bought in, by the company's labour, skills and capital. Added value can be determined by totalling net profit before tax and the wages of all employees and depreciation. So the productivity or effective use of all personnel can be measured using the index:

$$\frac{\text{Added value}}{\text{Total wages}}$$

The higher the resultant index, the greater the added value generated per £1 of wage and so the greater the efficiency of the organisation.

The effective use of administration might be measured by the index:

$$\frac{\text{Added value}}{\text{Administrative cost}}$$

Again the higher the resulting figure, the more efficiently administration is being used.

Figure 2.1 gives some representative tabulated figures which might be used to determine the relationship between added value and administration cost. In the three years quoted, added value has risen from £8.3 to £11.8 million with total administrative costs rising from £1.275 to £1.8 million. When compared with added value, there is an improvement at the end of the second year, but in a further year, the figure has returned to its original level. There has been no improvement in administrative productivity in the three years if measured in the way described.

Some of the individual functional costs tell a different story. If the relationship between functional costs and added value suggests that the higher the figure the better, then general management, management services and personnel functions have all improved their relationships. Accounting and general office services have seen a deterioration in their relationships with added value.

Yet these figures can be misleading. Perhaps management services people have been reduced because the need for systems development has receded. Conversely, 'accounting' has increased because of the need to advance inflation accounting. It is the end result of incurring cost that really matters. Even so, setting out data in the way suggested in Figure 2.1 does indicate where administrative costs appear to be getting out of line.

A crude measure of the effectiveness of office equipment, including computers and word processors, might be determined by using the index:

$$\frac{\text{Added value}}{\text{Annual cost of equipment}}$$

2.3 Relationships between functional cost and output

Section 2.2 suggested that one way in which functional efficiency might be judged is to relate the cost of a function and the number of people involved in it, and the output from the function. However like using added value relationships, this process can also give over-simplified results. For example, it seems logical to relate the cost of the purchasing function with the number of orders it has placed over, say, three or more years. If the cost of placing orders has increased beyond the rate of inflation, it might seem that the purchasing function has become less rather than more efficient. But the figures may be misleading – it may have become progressively more difficult to place certain contracts with considerably more negotiation being necessary

Figure 2.1 *Added value indices*

Data	1980	1981	1982
Number of admin. employees	1,300	1,500	1,545
Net sales	17,600,000	21,420,000	26,411,000
Net margin	1,800,000	2,300,000	2,100,000
Wages/salaries	6,500,000	8,600,000	9,700,000
Depreciation	790,000	1,200,000	1,350,000
Administrative cost, total	1,270,000	1,518,000	1,800,000
General management	185,000	463,000	320,000
Accounting	112,000	140,000	180,000
Management services	212,000	260,000	204,000
General office services	168,000	252,000	375,000
Personnel	123,000	136,000	107,000
General ratios			
Added value	8,300,000	10,900,000	11,800,000
Added value per employee	4,716	7,266	8,107
Average wage per employee	5,000	5,733	6,278
Added value per £1 wage	1,660	1,901	1,879
Net margin per employee	1,384	1,533	1,359
Sales per employee	1,353	1,428	1,709
Wages as % of added value	78%	79%	82%
Admin./added value ratios	6.54	7.18	6.55
Added value per £1 admin. cost:			
General management	44.80	23.50	56.25
Accounting	74.10	77.85	62.43
Management services	39.15	41.92	57.84
General office services	49.40	43.25	31.46
Personnel	67.47	73.52	110.28

Figure 2.2 *Input/output analysis*

Administrative function	End result	Cost of function	Number of people	Cost per unit of output	People per unit
Purchasing	Orders placed Value of total orders				
Management services	Systems developed Savings made				
Sales order processing	Orders processed Records completed Value of orders				
Production control	Stock level reduction Stock service levels Work order cards processed Production programmes written Delivery service				
Accounting	Invoices issued Statements issued Creditor position Debtor position Ledgers produced				
Personnel	Personnel records Reports produced				
General office	Letters typed Reports typed				
Office services	Repairs carried out Cleanliness of offices				

before achieving a satisfactory outcome. Through the extended discussions that will take more and more purchasing people's time the discounts received and service generally from suppliers improve considerably. The basic data which might be shown as in Figure 2.2 must be seen in this light. However, it is too easy to suggest that unmeasurable factors, like better supplier service, have improved by employing more purchasing people.

The form of Figure 2.2 is important, however, in suggesting where some functions are out of step when related to others. The cost of processing a customer's order is always a salutory step in determining whether the function is effective. This debate is carried further in Chapter 21.

2.4   Functional efficiency and change

Chapter 24 suggests how analysis of individual functional efficiency might be carried out. This chapter is concerned with the necessary internal response that an administrative unit must make to its environment and the changes occurring there.

The broad measurements suggested in Section 2.2 and 2.3 will give some indication of the changes that have taken place in administrative productivity. They will not tell the whole story, but indicate significant parts of it. Any response to changing circumstances should be based on:

1   Events outside the organisation – largely the analysis might follow that set out in Chapter 1.
2   The response made – basically the financial response set out in Sections 2.2 and 2.3.
3   The responses that still need to be made.

Past 'response' might include changes made in the last four or five years in:

1   *Policy and strategy:*
  ■   employment
  ■   functions offered or discontinued
  ■   cost efficiency requirements
  ■   redefinition of need for administration and its relationship with the rest of the organisation
  ■   profit or corporate planning
2   *Organisation:*
  ■   structural changes, if any
  ■   redefinition of authorities, responsibilities and power
  ■   participation procedures
  ■   attitude surveys
  ■   line and staff
  ■   span of control
  ■   centralisation *versus* decentralisation
3   *People:*
  ■   training

- recruitment
- skills analysis
- flexibility
- motivational processes
- career pathing
- job study

4 *Financial controls:*
- budgets and budget validations
- reporting systems
- relationships between input and output from each function

5 *Procedures:*
- objectives and targets
- management information improvement and control

6 *Efficiency activities:*
- use of management services and other specialists
- improvements in office routines through systems analysis and work simplification
- work measurement and incentive payment schemes
- mathematical techniques
- functional analysis and performance improvement

7 *Equipment*
- computers
- word processors
- data transmission
- copying, etc.
- return on investment – DCF

Under the various headings quoted the following information needs to be collected:

1 The requirement – in the light of the external environment and the financial evaluation of administration, what should have been done?
2 What actually happened – give cost and benefits – why things went wrong might be the subject of a separate study.
3 What still needs to happen?

A fundamental analysis of the reasons why necessary change has not occurred might be needed:

a The nature, skills and allocated role of management services might have been inadequate.
b Available funds to support a necessary equipment acquisition might not have been available.
c Lack of will and energy on the part of line management.
d External circumstances went too quickly.
e Other parts of the organisation got out of step.

The plan   In broad terms the plan that needs to be made should be as shown in Figure 2.3.

Figure 2.3 *The internal response plan*

Environmental problem	Response and comment	Personnel involved	Cost	Benefit	Time scale
1 Need to communicate with and involve staff more than in past	Participation improvements, but not stereotyped from other organisations, may be necessary	Training office KED and MEF line managers seconded for duration of assignment	At least two man-years of line management and training time: £20,000	Better industrial relations and faster change	1982–3
2 Reduce cost of clerical personnel to take account of inflation	Two procedures: better budgeting and general control; better use of people generally	Management services and local line management with some help from financial accounts	Up to £50,000 in equipment and labour cost	Improvement of admin. to added value ratio of 40%	1982–3 and from then on as an on-going activity by line management
3 Speed up information flow to enable decisions to be taken faster	Better use of current data processing equipment but enhanced data transmission required	Management services	Up to £250,000 per year now and in the future	Difficult to say, but converse of running down of organisation generally could occur	Review and introduction of new data communication June–December 1983

2.5   Conclusions

Anyone who either controls an administrative function or has been asked to investigate 'administration' needs to be armed with an analysis routine of the type suggested in this chapter. Perhaps the most important information that should be produced will relate to money spent and value obtained as a result. Determining this relationship is not easy, but even when only partially successful it will indicate where money being spent on administration is not worthwhile.

2.6   Further reading

1   B.H. Walley, *Efficiency Auditing,* Macmillan (1974).
2   E.G. Wood, *Added Value – the key to prosperity,* Business Books (1977).
3   M.F. Morley, *The Value Added Statement,* Gee (1977).

Three

Office Working Conditions

3.1 Introduction

Health and safety is not something that immediately springs to mind when offices are being considered. Compared to coal mines, or quarries, or some factories using hazardous materials, safety seems complacently a non-event. Accidents, however, do happen and about 5,000 or so are reported each year to the Health and Safety Executive. The main cause is, apparently, falls.

The two Acts of Parliament that legislate for office working conditions are *The Offices, Shops and Railway Premises Act 1963* and *The Health and Safety at Work etc. Act 1974.* The former is often couched in vague generalisations that might have been written by a 19th Century liberal opposed to children working in coal mines. It only codifies standards that have been generally accepted in the UK for many years. Most office managers were already aware of the effect that a reasonably pleasant and healthy office environment has on morale, fatigue, labour turnover and productivity and were, in fact, providing better working conditions than those required by the Act. This can, therefore, be regarded as a spur to those who had not previously realised that office working conditions could have a considerable impact on productivity.

The relevant sections of both these Acts are quoted in this chapter when discussing various environmental factors such as lighting or washroom services, but only because they specify the minimum conditions.

3.2 Health and safety at work

The 1974 Act is as specific for work carried out in offices as that performed in factories. It does not make detailed provisions, but gives powers to the Secretary of State for Employment, acting through the Health and Safety Commission, to design any safety or health regulations that from time to time appear necessary. The Act gives trade unions the right to form safety committees which can make recommendations to management on how to improve the office environment. It is likely that most employers would like to carry out an analysis as set out in Figure 3.1, so that if the Environmental

Figure 3.1 *Health and safety at work analysis*

Activity	Standard	Control mechanism
Government legislation	Full compliance with relevant Acts of Parliament	Factory inspector's reports. In-company audits
Company policy and responsibility	Health and safety policy and rules Responsibilities for carrying company rules	Job descriptions Performance appraisals
Office equipment	Equipment is designed, constructed and maintained so as to be safe	Purchasing/lease approval Safety audit Investigation of accidents
Methods of work	As laid down in policy documentation	Job safety analysis Accident and subsequent investigation
Health and environment	Threshold limits to meet local conditions	Measurements of various kinds
Fire	Elimination of fire hazards Means of escape	Report of fires Local fire brigade surveys Fire drills
Chemicals and toxic materials	Standards of use, fume extraction, etc.	Safety inspections
Attitudes	All employees following described practices	Safety sampling/audits Accidents
Training	Standards laid down by policy	Training plans and their achievement

Health Officer does call, it can be seen that health and safety is an important part of office conditions.

By law the employer is required to publish a health and safety policy document, which might cover the following aspects:

1   The preamble of the policy, perhaps stating that the organisation will provide a safe and healthy working environment. Efficiency will never override health and safety.
2   Responsibility – those responsible for ensuring that safety rules are obeyed in each area.
3   Advice – where managers or supervisors can gain advice.
4   Method – how safety is to be organised; the role of safety representatives and non-trade union employees.
5   Training in safety procedures.
6   Hazards and safety operating practices.
7   Records of safety and audits.

Company rules, regulations, procedures and safe working practices should be carefully set out. While all employees should be aware of appropriate safe working practices, they should also report all unsafe equipment or conditions. An agreement covering the activity of safety representatives will be an important part of the policy statement.

Responsibility for people not employed by the company is important. Visitors or temporary people must be informed of and comply with the company's safety regulation's.

3.2.1   Job descriptions

The following activities might be included in the job descriptions of persons appointed by the company to implement health and safety routines.

The fire and security officer will be responsible for advising on fire prevention and control:

- provision of suitable fire-fighting equipment
- training fire-fighters
- advising on fire prevention
- advising on fire hazards
- compliance with statutory and insurance requirements relating to fire
- arranging fire drills and alarm tests

The safety and environmental control officer should be responsible for ensuring that requisite environmental standards are achieved within the company. He should:

- ensure compliance with health and safety legislation
- formulate codes of practice
- establish company safety standards

- liaise with Health and Safety Executive inspectors
- carry out investigations into health and safety when necessary
- identify hazards
- ensure all machinery is safe
- organise training when necessary
- distribute safety literature
- report annually on safety and any serious accidents that have occurred

3.3   Safety and accident prevention

Safety and accident prevention will cover all office equipment from in-house printing machines to copying and word processing equipment. All such machines should have a written undertaking from the supplier that they have been tested prior to installation, installed appropriately and are safe in operation. Where necessary, machinery should be guarded and full records of maintenance carried out. Training is especially important.

New office equipment should be inspected by the company safety officer and be periodically reviewed. Amateurs should not be allowed to repair electrically driven machines. Machines should be properly earthed and ventilated. No toxic fumes should be allowed into the office. All electrically driven machinery should be disconnected from the mains supply while being cleaned. Initial training in the use and maintenance of machinery should be given by qualified personnel. The position of cut-off switches is important.

Apart from office equipment there are many other facets of safety and accident prevention that need to be considered:

- Safety should begin outside the building. If possible, vehicular and pedestrian traffic should be segregated.
- Pedestrian routes should be kept clear of obstructions.
- Swing doors and gates should not be so placed that they create a hazard.
- It should always be apparent which way a door moves.
- Glass partitions should be patterned in some way to ensure that people know they are there.
- Full plate-glass windows or dividers should be protected by the use of plant troughs or some other means of warning people about the window.
- Storage facilities should always be in areas where they will not be a nuisance and where, in particular, people will not trip over items being extracted.
- In high office blocks all opening windows should be at least 1.3 m from the floor – if window opening is allowed at all.
- Non-slip floor finishes should be stipulated at the time of building or occupation and changes in floor composition should be as few as possible.
- Good lighting should be provided on stairs and in all ancillary rooms.
- Maintenance – the Offices, Shops and Railway Premises Act requires floors, passages and stairs to be soundly constructed and properly maintained. Damaged stair rails, torn carpets and linoleum are all accident hazards.

- Electrical fittings should only be installed by qualified personnel; multi-way adaptors should be avoided.
- Filing cabinets, desks, chairs and other office equipment should be well maintained and free from sharp edges; wooden furniture should be so finished that it does not splinter.
- Heavy weights should not be lifted by female staff; no lifting at all should be done without regard to the possibility of strains or ruptures.
- Chairs should be well balanced.
- No furniture or pieces of equipment, such as waste paper baskets, should be placed where people can trip over them; filing drawers should not be left open or cupboard doors left ajar.
- Horseplay should not be allowed, nor running along corridors or in offices.
- Chairs should not be used to reach high shelves – steps should be provided.
- Trailing telephone wires and electric flexes should be avoided.
- Guillotines should be properly guarded, used and supervised.
- Floors should not be highly polished and only non-slip polishes should be used.

3.3.1 Environmental Health Officers

Environmental Health Officers enforce the Health and Safety at Work Act. On a visit to offices, they are likely to check the following:

- All office or service areas will be visited including toilets, lifts and other non-working sections of the building.
- Hazards of all kinds will be critically regarded – obstructions on floors or stairways, safety of all electrical equipment, storage and use of chemical substances; anything that might cause an accident.
- Whether employees have adequate working space.
- What ventilation is used and how effective it is.
- Adequacy of lighting and heating.
- Fire precautions.
- First aid facilities.
- Welfare facilities.

3.3.2 First aid facilities

It is stipulated in the Health and Safety at Work Act that at least one person qualified in first aid is required for every 150 people. First-aid equipment has to be reasonably accessible and always ready for use. The St John's Ambulance organise a range of courses and will run in-company courses for at least ten people.

The first-aid box should contain, amongst other things, a stock of small and medium bandages, splints, triangular bandages, adhesive plaster, cotton wool, disinfectant, eye bath, pads and solution, aspirin, codeine, paracetamol, large dressings.

3.3.3 Over-crowding

Over-crowding or adequate space for working are difficult to define. The Offices, Shops and Railway Premises Act states that each person in an office must have 11.5 m³ of space and 3.75 m² of floor area. When calculating the space required, space occupied by desks, chairs, filing equipment, office machinery and general office fittings must be taken into account.

3.3.4 Dust control

Once dust was part and parcel of any office. Now, at least as far as the computer room is concerned, absence of dust is one of the most important factors in trouble-free operation. The faster the design speed of the computer, the more likely that it will be increasingly sensitive to dust in the atmosphere. Most, if not all, computer rooms have a built-in ventilation system but, unfortunately, this will not ensure a dust-free atmosphere. It is still possible to have a reduction in computer and peripheral efficiency of up to 15 per cent due to dust.

Dust can play havoc in all sorts of ways. It can scour magnetic tapes, obliterate stored data, create signal loss and short circuits, and block air filters causing overheating. Dust can be introduced by the hardware itself, by people entering the computer room, and from the room itself, especially if there is glass fibre insulation in the roof. The walls and room generally may deteriorate causing dust.

Paper is one of the worst offenders in dust control. If paper dust is left to be continually recycled through the ventilation system, it will cause increasing harm.

Absolute cleanliness is essential. The computer room has to be cleaned rigorously, but even this may add to the contamination if workmen are allowed into the room. They may be a prime cause of further contamination. Obviously the fewer people who have access to the computer room the better.

It may be necessary to use dust-absorbent mats and dusters that will also collect moisture. Aerosols are marketed containing special cleaning solvent for use on solvent-sensitive materials or surfaces.

An independent dust analysis may be needed to determine the dust level and the causes of contamination.

3.4 Fire

Fire is perhaps the major hazard to safety in the office and the Act is particularly strict about fire precautions. It states: 'In all premises to which the

Act applies, there shall be provided and maintained an appropriate means for fighting fires which shall be so placed as to be readily available for use'.

The following checklist is a useful guide to fire prevention and fire fighting:

- Fire certificates are needed if more than 20 people are employed (10 if above ground level) or if the work carried on uses flammable materials. Employers must apply to the local Fire Officer for a certificate, which will show a plan of the areas covered, with all the fire exits clearly marked. The Fire Officer must be notified if any changes occur.
- Are the means of escape adequate for the number of employees in the building? Are they free from obstruction? An inspector may accept that a fire exit is kept locked if a key, perhaps in a glass case, is kept in a conspicuous place nearby.
- Are there two ways out of every work area? In multi-storey buildings at least two staircases, separated from working areas by fire-resistant doors, are required.
- Are the fire exits always free from obstruction?
- Are regular fire drills held? Employers must ensure that their staff know what to do when a fire occurs.
- Is the fire bell sounded regularly and can it be heard in all parts of the building, even above noisy machinery or equipment?
- Is there a squad trained to tackle simple fires?
- Is suitable fire-fighting equipment available, ready for use and inspected regularly, including hose reels, extinguishers and buckets of sand? Dry-powder extinguishers are the most effective means against fires caused by flammable liquids.
- Have senior personnel been nominated as fire wardens to control escape routes and help to fight fires?
- Has all worn electrical wiring, badly maintained equipment or anything else likely to be a fire risk been eliminated? Is the wiring circuit over-loaded?
- Are open coal, electric or gas fires avoided as far as possible?
- Are warnings displayed against fire hazards, such as putting cigarette ends into wastepaper baskets?
- Are gas rings and other cooking facilities strictly supervised?
- Are the premises clean and free from piles of combustible material?
- Is there a fire-detecting system linked to the local fire station?
- As far as possible, are fire-resistant fabrics used in the office?
- Can the 'chimney effect' which often exists in tall office buildings be reduced? Can one floor be easily shut off from another?
- Some fire doors automatically close in the event of fire – have these been installed?
- Foam rubber is widely used in office chairs and other furniture. It ignites easily and gives off highly toxic fumes. Are employees aware of the dangers?

3.5   Lighting

The Offices, Shops and Railway Premises Act stresses that suitable and sufficient lighting, either natural or artificial, should be available in offices and that windows and skylights should be kept clean. The definition of suitable and sufficient lighting is not given and it has been left to various bodies to suggest standards, but the effect of poor lighting is obvious.

The first task in any review of lighting is to determine the needs of the people in the office and, secondly, the actual or potential cost. Differing tasks have differing lighting requirements. Detailed work from carbon copies or other vague impressions is much more demanding of light than reading from a well printed book. Most tabulations from computers have, of necessity, to be carbon copies and when these are photocopied good lighting is required.

Many office workers suffer from some degree of eye strain caused or aggravated by inadequate lighting. Any lighting system should be evaluated in terms of its effect on people and productivity. A good system enhances employees' ability to see visual tasks, so increasing speed and accuracy. By improving the office environment with good lighting, morale improves and performance improvements should follow. *American Standard Practice for Office Lighting* gives good practice in this field (see Section 3.10 for details).

3.5.1   Natural light and office design

Natural light is considered to be superior to artificial lighting and is more likely to be attainable in a fairly narrow, multistorey office block which is not hemmed in by other equally tall buildings. Design and layout should determine that the offices needing most light are located on the outside of the building, with stairs, lifts, cloakrooms and lavatories all placed in the centre.

A drawing office will not only need reasonably high illumination, but also a shadowless north light. The business machine room and the accounting and general offices should all be placed where most natural light is available as their occupants need high illumination for their work.

3.5.2   Quantity of light

The quantity of light needed in an office or adjuncts is determined by three factors:

1   The tasks being performed – the degree of contrast between documents and background and the speed and accuracy required.
2   The office environment – colour of the walls, etc.
3   The age of the occupants.

The standard measurement of illumination is the lumen per square metre, or lux. Measurement can be made by means of a lightmeter which can be obtained from the British Lighting Council, or purchased for about £30. Current standards for various tasks are:

	Lux
Business machine rooms, drawing offices	450–1,000
Accounting, general office work, executive offices	400–800
Staffrooms, washrooms, lavatories, cloakrooms, reception rooms, stairs, lifts	250

These illumination standards need to be discounted for dirt and deterioration and a correction factor of approximately 1.75 should be added. Regular cleaning of lighting equipment will vastly improve lighting economics.

Further correction should be made for the age of the office's occupants. If the average age is over 40, then the standards quoted should be raised by 50 per cent. Correction factors should also be applied for especially accurate and speedy work.

The American Illuminating Engineering Society, in contrast to its British counterpart, is already recommending standards higher than 1,000 lux and it is likely that good employers in Britain will follow this example. Nowhere, it is stated, should be lower than 400 lux.

3.5.3 Quality of illumination

Quantity of illumination is insufficient if quality is absent. Quality largely depends upon absence of glare from lighting and also upon good reflection. The IES code incorporates a 'limiting glare index' and, using their calculations, the acceptable glare has given a rating of 19. It is possible to calculate the potential glare rating of any theoretical lighting arrangements to see whether visual discomfort from glare will occur.

Some factors to take into account when considering glare are:

1 It can be reduced by an even distribution of lighting that does not produce shadows.
2 Large fittings shining upwards on to a near-white ceiling will produce diffused non-glare lighting and even illumination.
3 Shiny surfaces, such as high-gloss painted walls or shiny desks, should be avoided as these reflect glare rather then absorb it. Bright, light colours reflect better than dark colours.
4 Many small light fittings will tend to cause more shadows than fewer large fittings.
5 Light fittings which have proved suitable in large rooms may not be suitable in small offices. Different offices may require different-sized light fittings.
6 A light fitting with a louvred or prismatic base and opaque or semi-opaque side panels, which directs most of its light to the ceiling, usually causes the least amount of glare.
7 Concealed lighting will not cause glare, but may not be the most

economical method of obtaining the required degree of illumination.
8   Glare from lights may be compounded by light from outside the building
    and screens may be needed.

3.5.4   *Lighting systems*

Artificial light should be of good colour, free from flickering, heat or fumes,
reliable and safe. Economy alone suggests that some form of fluorescent
lighting is best. Fluorescent tubes have been considerably improved over the
last few years and 'de luxe' colours have been developed that are much more
pleasant than the earlier ones, though the actual lighting may be less efficient.
Most manufacturers still have high-efficiency types such as warm white or
daylight.
    A low-loaded range of fluorescent lamps has also been produced and
though these have a higher efficiency than high-loaded ones, they do not give
quite the same degree of illumination.
    Other factors to consider in choosing a lighting system are:

a   Where offices have sufficient natural light near outside windows, the back
      of the office will often be in semi-darkness. The most economical answer to
      this problem is to have permanent supplementary artificial lighting of the
      interior (PSALI) in the back of the office. This kind of lighting may be
      permanently on irrespective of time or type of day. The calculation of the
      lux required would depend upon the distance the office stretches from the
      windows, the size of the office and the tasks being undertaken.
      Photoelectric cells can be used to control on/off switches.
b   Desks and office furniture should be capable of rearrangement without
      changing the lighting system. General rather than localised lighting might,
      therefore, be preferable if flexibility is required.
c   Filament lamps suffer from high cost per lux produced and often the
      shading used is not as effective as fluorescent lighting in reducing glare.
d   Areas of light from lamps should overlap so as to provide uniform
      illumination.
e   Light fittings should be placed as high as possible so as to be out of the line
      of sight, on either side of and behind workers.
f   Lighting should be wired so that lights in the darkest section of the office
      can be switched on first, then the next darkest section, and so on.
g   Blinds should be used on windows after dark to conserve illumination by
      reflection.
h   Lighting units can be:
      * direct – these project all light downwards and are often shielded
        by plastic louvres
      * indirect – these direct most or all of the illumination upwards
        to the ceiling; this type tends to throw the least shadow and to
        minimise glare
      * semi-indirect – 60 to 90 per cent of the illumination is directed

upwards to the ceiling; higher total illumination is possible than with direct lighting

- general diffuse types – these have an equal amount of light shining up and down; glare and shadows may be troublesome
- semi-direct types – most of the light is directed downwards

Most of the lighting equipment now available can be categorised as above. The more direct the light, the higher the illumination and the greater the risk of glare and shadows.

i Planned perimeter lighting should be provided as it ensures more equitable levels of illumination. It reduces ceiling reflections by providing lighting from several different directions. Higher loading of lamps should be provided for perimeter lighting.

j The mixture of daylight and electric light provides an interaction that could make a good visual environment. Glare from windows has to be compensated by extra internal lighting if an appropriate environment is required.

k Lighting from external sources should be encouraged, as it tends to change in quality and quantity throughout the day, so avoiding boredom.

l Two lighting installations may be required, one for daylight and one for after dark.

m Colour and colour-rendering can influence people's moods and job performance. Surfaces will appear to change colour under different kinds of lights. Warm colours will appear stronger under electric light, cool colours weaker. Colour-matching or northlight fluorescent lamps have a colour effect similar to north sky daylight.

3.5.5 Lamps

Fluorescent lamps are usually preferred for the functional lighting of general working areas. Filament lamps provide decorative interest and are more useful where lighting is needed only for short periods.

Fluorescent lamps can be from 150 mm to 2.4 m long. Lamp efficiency depends upon colour and size – rated life of most types is up to 7,500 hr.

While fluorescent lamps are cheaper in use than filament types, the associated fittings can be expensive. Conventional control gear consumes energy equal to about one-fifth of lamp wattage. At the end of its useful life, a fluorescent lamp will probably be giving 10 to 15 per cent less light than when it was new. There seems a strong case for replacing lamps at the end of their useful rather than their active life, which would avoid a 'panic' measure to replace a failed lamp when work might have to stop. Scheduled replacement is recommended.

All lamps should be cleaned at regular intervals. Lamps and fittings that provide simple access for cleaning should be chosen. Fittings should be so placed as to facilitate cleaning.

3.5.6   Visual comfort probability

Visual comfort probability (VCP) is an evaluation method that can be used in the choice of suitable lighting fixtures. The measurement indicates the percentage of people who consider the lighting system to be acceptable when sitting in the most undesirable position in the office.

3.5.7   Emergency lighting

In an era of social and economic disturbance, it is important to consider whether emergency lighting is worthwhile and, if so, on what scale. There are various means by which emergencies can be provided for, including having a private stand-by generator. Battery, oil or gas cartridge lamps for key work stations may be a more economical and reasonable method.

Most offices will have some outside light. It may be better to consider whether staff whose work permits it should work at home during emergencies.

Further information, including a free advisory service about lighting, can be obtained from the British Lighting Council, Lancaster Place, London, WC2. From a rough office plan, the Council's experts will advise on a suitable lighting scheme. They also organise exhibitions of modern lighting equipment.

3.5.8   Lighting and morale

It is frequently said by writers on office design that lighting is a potent factor in raising office productivity. This is difficult to determine precisely, as separating lighting from any other factor in the office is difficult. Poor supervision and good lighting will rarely raise productivity. Office managers should be wary, therefore, of promises that cannot be fulfilled. It may be interesting, however, to consider these factors:

- Desks may be moved and retained in positions where light shines down directly onto the tasks being performed.
- Lighting can be used to improve the aesthetic condition within the office. Lighting might define space or working areas. A service area in an open-plan office, for example, may have noticeably less brilliant light than a working area.
- Lighting produces heat which occasionally has to be offset by cooling. Lighting can be used as part of the central heating system.
- Lighting, say office designers, can affect the mood and morale of office employees.

3.6   Heating

3.6.1   Requirements

The Offices, Shops and Railway Premises Act states that a reasonable temperature for all offices, other than those where people are employed only for a short time or where considerable physical effort is made, should be at least 15.5°C after the first hour of work. This appears to be low and the usually acceptable temperature, for general clerical work without any physical effort, is 20°C.

Anyone who has worked in a medium-sized office will be well aware of the clash of opinions about what is a desirable temperature, and views will vary with the age, sex and temperment of the occupants. Generally acceptable temperatures do, however, tend to be rising as more people become accustomed to central heating in their homes, though heating, however effective in itself, will only improve the physical environment if accompanied by an adequate ventilation system.

Heating engineers are able to make reasonably accurate calculation of the amount of heat required to maintain a particular temperature. Their calculations are made with the following factors in mind:

- *Heat losses* – these are due to conduction through walls and windows, with outside walls losing most heat. Ventilation, too, is a factor in heat loss.
- *Heat gains* – these will vary with the number of people in the office and the number and type of machines and lighting units installed.

Other factors that need to be known when calculating the required heat for a specific temperature are the size of the office, the site of the office, e.g. north- or south-facing, the degree of insulation in the roof, exterior cavity walls and under the floor, and also whether double glazing is used.

3.6.2   Types of heating system

Hot water systems have always been widely used and are now even more popular for domestic installations, following the introduction of small-bore piping. The system is usually a pumped circuit serving radiators, and fuel used may be gas, solid fuel or oil. Radiators are usually placed under the windows where they have a convective output that both lessens the downdraught effect from cold windows and compensates for radiant heat loss by the people nearest to the cold window surface. Perimeter skirting heaters are also used and help to prevent across-the-floor draughts.

Underfloor heating is produced either by means of embedded electrical wiring or hot water piping, usually the former. The advantages are that the heat given off is at ground level, so giving warm feet and a cool head, and draughts at floor level are stopped. The system has an enhanced capacity for thermal storage and only intermittent boosts of power are needed to maintain an even temperature. Unlike the convected heat from radiators, dust is not unduly disturbed by the gentle heat given off and no dirt mark problems arise.

Structural alterations are usually necessary to install this type of heating so it is more conveniently put into a new building than an old one. The cost of electric underfloor heating is often considerable, and certainly higher than solid fuel, gas or oil hot water systems.

Oil or electric convector heaters   Temperature distribution tends to be uneven with these appliances. Hot air rises and gives higher temperatures in the top half of the room than in the bottom half, which goes against the accepted rule of warm feet and cool head. Fan-driven heaters can increase the circulation of hot air and tend to even-out temperature distribution.

Ducted warm air   With this system, warm air is distributed through outlets. Air temperature can usually be regulated and draughts can be controlled. Filters can be fitted to the outlets to lessen the problem of dirtying walls and ceilings. The thermal capacity of such systems is small and can be fully regulated by manual or automatic controls.

There are other fairly well known methods of heating. Steam instead of water has been used in the past for circulatory radiator systems. Open fires, stoves, electric fires, oil-filled, thermostatically controlled radiators can all be used, but either inconvenience or economics make them unacceptable for medium- or large-scale use.

3.6.3   Considerations in choosing a heating system

1   Many systems such as underfloor electric heating and hot air ducting need comprehensive structural alterations and are unsuitable for any office that is in a building shared with other organisations.
2   Hot water systems normally have an inbuilt 'extra' capacity of approximately 25 per cent to cope with severe climatic conditions. No other system has this extra output when required.
3   Unless the system is very sophisticated, there will always be a variation in temperature from one office to another.
4   The provisions of the Offices, Shops and Railway Premises Act make it necessary for office heating to be flexible. There will be a need to build up temperatures rapidly, early in the day.
5   Unflued combustion heaters are dangerous, and this includes paraffin heaters.
6   Control of heat losses is as important as providing heat gains.
7   Air infiltration from large window surfaces facing into the prevailing wind should be eliminated as far as possible.
8   Small-bore central heating is probably the easiest to install in existing premises.

9   Solid-fuel boilers have an efficiency of 65 to 80 per cent but this will deteriorate without good maintenance. Waste problems may present trouble and fuel supplies may be difficult to deliver to some sites.

3.6.4   Economics and convenience

The difficulties of forecasting future energy costs and availability make an economic assessment of heating of all kinds speculative. Wherever a choice in heating methods is presented, current trends in costs and availability should be determined. The best the office administrator can then do is accept the best cost estimates for now and in the future and take advice.

3.7   Ventilation

The impurities in the air of offices will be directly related to the number of people per square metre, whether they smoke, the temperature of the office and the moisture given off by people. Heat will be generated by the people and office machines. Good ventilation will not only provide a suitable working environment, but also diminish the possibility of disease spreading.

Carbon dioxide build-up will cause drowsiness, headaches and lead to low productivity. The Heating and Ventilation Engineers Guide (see page 000) suggests that CO_2 should not rise above 0.5 per cent. Natural ventilation through open windows would clear carbon dioxide, but it is often impossible because of noise, dirt, smoke and fumes being brought in. The problem of air change and humidity control is therefore left to electromechanical methods. For big cities it is likely that air conditioning will be essential, or a recirculatory system may be more suitable. The noise from ventilation/air conditioning equipment could be troublesome in some quiet offices unless properly installed and muffled.

The accepted rate of air change was at one time two complete changes per hour of outside air to replace that already in the building, with discounting factors for winter and summer external temperatures. Office architects and ventilation equipment suppliers now suggest that up to six changes per hour are required to provide the light, airy atmosphere conducive to high productivity.

3.7.1   Choosing a ventiliation system

Reliable ventiliation can only be achieved through electromechanical means, though wide-open windows and cross ventilation is a possibility when outside temperatures are high and wind is slight. In choosing a system noise might be a problem. Offices facing south-south west are most likely to need ventilation.

Thermostatic and humidity control over temperature and ventilation is probably essential. If mechanical ventilation is not installed there should be at least $0.5 \, m^2$ of openable windows, either in the walls or the roof, for each $10 \, m^2$ of floor area.

Extractor fans should be sited at a high level and as far from the part where fresh air enters the office as possible. In large offices several fans will be needed to distribute air flow evenly. Some fans are able to reverse air flow. Light-weight ducting in the ceiling connected to extractor fans might be considered.

Amongst the equipment that might be included in the system is:

■ *Air conditioning* – whilst fresh air is obviously needed, it will frequently need to be cooled. Systems are available even for comparatively small offices which can utilise equipment with cooling capacity of 12,000–23,500 BTU/hr. Each system should have a ventilation unit that is independent of the air-conditioning function.

■ *Clean air* – to conserve heat and avoid draughts, it is possible to fit electric air-cleaning equipment that will remove tobacco smoke, dust fumes, etc.

■ *Modular design equipment* – some equipment has a modular construction starting with a fan unit, to which other units or modules can be added such as air purifiers, air sterilisers, heaters and humidifiers, as required.

3.7.2   Humidity

Central heating and air conditioning can cause numerous ill-effects if controlled humidification is not provided. Warming air from 0 to 22°C results in the air's capacity to hold moisture being increased four-fold. In the warming process, water will be taken from plants, flowers and people. People who feel cold at office temperatures of 22°C are most likely suffering from heat loss due to evaporation. Turning the heat up further will only cause increased discomfort. Drying out the respiratory system, according to medical opinions, enhances the risk that bacteria will stay longer in nose, throat and lungs, so causing sore throats and colds.

The effect on fabrics is often apparent. Both natural fibre and synthetic carpets and curtains dry out rapidly and become brittle where no humidification has been introduced. Extra dust and static electricity are also caused.

Britain has, on average, fairly high levels of humidity, coupled with comparatively low temperatures. High indoor temperatures with low humidity result in an environment which could be uncomfortable and unhealthy. The change between outside and inside environments can be extreme.

Measurement of humidity   Humidity refers to the general moisture in the air. Absolute humidity is the weight of water vapour contained in a predetermined volume of dry air. Relative humidity includes temperatures and measures the degree of vapour at a given temperature. Relative humidity is the percentage of water vapour present, compared with the maximum that could be held at a given temperature. In air-conditioned offices it is recommended that levels of relative humidity should be between 50 and 60 per cent. A sling psychrometer or swivel hygrometer are used to measure relative humidity.

Humidifiers   Humidifiers normally work by either atomising or evaporating moisture, or turning it into steam.

Atomisation – water from a reservoir is sucked up onto a spinning disc and passed out into the atmosphere as a fine spray by centrifugal force. They are used more in industrial rather than office environments.

Evaporation – this type operates by allowing an electric fan to draw in dry air which passes over a saturated wick, pad, or roll and absorbs water vapour. The moist air is then expelled into the atmosphere.

Steam evaporation – water is heated with a thermostatically controlled element. The water does not boil, but is heated sufficiently to be absorbed into the dry air.

Warm air ducting – provides a means of spreading water vapour and systems of humidification might be used to ensure free and balanced distribution of water vapour.

3.8   Noise

No one needs to be told that noise is a growing problem, not only in domestic life but also in streets and offices. One supposes that there were once nearly noiseless offices where only the scratch of quill pens broke the silence. Now noise in offices is on the increase, not only from inside buildings, but also from outside. People seem noisier than they used to be. A slackening in discipline has brought more chatter and less considerate behaviour in some instances. Noisy equipment is on the increase.

Noise has a direct and deleterious effect on office work. In a noisy office, mistakes occur more often, productivity is lower, morale droops, absenteeism and labour turnover increase. Even a well planned office with up-to-date furniture and fittings will not improve productivity if the noise level is too high.

What is an acceptable level of noise? Noise is measured in decibels or phons. Phons are units of sound output as it affects the human ear. A decibel is a measurement on a logarithmic scale designed to measure the pressure of sound waves. On the decibel/logarithmic scale, up to 45 dB is considered normal. About 60 to 70 is the level of most large offices with telephone and machine noises. Above 70 dB is considered unacceptable and it is at this stage that a serious noise incursion into mental activity occurs. But where absolute quiet is needed, noise levels of more than 50 will start to impinge. Measuring sound in decibels needs special equipment and the services of an acoustic engineer will probably be required.

Phons provide a measurement for comparison purposes. When using a dimensionless unit, a 'sone scale' has been devised to give numbers proportional to loudness level, namely:

$$S = 2(P - 40)/10$$

Using logarithms to the base 2, this formula is more easily handled in the form:

$$P = 40 + 10 \log_2 s$$

In Britain, employers are not bound to reduce noise that merely irritates but does no damage. However, 55 dB is considered to be an office standard.

It is occasionally difficult to get noise readings. The simplest way to determine noise levels is to check whether normal conversation can be carried on at all times – both near and at a distance from equipment. Some electric typewriters and word processors produce noise rated at greater than 80 dB. If more than one machine is in operation, noise levels will increase in line with logarithmic scale.

What, then, can be done to restrict noise? Some of the following suggestions should be considered.

3.8.1   Noise from outside sources

1   Choice of site will largely determine the level of outside interference. Noisy main roads should be avoided – a traffic count, especially of heavy lorries or buses, should be made. Hills or gradients where lorries and buses change gear and rev engines should also be avoided. Similarly, sites where large-scale building or road improvements are due should be avoided.
2   If the site has already been chosen or if there is no other, an earth baffle will reduce road noise, especially if the office block is built as far to the rear of the site as possible. It has been found that noise is still a problem in very tall buildings.
3   A logical layout of offices should locate those departments that need a quiet environment on the quietest side of the building.
4   Insulation from the outside environment can be improved by double glazing, ventilation systems that do not need open windows, extra-thick walls, acoustic tiling on interior walls, and/or sound-insulating materials in cavity walls.

It is possible to give the 'quiet offices' extra sound-proofing. The Noise Advisory Council has recommended that no residential building should be subject to a noise level greater than 10 dB(A).

3.8.2   Noise from inside the building

Layout – 'quiet offices' should be kept away from noise-making areas of the building such as stairs, lifts, canteens, main corridors and machine rooms.

Noise elimination – a determined effort should be made to eliminate noise originating from inside the building and the following steps might be considered:

- Ask staff to speak quietly and to avoid running about.
- Arrange office layouts so that excessive walking and the need to converse across several desks are eliminated.
- Put non-slam springs on all doors and keep doors facing into main corridors shut.
- Segregate noisy machinery into one room or one corner of the general office, where it can be partitioned off.
- Oil all squeaky tilt chairs.
- Make drawers open and close quietly.
- Mute telephone bells, or substitute signal lamps.
- Fix castors on all chairs, boxes and tables that need to be moved frequently.
- Use wooden rather than steel desks.
- Use extra-thick floor covering to lessen noise from walking.
- Eliminate doors opening into noisy offices or corridors.

3.8.3 Noise reduction

Various methods can be used to lessen noise if it cannot be eliminated. In most of the following suggestions the effect of a quiet atmosphere on morale and productivity has to be weighed against the cost of the insulation required to achieve it. Good morale and high productivity are the result of many factors and it is difficult to separate the effects of any one, such as noise, from other environmental factors:

1 Ceilings should have acoustic tiles or noise baffles of some kind. Acoustic tiling can be made of glass fibre, asbestos or perforated aluminium. Wood is a reasonable non-reflector of sound.
2 Walls, too, should be fitted with acoustic materials above a height of about 2 m. Plasterboard walls or wood panelling are not sound reflecting.
3 Using sound-absorbent materials on floors, such as thick cork or linoleum with a good underlay, should be considered.
4 Noisy machinery and telephones in busy offices should have noise hoods fitted to them.
5 Non-vibration feet should be fitted to office machinery. Typewriters should stand on thick felt or rubber noise-absorbent pads.

3.8.4 Noise – general

Contrary to popular opinion, trees do not act very effectively as a noise screen. Offices on the side of a building away from the road often have noise levels up to 15 dB(A) lower than units facing onto a main road, the building itself acting as a screen.

Wind can sometimes affect noise propagation considerably – there can be up to 10 dB(A) difference between an up-wind and a down-wind office.

The internal sound insulation of office buildings will always incur some penalties, not just in cost but in flexibility, ventilation and perhaps lighting.

3.8.5 Some data on noise

On concrete floors:
- 3 mm lino reduces noise by 5 phons
- boarding on a slug wool quilt reduces noise by 10 to 20 phons

On timber floors:
- carpet on underfelt reduces noise by 10 phons
- 98 kg/m$_2$ of plugging sand or ashes reduces noise by 10 phons

The following figures give the reduction in decibels of airborne sound achieved with the use of various insulating materials:

Glass fibre, 12.7 mm	25
Normal window glass	25
Plate glass, 64 mm	30
Timber joist floor plus 98 kg/m$_2$ plugging	40
Noise hoods on noisy machines	6

The recommended noise levels, in dB(A), for various areas are as follows:

Typing pool, punch room, canteen	65–70
Open-plan offices	63–65
Private offices and conference rooms	60
Rest rooms, quiet offices	58 or less

3.9 General amenities

This chapter has been concerned with the various environmental factors that impinge upon the office administrator and his staff. Many of these factors are governed by legislation, others by good housekeeping and what is considered proper or reasonable. This latter point covers most of the general amenities which offices of any kind should have. However, the Offices, Shops and Railway Premises Act makes the following general remarks:

1 Seating requirements are covered by Sections 13–14. Employers must provide seats if employees can sit without detriment to the job they are doing, or if a large part of the work they do can be done sitting down.

2 Cloackrooms and changing rooms Section 12 covers the provision of suitable and adequate cloakroom space. Arrangements for drying wet clothing must also be provided.

3 Lavatories and washing facilities are covered by Section 9. Suitable and sufficient washing and sanitary equipment must be available and soap, towels and warm water are essential. An adequate supply of drinking water, with either jets of water or suitable drinking vessels, preferably disposable, is also needed. The Act does not give precise requirements, i.e. the number of facilities per person, but there have been several suggestions on minimum requirements. The Gowers Report suggests one lavatory for every 25 people, but this seems to be ungenerous.

Other considerations to be borne in mind when considering washing, drinking and lavatory facilities are:

a   The better the facilities, the more likely they will not be abused.
b   No one should have to go more than one floor higher or lower for the facilities. Centralisation will tend to lengthen the time staff have to be away from their desks.
c   Soap dispensers and automatic roller towels are the most economical.
d   Disposable paper cups seem to be more popular than glasses or non-disposable drinking cups. Fountains can spread disease if not properly designed.
e   Foot-controlled water outlets conserve hot water.
f   To avoid congestion, drinking water, lavatories and cloakrooms should be separated, though drinking water should be available in the cloakroom.
g   The number of wash basins suggested by various bodies is 2 for up to 20 workers, 3 for 41–60 workers, and 4 for 61–80 workers. Again this seems ungenerous.

3.10   Further reading

1   *Health and Safety at Work Series,* HMSO:
    No. 19: *The Ventilation of Buildings, Fresh Air Requirements,* HMFI.
    No. 25: *Noise and the Worker.*
    No. 39: *Lighting in Offices, Shops and Railway Premises.*
    No. 40: *Means of Escape in Case of Fire in Offices, Shops and Railway Premises.*
    No. 48: *First Aid in Offices, Shops and Railway Premises.*
2   *The IES Code,* Illuminating Engineering Society.
3   *American Standard Practice for Office Lighting,* IES (1974).
4   *Safety in Offices and Shops,* and *Care in the Office,* ROSPA.
5   G. Salmon, *The Working Office Design Council,* Heinemann (1979).
6   J. Harris, *Employment Protection,* Oyez (1976).
7   *Health and Safety at Work Act,* TUC (1975).
8   J. Jackson, *Health and Safety and the Law,* New Commercial (1979).
9   G. Janner, *Janner's Compendium of Health and Safety Law,* Business Books (1982).
10 G.W. Underdown, *Practical Fire Precautions,* Gower (1979).
11 Building Research Station Digests.
12 R.H. Fox, *Thermal Comfort in Industry,* Ministry of Technology, HMSO (1962).
13 *Better Offices,* Institute of Directors.
14 Peter Manning (Editor), *Office Design – a study in environment,*

Pilkington Research Unit, Department of Building Science, University of
Liverpool (1965).
15 The Architectural Association has an information library and publishes
office architecture information sheets.

3.11   Useful addresses

Architectural Association, 32 Bedford Square, London WC1.
Building Centre, 26 Store Street, Tottenham Court Road, London WC1.
Building Research Station, Bucknoils Lane, Garston, Watford, Herts.
Council of Industrial Design, 28 Haymarket, London SW1.
The Illuminating Engineering Society, York House, 199 Westminster Bridge
Road, London SE1.
The Institute of Building, 48 Bedford Square, London WC1.

Four

Reducing the Cost of the Office Environment

4.1 Introduction

All office managers should be interested in trying to reduce the cost of the office environment – lighting, heating, cleaning and so on. However, there is a limit to which such cost reduction should go before it materially affects people's performance. Cost-consciousness can quickly develop into tight-fisted skimping which is resented.

However, the calculation of office environment costs and their planned reduction – or even containment, if this is possible – is to be applauded.

4.2 Operating costs

Building Research Station Digest No. 138 (February 1972) suggested even then that the annual cost of providing user services amounted to 30 to 45 per cent of the marginal capital expenditure of an office building. Various government departments have calculated that energy can account for 17 per cent or more of all occupancy costs.

The Building Research Establishment calculated that, by the mid-1970s, annual energy costs were approximately £1.50/m_2 for larger offices and £2.10 for smaller ones. Where air conditioning had been installed costs tended to rise by about 45 per cent.

Maintenance costs vary depending upon the type of office being considered, its functional floor area and whether air conditioning is in use, or heating only. For heated offices the annual cost of maintenance is currently about £3.30/m^2 of functional floor space. These figures could obviously vary depending on the range of facilities and services which the office provides. It could be useful to break down the budget for office costs as follows:

- Energy: oil, electricity and gas, each broken down as a cost in £/m_2 of functional floor area, by season, by department or floor if required. Note that suitable metering and thermostats are then needed on each floor.

- Maintenance costs broken down by office equipment:
    data processing
    correspondence
    copytyping/word processing
    transmission
    communication
  and general services:
    lifts
    building infrastructure
    lighting
    air conditioning
    plumbing and drainage
    fire fighting
    general electrical apparatus
    water pumps and valves
    boilers
    supervision
  Each item should be broken down to show:
    direct labour cost
    materials cost
    capital expenditure.
- Cleaning: direct labour and materials.
- Replacement of office furniture.
- Rates and insurance.
- Security.
- Painting and decorating – this might come under general maintenance but would offer better control if it was budgeted separately.
- Telephones and telex charges – broken down by department if possible.

Budgets should be established for each item and the highest or key costs should undergo a budget validation appraisal. Monthly control data is required to ensure that the budget is not being overspent. Budget comparisons with other similar offices in the same area and in different areas should be obtained if at all possible, so as to help the budget validation procedure. Each budget should be related to the functional floor area.

4.3 Lighting

The following indicates where savings on lighting might occur:

1 Mercury lamps are twice as efficient as incandescent lamps, although initial costs will usually be higher because of the ballast required.
2 Separate convenient switches should be provided for parts of offices that have differing patterns of lighting. Main switches that switch off whole floors could also reduce light usage.
3 Lighting should illuminate the task, otherwise it is wasted. All lights should be so fixed that they help to improve office performance.

4   Much light is absorbed by dark colours and as much as 15 per cent of all light produced is wasted. Changing from dark to light colours in an office could decrease light usage considerably.

5   There is often enough heat generated by lighting equipment to supply a considerable part of an office's requirements. Unfortunately the heat is generated where light is needed, not where the heat is required. A possibility is a system of heat transfer from the middle of the office to the periphery.

   Conversely it may be possible to fit recessed troughs with air returns to remove lighting heat before it enters the office. The returned air can be introduced into the ventilation system so reducing the amount of energy needed for that service.

6   Turning lights on and off for short periods may not be economical. Each time a fluorescent light is switched off it loses some of its life. It is a moot point over what length of time it will become economic to switch off. At current cost levels, it seems that to switch off a fluorescent light for less than half-an-hour may not be worthwhile.

7   Dirt is the all-important enemy to light in achieving maximum light for minimum money. In some dusty offices it is likely that light efficiency can deteriorate by up to 30 per cent in six months.

8   Some prismatic panels and diffusers made of certain plastics will yellow with exposure to light. On average this may mean a loss of 50 per cent in lighting efficiency by light absorption.

9   Automatic dimmers and switches may be worthwhile in some instances.

10   Microprocessors are now being used to monitor and program all energy loads within a building. They can be set to switch off units from one period to another. It is claimed that such equipment has a payback period from 12 to 18 months.

11   More sophisticated microprocessor-based equipment load sheds to keep within a predetermined energy level when demand for lighting in some areas increases.

12   The number of light fittings required (and thus the lighting cost) should be governed by a mounting height/space between fittings/light required ratio. The greater the light output per unit the fewer the units required.

13   In the late 1970s, the use of krypton to increase lamp efficiencies was proved. Krypton enabled tube diameters to be reduced which led to tube fittings where lamp watts were decreased, but lumens produced increased.

14   A new phosphor technique based on television-tube technology, known as 'polylux', provides an extremely economical replacement for conventional tubes.

15   Small-diameter lighting tubes should provide the additional economy of smaller light fittings, taking up less space.

16   Maximum use of natural light is, of course, important. Windows should be kept clean, while curtains or blinds should be so installed that, even when open, they do not obstruct natural daylight.

4.4   Space heating

Heating is one of the largest costs incurred in an office building. Once a building is erected its structure will largely determine the amount of heating required. Unfortunately until recently architects have paid little attention to minimising energy costs in designing office buildings and few, if any, built before 1972 are adequate in this respect.

1   *Insulation* is an obvious consideration. What insulation is possible?

- Double glazing – this tends to reduce heat requirements by approximately 10 per cent.
- Cavity wall insulation – this could reduce heat requirements by 25 per cent.
- Roof insulation – perhaps the most important insulation factor of all depending upon the number of stories in the building. Single- and double-storied buildings should gain considerably. Single-storey buildings might save 30 per cent or more on heating bills.

It is difficult to determine the exact savings as these will depend upon the building's structure, its position, the area of glass, the prevailing wind, etc. The Government will help:

- A 25 per cent Department of Industry grant is available towards structural insulation or boiler replacement. Qualifying factors include a project cost of £3,000 or more.
- A 100 per cent write-off against corporation tax in the first year after installing insulation.

In assisted areas the total grant may work out at more than 20 per cent.

2   *Reducing heat*   Thermostats on each floor are useful if they can be made tamperproof. Expectations of what is a suitable working temperature have increased in the last two decades as central heating has become widespread. Expectations can be directed downwards as well as upwards. Once 19°C was considered satisfactory, now 22 or even 23°C is preferred – though current legislation requires offices to be heated to at least 16°C (60.8°F). Many parts of a building do not need temperatures on this scale and thermostats, strategically placed, will help to maintain differential heating.

3   *Later starting-up times for boilers*   A more rigorous attitude towards lighting boilers, etc., might be tried. Build-up times to appropriate temperature might be reduced.

4   *Use of heat other than that provided by the heating system*   This is becoming more and more important in the minds of energy conservationists. It is possible to utilise heat from lighting, from the sun, even from the people in an office, to ensure equitable temperatures.

5   *Switching off heat*   Often flexible working hours will add to space heating bills. A few people working overtime on one floor may necessitate the

whole office building being heated. Is it worth it, or could parts of the building be switched off completely?

6   *Types of heating and fuel used*   Once the type of heating that would be most economical was fairly easy to determine. Now, with inflation and energy price rises it is more difficult. Some fuels still seem to give greater advantages than others.

7   As temperatures in offices have risen, people have responded by wearing light summer clothes even in winter. No coats, jerseys, or cardigans is the rule. Wearing more clothes is an obvious way of keeping warm.

8   *Stopping air movement* often has a potent effect on reducing the apparent chill in the air. Double doors, or at least doors that have automatic closing mechanisms, are important. Gaps around doors or windows should be sealed. Radiators should be placed beneath windows. Double glaze where this is economical.

9   *Heat loss* can be reduced by restricting window area, but this will reduce natural light and cause extra artificial lighting requirements.

10   The more stories in an office building, the less the energy requirement per square metre of usable space will be.

11   Reducing ceiling heights or increasing the number of people in an office will decrease energy requirements (though have in mind the Offices, Shops and Railways Premises legislation).

4.5   Energy management systems

Such systems collect environmental and operational information within an office building. Remote control of energy use can be carried out from one central point. The equipment can facilitate time/load cycling, humidity control and compensate for outside conditions. Censors are installed in the building and control local heat and humidity generation through feedback mechanisms.

4.6   Integrated environmental design (IED)

Somewhat of a cult developed in the 1970s, IED is an integrated system of lighting, heating and air conditioning based on an ability to reclaim heat that would normally be wasted. Instead of each service – lighting and heating – being looked at separately, they are considered to be parts of a total heating environment. Heat from the lighting units is channelled to help to heat the office rather than expelled.

The heat recovery, it was stated, resulted in 60 per cent of the heat needed to keep an office at an equitable temperature being recycled from the light fittings, cooling plant and occupants of the office. Unfortunately, in many cases, the additional costs of new lighting and air conditioning have proved more than the savings in heat requirements.

4.7   Office cleaning and maintenance

Maintenance can be costly, but it can be extremely cost-effective. e.g. two similar space-heating boilers can be operating at a 20 per cent efficiency differential. Thermal efficiency of boilers is largely affected by the fuel-air ratio, which will often be corrected by proper tube cleaning.

Where maintenance costs absorb a high degree of office operating costs, adequate control is required. Budgeting, budget validation, job time calculations and labour control are all needed if maintenance costs are to be minimised yet maximum benefit gained.

Cleaning and other services may be economically achieved by using various contract services. The potential cost of the service will be known and standards of cleanliness more or less guaranteed.

4.8   Location of offices

There have been various reports produced on the economics of location. These tend to show that it is cheaper to rent office accommodation away from the centre of a big city, particularly London, and cheapest of all to move to a small town.

It seems particularly illogical, if not perverse, to want an office in the centre of a major city, rather than have a site in a suburb or small town. There is always, of course, the need to recruit good staff and life in a small isolated town can often be parochial and the catchment area for recruitment too small to yield a satisfactory staff. Suburbs of major cities have obvious advantages – Wilmslow or Altrincham for Manchester; Jesmond for Newcastle; Solihull for Birmingham.

A city-centre office might provide the opportunity for lunch-hour shopping, but also the weary and costly problem of commuting. A city centre can be expensive in staff time and stress as well as in renting costs.

In 1980 the *Financial Times,* in a review on office property, gave the following guide to office rents (in £/ft^2) for new, high-specification offices:

Central London:
Bank EC2	23.50
Holborn	16.50
Southwark	12.50

Surburban London:
Croydon	10.00
Putney	11.00
Crawley/Gatwick	7.50
Redhill/Reigate	8.00

Provinces

Birmingham, Central	6.00
Birmingham, Suburban	4.00
Bristol	5.00
Derby	2.75
Hull	3.50
Liverpool	4.50
Manchester, Central	4.50
Manchester, Suburban	4.00
Newcastle-on-Tyne	4.00
Norwich	3.00
Sheffield	4.75

4.9   Further reading

1   A.S. Windell, *Reducing the Cost of Electricity Supply for the Industrial and Commercial User,* Gower (1981).
2   Building Research Station Digests.
3   R. Dick Larkham, *Cutting Energy Costs,* Gower (1978).
4   P.W. Daniels, *Office Location and the Journey to Work,* Gower (1980).
5   G. Newton, 'How to set about trimming your energy bill', *Works Management* (May 1980).
6   *How to cut energy costs,* Anbar (1981).

Five

Office Layout

5.1 Introduction

An office layout study is the analysis of all the factors involved in the siting of work office equipment, ancillary services, storage areas, functional relationships and work flow, plus the design of the functional aspects of the buildings which house them. By any standards this can be a highly complex activity. The benefits of good office layout will be:

1 The best use will be made of office space – when costed in square metres.
2 Capital investment in the office building will be limited.
3 There will be savings in the services needed within the office – ventilation, lighting, heating, communication equipment.
4 The movement of documents between processes will be limited.
5 Departmental and functional efficiency will be enhanced through good communications.
6 The workforce should be well motivated through a good and well designed environment. Noise, for example, should be minimised. The environment produced should lessen staff turnover, improve morale and help recruitment.
7 Movement of staff will be limited.
8 Fatigue should be lessened.
9 Planning and control of work should be enhanced.
10 Opportunities to achieve better housekeeping should ensue.

Even if some of these benefits are mutually exclusive, they add up to a formidable list which powerfully emphasises the need for a good office layout.

5.2 Constraints

Making a technologically perfect layout will rarely be possible. A series of compromises will normally be needed which will encompass various constraints:

1   The site and structure of the office building will be paramount, single or multi-storey, oblong or square, adjacent to a main road or in a side road, etc.
2   Environmental constraints will come second in importance to the site and office structure.
3   Good work organisation is recognised as a valuable aid to improving productivity. The primary working group in particular could have major importance. Office layout may need to accommodate specific group-job designs as this may be more important to productivity than the technical excellence of the layout.
4   The cost of improving the office layout should be subject to the conventional discounted cash flow criteria or other suitable means of ensuring that an appropriate return will be obtained.

5.3   Principles of office layout

Anyone who becomes involved with office layout should have a set of basic principles to work from. These in some instances may appear trite, but together they provide a set of working procedures that should lead to a good office layout.

a   The least possible space, consistent with good working conditions, should be used. Any comparison of one layout with another should start with the number of people and space used.
b   Working conditions should be conducive to high work activity and morale. These factors may be difficult to measure accurately but more often than not some judgement can be made.
c   The layout should minimise service costs – lighting, heating, ventilation and all ancillary services, such as telephones, lifts, etc.
d   Interdependent operations, processes, activities and departments should be placed in proximity to each other with as little work and clerk travel as possible.
e   The layout should facilitate work flow and service.
f   There should be centralisation of the most widely used services – typing, mailing, photocopying.
g   There should be a logical position of all stores and service areas based on least travel between service and point of use.
h   Service areas, such as corridors, stairs, lavatories, rest rooms, reception, etc., usually take up approximately one-third of the floor area.
i   Standard floor space requirements for clerks, supervisors and managers need to be established as well as spacing for filing and other equipment. It is likely that clerks will need 13–19 m^2 and managers 25–60 m^2. Supervisors rarely have an office of their own. There is no simple answer to the question of space allocation – each organisation will answer the problem differently.
j   When an office layout is conceived consideration must be given to future expansion.

k Delicate or mentally arduous work should be isolated if possible.

l Work stations or departments demanding most light should be sited on the outside of the building.

m Garage and parking space should be adequate.

n All heating, lighting, ventilation, decorations and cleanliness should be checked against standards suggested in other chapters.

o Main gangways should be from 914 to 1,220 mm wide; subsidiary gangways from 800 mm.

p Floor loading, power and telephone points, security arrangements for vital documents, fire proofing, all need to be considered.

q Supervisors should have an uninterrupted view of the people they control.

5.4 Information requirements

1 A list of the main departments, their functions, relationships with other

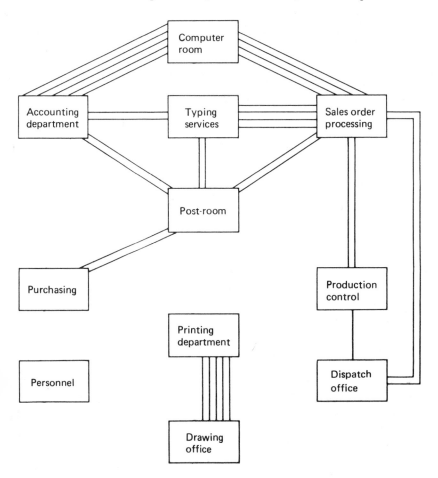

Figure 5.1 *Functional relationships*

departments and outside companies and their place in the organisation. This will help to determine the internal office arrangements, e.g. which offices need to be next to one another (see Figure 5.1).

2   Complete lists of work specifications, the number of people and their grades (status) plus departmental furniture and equipment. These will help to determine the amount of floor space each department needs. A numeric system can then be used to indicate the amounts and importance of who and what travels where.

3   A specification sheet is then required listing:

- department
- name
- status
- separate offices required
- filing equipment
- other equipment
- telephone points
- total space required

Particular attention needs to be paid to power and telephone points, ventilation equipment for the office in general and for machinery.

4   A list of required space and separate offices, etc., can then be drawn up and compared with space available.

5   Activity sampling will assist in determining the location of equipment and desks not completely settled by the flowchart.

6   Various scale plans of the new offices are then needed.

5.5   Working methods

The methods likely to produce a good office layout will include the following:

a   A string diagram of document and clerk travel for the whole office building. When related to the plan of the building it will assist in allocating office areas or locations. Figure 5.2 is a typical example.

b   Another standard method of indicating functional relationships is to prepare a travel chart or diagram. Each area or unit which receives or despatches work, and the number of personnel who have to travel between various points in the same office and also between different offices is listed.

c   A three-dimensional model will help to establish the layout and then to sell it when it is completed.

d   One of the simplest and cheapest methods of preparing a layout is to use

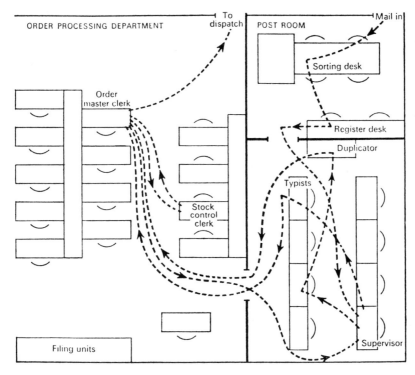

Figure 5.2 *Document flowchart*

squared paper on which a scale plan can be drawn. Each desk and piece of equipment can then be cut to scale in coloured card and juggled until the optimum layout has apparently been made.

5.6 Layouts

This section suggests some of the many alternative designs that an office layout team will have to consider.

1 Information, document, workflow The type of information or workflow should condition the layout of work stations, i.e. whether information runs in straight or parallel lines, diverges or converges, or is circular. The flow will produce layouts of the kind shown in Figures 5.3 and 5.4.

2 Modular layouts of the type shown in Figure 5.5 are useful in conserving space and providing uniformity and some flexibility in design. Occasionally where a flow line principle can be established, it may be possible to introduce the kind of layout shown in Figure 5.6.

3 Functional layouts The layouts of departments are often established to

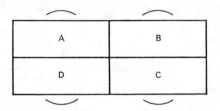

Figure 5.3   *Circular information flow*

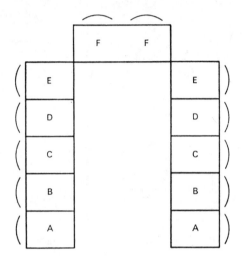

Figure 5.4   *Converging parallel flow*

reflect functional activities and perhaps hierarchies. Figure 5.7 shows a purchasing department set out in this way.

4   The main corridor principle   Many office blocks are built on a rectangular base with a central core of service areas such as lifts. The need to establish maximum use of external light suggests that a main and subsidiary corridor principle is applied. Activities such as filing and typing can be established near the service areas. Figure 5.8 shows how the main corridor principle might apply in a rectangular office block.

5   Maximum space usage   Occasionally it is necessary to make the absolute maximum use of available space. People may complain of cramped conditions, but 'facilities' rarely will. So such activities as filing may need to be compressed into the smallest possible floor area. Figure 5.9 suggests how this might be done.

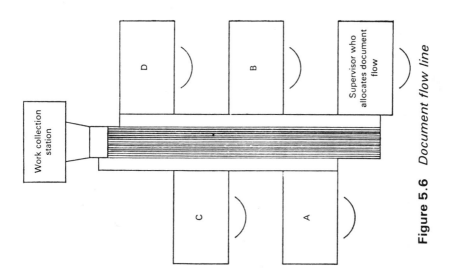

Figure 5.6 *Document flow line*

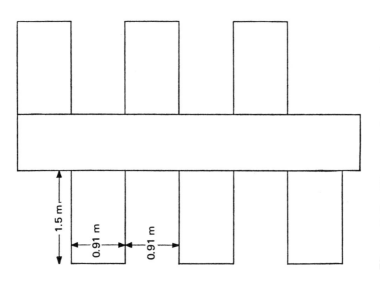

Figure 5.5 *Diagram of a modular layout*

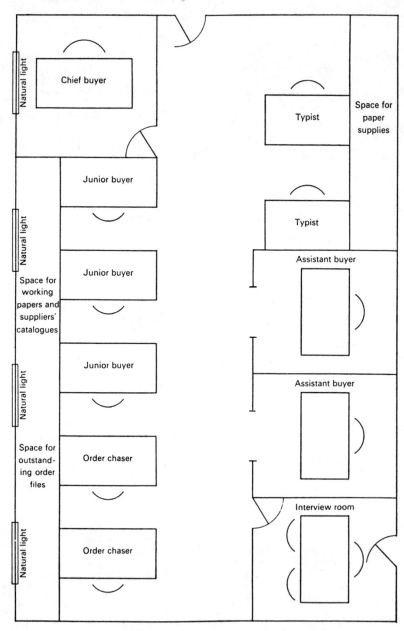

Figure 5.7 *Purchasing department layout on functional lines*

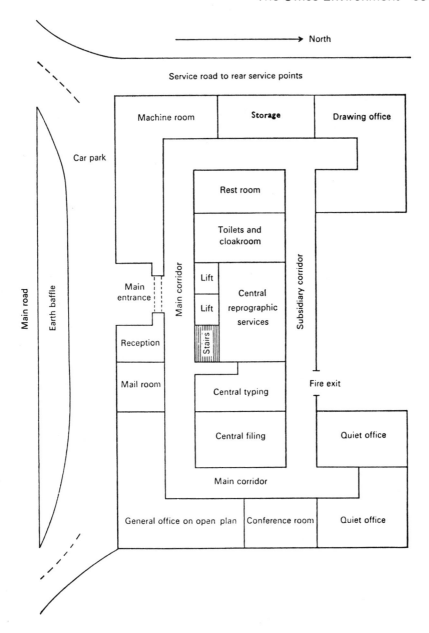

Figure 5.8 *The main corridor principle*

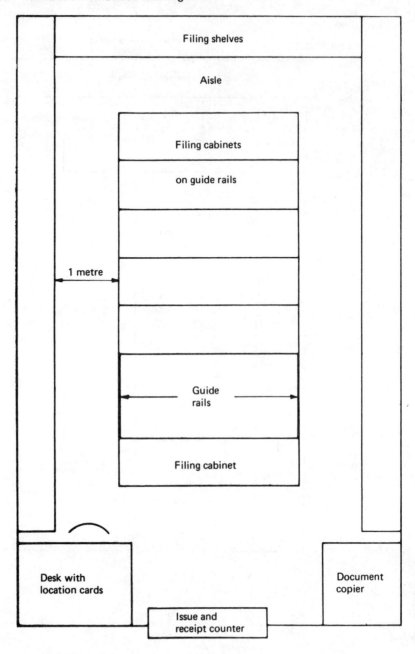

Figure 5.9   *Maximum space usage*

5.7   Open-plan offices

In the past decade many new office designs have been established which use *Bürolandschaft,* or open plan, as the basis. Office landscaping has been part of the design, but not always.

An open-plan office is a place where clerical work is performed and is typified by a lack of closed and private offices. Work stations can be screened, but screens are usually only shoulder-high. There is some justification in suggestions that open-plan offices without landscaping will lose many of the benefits that are said to accrue from their use.

Size of open-plan offices tends to vary but rarely are they less than 200 m². Some architects suggest 600–800 m² is required before open-plan offices justify themselves. The upper limit could be about 1,300–1,500 m².

5.7.1   Elements of an open-plan office

From the experiences gained in designing open-plan offices, these features seem practically essential:

a   The full office should not be seen. It should be subdivided by screens, partitions, furniture and other fittings. The screens should be interchangable and must not reach to the ceiling.
b   Air conditioning is essential. Natural ventilation will cause dust, frequent changes of temperature and draughts and it will enable outside noise to enter.
c   Maximum use of noise-deadening and absorption equipment is needed, including acoustic ceiling and wall tiles, carpets or other sound-deadening floor covering and sound-absorbing office furniture.
d   Lighting should be appropriate and even across the whole of the open-plan office. Dependence upon outside light should be minimal. Light should be non-glare and output-promoting.
e   Work stations should be distributed freely. An asymmetrical working space utilisation should be the rule rather than the exception.
f   The provision of services – electricity points, light fittings, telephone cables, communication conduits, etc. – should allow complete flexibility.
g   Work stations should be at least 8 m² plus some reserve.
h   Depth of noise should never exceed 50 phons. The range of understanding of normal conversation should be restricted to 5 m.
i   Noise-generating machines should be located so that, as far as possible, sound is absorbed without annoying staff.

5.7.2   Advantages of open-plan offices

There are many advantages to open-plan offices, as can be seen from Figures 5.10 and 5.11. For example:

1   Flexibility – personnel, departments, sections can all be moved around

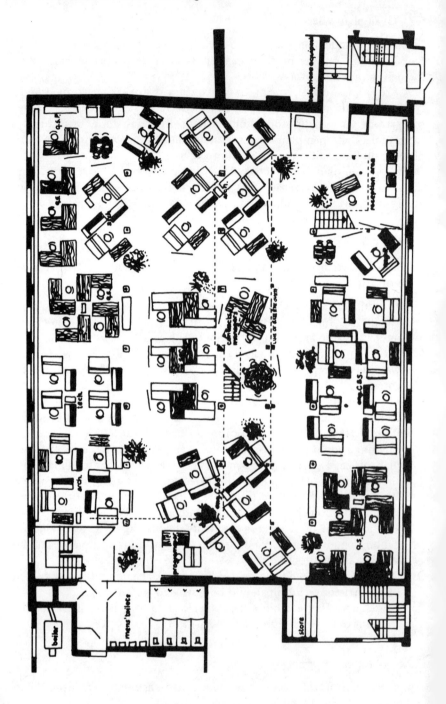

Figure 5.10 *Main ground-floor plan*

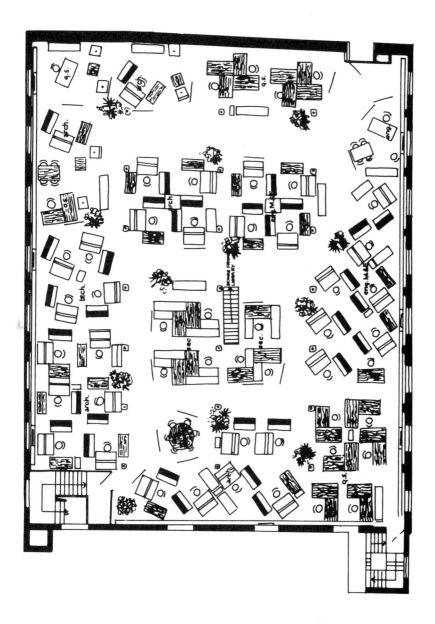

Figure 5.11   *First-floor plan*

easily. The office layout can be adopted to suit organisational development or new trading conditions.

2   Communications are much improved. The possibility of conversing easily and frequently, without having to see if the person to be contacted is busy or has visitors, is an advantage.

3   Team efficiency should improve.

4   There should be a decline in status symbols. Open-plan offices should engender a much more democratic organisation. If work spaces are the same, common ground between manager and employees will have been formed.

5   Conduct and behaviour should improve. Personnel should feel that they have to conform to a high standard – if the observable manager sets it.

6   There should be greater self-discipline.

7   A greater understanding of the work of other groups in the office should ensue.

8   The flow of work between individuals, sections and depatments will improve because of the shorter and less obstructed 'clerk travel'.

9   There should be a saving in heat and light.

10   There will be an overall saving in the cost per square metre of usable office space.

11   As the floor area will not be taken up by non-essential fittings such as partitions, more clerks can be accommodated in a given area.

12   Joint use of office equipment, such as calculators, photocopiers, telephones, will be easier.

The published data on open-plan offices suggests that clerical efficiency is better than in closed offices. For most senior office personnel, however, limiting the office cost per clerk employed will be the overriding benefit to be gained from open plan-offices.

5.7.3   Main disadvantages of open-plan offices

a   The background of low noise could restrict confidential discussions, especially interviews. Special conference and interview rooms may have to be provided.

b   People doing mental work may be distracted by movement in the office, if screening is not good enough. Visitors can be very distracting.

c   The office can quickly degenerate if it is not well looked after.

d   Appropriate lighting, air conditioning, sound absorption and humidity control are essential, otherwise the benefits will not accrue.

e   The morale of the primary working group may be affected by having an open-plan office. The close-knit community may – for many months – feel that their sense of unity has been eroded.

f   The amount of heat, light and ventilation required varies from person to person. Open and large offices always increase the number of squabbles about window opening and closing, and whether radiators should be turned on or off.

g   With economy-minded employers (and these are the ones who would consider the advantages of open-plan offices), there may be a tendency to squeeze too many people into an office and try and get too much in economy from joint machine usage and savings in heating and lighting.

5.7.4   Use of open-plan offices

Except where work is confidential, there are many visitors, office personnel have to speak loudly for some reason and/or there are jobs that need complete and undivided attention, the open-plan office seems to have a use. There could be occasions when prestige may dictate single or closed offices, but these should be rare.

Electronic data processing may be excluded from a general open-plan office, but most other office functions should be absorbed. Security may be one risk that should be taken into account. For example, should the cashier and his money be in the open office? Local government, nationalised industries, private enterprise, all use open-plan offices to some extent.

5.7.5   Psychology and the open-plan office

The use of open-plan offices is still very emotive and 'selling' them is difficult. Precise information must be given to potential occupants about accommodation and its benefits at an early stage. Models might be used to indicate the type of accommodation that could be provided. Experience has proved that getting staff involved in actually planning the office has a beneficial effect.

The literature on open-plan offices suggests that after installation most office staff prefer their new environment to their old.

5.8   Further reading

1   'Don't forget the people in the electronic office', *Office Equipment Index* (September 1981).
2   *The Planned Open Office – a primer for management,* HMSO (1971).
3   Axel Boje, *Open-plan Offices,* Business Books (1968).
4   *Planned Open Offices – cost-benefit analysis,* DoE (1971).
5   *Better Offices,* Institute of Directors (1960).
6   M. Saphier, *Office Planning and Design,* McGraw-Hill (1978).
7   M. Saphier, *Planning the New Office,* McGraw-Hill (1978).
8   *Planned Open Offices,* DoE (1976).
9   K.H. Ripnen, *Office Space Administration,* McGraw-Hill (1974).

Six

Office Furniture

6.1 Introduction

Office furniture should be selected using four basic criteria – cost, size, efficiency and whether it is ergonomically acceptable. Status should be a minor consideration.

Various measurements can be obtained by applying ergonomics and anthropometry to office equipment design. (Ergonomics is defined as the study of how to fit the job to the person; anthropometry is the measurement of the human body.) From these measurements various averages can be found which form the basis of standard equipment to fit average-sized people.

The British Standards Institution has published three booklets – BS3044 (1958); BS3079 (1959); and BS3404 (1961) – listing the anatomical, physiological and anthropometric recommendations for use in the design of office chairs and desks. BS3983 (1965) gives specifications of office desks, tables and chairs. The dimensions and design details accepted in these booklets and also by various authorities in the United States are as follows.

6.2 Chairs

1   The chair should suit the individual for whom it was bought and the function which the individual will carry out. The type likely to fit most users is a posture chair which can be adjusted in height and back support, so encouraging good posture. The seat should be made of a strong resilient material, slope down towards the back support and permit some variation of the good posture position so that its user may relax and avoid muscle fatigue. Chairs should be chosen only after testing by individuals in the organisation. Comfort and adjustability to all sizes of personnel, and resistance to wear, should be the criteria for purchase. Upholstery should be easily cleanable.

2   A height of 432 mm from the seat to the floor is likely to suit most people, but this should be adjustable.

3   The depth of the seat should be 381 mm, short enough for the edge of the chair not to press against the back of the knees.

4   A width of 406 mm will accommodate most well-built office workers. If arm rests are provided the seat width should be increased to at least 483 mm.

5   Armrests should be approximately 210 mm above the seat level, which should allow most people to rest their arms comfortably and without assuming a distorted posture.

6   The backrest should provide support for the small of the back but should not be so large as to hinder shoulder and arm movement when the occupant is leaning back.

7   The base of the chair should give complete stability over the range of tilt that has been built in. Suitable castors should be fitted to permit easy movement, preferably double-roller types.

8   Fabric coverings which are flameproof, or at least flame-retardant, are to be preferred.

6.3   Desks

After chairs, desks are the most important piece of office furniture, but they suffer from trying to reconcile what is basically incompatible – being functional and adaptive. A desk is designed for a typist, yet it is hoped that it can be a general clerk's desk also. The need to compromise has produced two distinct trends in desk design. One is the modular layout of a desk, as shown in Figure 6.1; the other is the single L-shaped desk that many secretaries now use (Figure 6.2).

In the modular layout, various units of working area or cupboard space can be substituted. Modular units can be built up and broken down to provide working and filing space for many types of clerical activity. Deep cupboards can replace a series of narrow drawers; single pedestal desks can replace those with double pedestals; in fact, any kind of layout can be devised and subsequently altered to meet changed circumstances.

The L-shaped desk – which could form part of a modular unit – is often used to combine two different functions, e.g. one side of the L can be used for general clerical work, and the other side for a specialist activity such as typing or machine calculating. The two sides of the L need not be the same height.

Metal desks, in general, are cheaper and last longer. They can be painted any colour to match an existing decoration scheme. *Wooden desks,* on the other hand, are comparatively expensive. They absorb sound and are poor conductors of heat and cold, and tend to scratch and mark easily.

It is possible to build a modular layout within one's own company by using components and this should be investigated if new office furniture is required.

Function often decides whether a desk needs to have one or two pedestals, i.e. desk supports housing drawers, or space for filing or office equipment. Most modular desk layouts, for example, have single-pedestal working

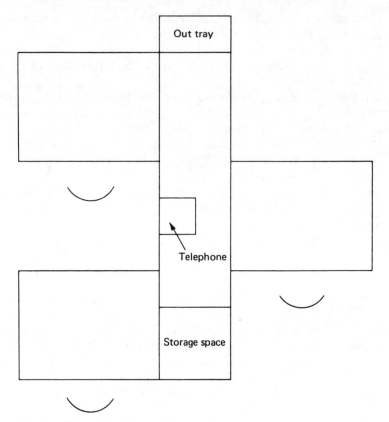

Figure 6.1 *Modular work station*

surfaces, with filing or drawer space beneath the central or work surface.

Function, too, will often dictate the *size of working surface*. Status creeps in here to the extent of tending to increase desk size for successive grades of managers, irrespective of their needs. For example, senior managers often have desks of 1,840 mm × 920 mm. Junior managers are usually satisfied with desks of 1,540 mm × 920 mm. Ordinary clerical grades find 1,390 mm × 770 mm sufficient.

Average desk reach is also relevant in deciding the size of the working surface. Very large desk tops are useless where normal forward reach will not be sufficient to use the desk-top's extremities – the edges of the desk will either remain unused or become depositories for files or unwanted clutter, which should be stored in the pedestal sections. A curved desk, which allows a greater working surface to be reached, is an obvious answer, but is not suitable for building into modular units.

The *underside of the desk* should not be so low that it obstructs knee clearance and the kneehole should end at least 660mm from the floor. Desks with a deep drawer above the knees should be avoided.

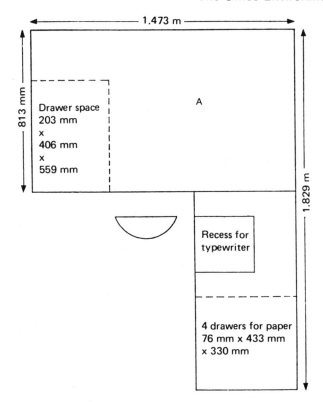

Figure 6.2 *Diagram of an L-shaped desk*

Completely adjustable desks have still to be produced and anthropometric-ergonomic design has been limited to the dimensions quoted and the curved desk. There are, however, many variations on the standard, largely in the type and number of pedestals, provision for specialised equipment, the degree of overhang at the edges of the desk and the material from which the desk is made. Function, therefore, should decide which kind of desk is acquired.

6.4 Work stations

Conventional pedestal desks tend to limit the capacity of the modern office to change because of their predetermined relationship of working surface and storage. Consequently some desks are designed to be part of a work station. Desk pedestals, for example, are often mounted on castors and not attached to the desk. When staff move from one work station to another the pedestal can be moved easily with them.

With the high cost of accommodation it is essential that maximum use is made of all floor space. The work station, built up from flexible desks, cupboards and partition units, is one way in which this can happen. The

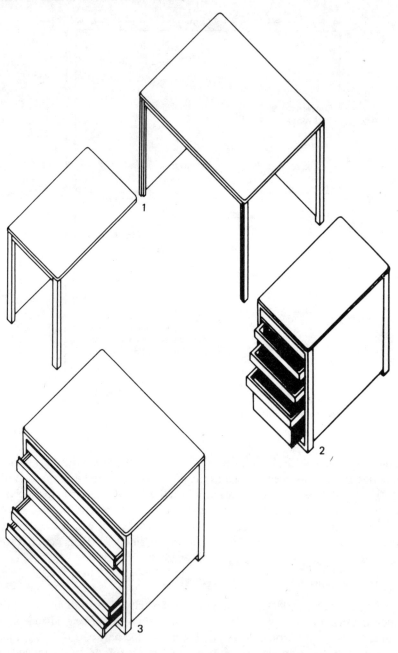

Figure 6.3   *Modular work units*

flexibility ensures that the L-shaped desk shown in Figure 6.2 can be built up to provide the work station for staff shown in Figure 6.1.

In most offices where change is nearly continuous, flexibility of layout and furniture can be provided by having functional units, which permit special groupings for specific tasks (see Figure 6.3).

The primary function of office furniture is to provide working surfaces at appropriate working height, e.g. writing height 711 mm, machine height 654 mm. Units have a personal drawer and can also have a series of options:

Surface units are supplied with:

- Depth, 508–812 mm
- Width, 610–1,321 mm
- No panels
- Panels front and left
- Panels left, front and right, slide and ring drawer

Extension units are supplied from:

- Depth, 508 mm
- Width, 812–1,321 mm

Machine units are supplied from:

- Depth, 508–812 mm
- Width, 610–1,321 mm

Pedestal units are supplied in sizes of:

- 508 × 508 × 711 mm
- 508 × 812 × 711 mm
- 508 × 508 × 654 mm
- 508 × 812 × 654 mm

with up to 19 interiors for each size.

Working surfaces can be supported by high storage units and also acoustic screens. Modular furniture is ideal for landscaped and conventional offices – it provides flexibility, colour and ability to replan quickly. It is convenient to move; various work functions, even psychological needs, can easily be met; colour according to taste can be supplied. Large open-plan offices can have different-coloured sections, planned in a different fashion.

A simulated layout is shown in Figure 6.4. Work station concepts are a dynamic and growing idea in office layout planning.

6.5   Furniture for office technology. Systems furniture

Office furniture needs to complement the latest office technology if it is to be

Figure 6.4 *A simulated layout*

used effectively. The technology of the past – dictating machines, calculators, listing machines – could all be accommodated fairly easily by conventional furniture. The advent of word processors and small computers that do not need expensive air conditioning suggest that a new look at furniture is needed.

The term 'systems furniture' was invented some 10 or more years ago to describe the integral working surfaces and storage units referred to earlier in this chapter, but it is now more appropriately used in relating the new technology to the people who will operate it, so that there will be an appropriate functional relationship between the two.

Some of the more important aspects of system furniture are:

1   Tables, drawer blocks, cabinets, filing systems, conference units, screens, working areas for VDUs, etc., interlock to provide work stations that improve communications, work flow and space utilisation.
2   It is highly flexible and can be changed around very quickly to suit new work routines.
3   It is usually of different heights that accommodate various technological work patterns.
4   Work stations can be isolated from each other for privacy.
5   It should provide the basis for both *Bürolandscaft* and cellular office designs.

6.6   The terminal

With the increasing use of computers of all kinds, on-line entry through a terminal has also increased. The visual display unit, which embodies a keyboard and a display screen, is now common in many offices. As numbers have grown, so trade unions have sought to ensure that VDU operators have the best possible working conditions – eye strain, back and arm ache have been fairly common complaints. How much of the problem is real or imaginery is still open to medical debate, but it is wise to minimise the potential problems.

6.6.1   Problems in handling a VDU

a   Unless a person's eyes have a limited field of vision they will soon become tired and perhaps misregister what they see. For example, where there is a wide gap between the documents being fed into the terminal and the keyboard and the screen, eye strain will be maximised.
b   Again to avoid eye strain, contrast needs to be well balanced. The VDU image should be sharp with good character height of at least 3 mm. Adequate distance between characters is needed – at least 30 per cent of the character height.
c   It should be possible to distinguish clearly between letters or characters that could be confused, i.e. O or Q, S or 5, U or V, etc.
d   Luminance – the light which reaches the eye from an illuminated surface – should contrast with surrounding surfaces in the ratio of at least 3:1. It may be necessary to have a black-topped working surface and dark walls and avoid direct sunlight shining onto the screen. Visual relief areas might be provided.
e   The angle of screen should be adjustable to ensure the correct distance from eye to screen. The screen should be restful in colour and image. The brightness should be adjustable with well focused characters.

f   Lighting needs to help the contrast between screen and background. Subdued lighting will often be necessary.

g   The keyboard needs to be detachable from the screen, but of sufficient weight to prevent unwanted movement. Key pressure should be minimal with a travel of no more than 4.5 mm. The characters shown on the keys should be deeply etched. Keyboard height should prevent undue strain on arms and neck – a slight inclination may be best.

h   The work station should be of two or more different heights, with an adjustable seat. Work stations should not be general-purpose but ergonomically designed to suit VDU operation and be adjustable to each person. Working surfaces should ensure that documentation is easily handled and filed after use. Documents should be positioned to give maximum ease in use.

i   Chairs need to be adjustable for height and have arm rests where these give greater comfort and do not detract from performance.

j   Other furniture possibilities include a sunken space for the VDU on the desk top, document stands to provide easy reading, ability of equipment to be used equally well by left- or right-handed people, while footrests might also be essential.

k   Noise should not be a nuisance, otherwise the VDU operator may be distracted.

6.7   Further reading

Readers are invited to look at the various publications, e.g. the journal *What to Buy for Business,* dedicated to propagating the use of office equipment and furniture. Most of these are free.

Seven

Office and Computer Security

7.1 Introduction

Modern office buildings with multiple occupancy are notoriously vulnerable to intrusion by outsiders. With increasingly sophisticated and expensive equipment in use the person who wants to steal must be sorely tempted. As the need for high technology in business, industry and product design increases so the possibility of industrial espionage grows. The general unrest evident in our society is another factor to consider. Office security is a vital subject which the office manager must take seriously.

In the late 1970s there were over 40,000 forced entries to property in the Metropolitan Police area, as well as 10,000 or so 'walk-in' thefts. The police say that the peak period for burglary of business property is between 2.00 and 7.00 p.m. on Fridays and Saturdays – mostly when offices have been closed.

Security might be a positive factor in the initial design of an office building. Architects are now gaining more and more commissions where security is a prime requirement in the design. These are not just commissions for government offices, but a whole range of commercial, industrial, banking and general administration buildings. The buildings will have limited access; their services – water, lighting, air conditioning, etc. – will be largely self-contained; the structure will be such that it can withstand a siege, even with missiles of various kinds being thrown at it; window area will be limited and walls specially thickened.

For those wishing to make an existing building more secure, the problem is acute. It is said (even by those who market security devices) that criminals who are determined to gain access to a building or gain knowledge of company plans will eventually do so. The determined thief still cannot be stopped completely. However, it should be possible to make his life extremely difficult and the opportunist thief should rarely, if ever, achieve his aims. Access to the office building should nearly be impossible to achieve except for *bona fide* employees or visitors under strict escort. Parts of the office building should be made high-security areas, regularly scrutinised by television monitors and

Figure 7.1 Vulnerability analysis

	Vulnerability point						Computer			
Type of security risk	General office equipment	Office processes	Office services	Information	Money	VDUs	Hardware	Software	Information	Telecommunications
Access and theft external										
External sabotage										
Internal sabotage										
Fraud or data manipulation for illegal purposes										
Theft, internal										
Flood										
Fire										
Destruction by neglect or accident										
Accidents to personnel										
Interruption by power failure										
Other external vulnerability, e.g. weather										
General Interference										

out-of-bounds to normal personnel. Anyone who has visited some high-risk IBM offices and buildings will appreciate what is being recommended.

While the views expressed may sound melodramatic, anyone who ignores the risks is closing his eyes to the dangers of running a business of any kind in the 1980s. The advent of the computer and especially large, central computers has only emphasised the need for tight security measures. If the major portion of this chapter is concerned with computer security it is because the computer seems to be the most vulnerable and the most likely target for anyone disposed to break an organisation's security and cause it harm.

7.2   The security review

Figure 7.1 shows a simple chart of the kind of analysis any security-conscious manager might undertake. The left-hand side of the figure shows the types of risk to be considered:

1   *External theft* covers the general theft of office equipment or cash.
2   *External sabotage* – it is possible that some political or other groups may wish to harm the organisation, particularly the computer. Latter-day Luddites are not unknown.
3   *Internal sabotage* which may stem from personnel within the organisation. Someone may have a grievance or belong to a political group, either of which could motivate internal sabotage. Occasionally employees may wish to gain information they could sell to competitors.
4   *Internal neglect* – damage can quickly be done to data files by misprocessing or general neglect. Files can become corrupted, information wiped out.
5   *Fire and flood* – fire is obviously the more likely of the two and, prevention being better than cure, fire prevention should be seen to be important.
6   *Fraud and data manipulation* for illegal purposes – computer fraud, if evidence from the USA is valid, is on the increase.
7   *Accidents to personnel* – must obviously be avoided where possible.
8   *External environment* – it is possible that an external power failure or even power reduction will bring chaos to a company heavily dependent on power-driven equipment. Weather may influence office efficiency, e.g. high humidity may be damaging.
9   *General interference* covers strikes or other industrial relations problems. What would happen if computer operators decided to 'down tools'? Or would the resignation of key systems analysts wreck the system development program?

Once the matrix of risk and function in Figure 7.1 has been established, it will be necessary to code the linking squares as suggested – vital, dangerous to company activities, important but acceptable – to set priorities for expenditure.

7.3   Access to the building and vital internal sections

Access can be restricted to a building, office, or area in many ways. The first consideration must be given to a good locking system. There is a British Standard (BS3621) for thief-resistant locks and responsible companies like Chubb Security Service will be able to advise on what is most suitable.

Key control is a vital component in a good locking system. Duplication of keys for convenience is the usual rule but occasionally these duplicates can get into the wrong hands. A key holder should be nominated and local police given the name of this person.

Windows are a major hazard in many old buildings and various companies such as Chubb or Ingersoll offer patent locking and window-protection devices.

Intruder alarms are essential in many cases. There are two types – passive and actice. The passive type includes listening and infra-red devices, while active equipment includes microwave and ultrasonic detection. The ultrasonic system usually comprises an intruder detector and a receiver/alarm placed in a strategic location and plugged into a mains supply. The equipment floods ultrasonic energy over a range of 35 m² or more. When an intruder is detected, a message is passed to the receiver/alarm which reacts by emitting a high-decibel shriek.

The microwave system also operates on the Doppler principle (which is the basis of the ultrasonic equipment) and long-distance coverage is possible – from, say, 50 to 500 ft². False alarms are obviously a problem and some equipment is designed to reduce such occurrences.

Passive systems use infra-red devices or photoelectric beams or TV surveillance. They record passers-by or intruders and report to a central control where a security officer can take action if it is considered necessary. Automatic 999 call devices can be installed.

Perhaps the most effective method of preventing access to key security areas is the 'key card system', but whereas a good lock will cost approximately £30, an electronic card key system could cost at least ten times as much. The system operates by a user inserting a personal plastic card carrying a magnetic strip into an electronic switch mounted on a door. The magnetic strip is read and the door opens on a signal. The code on the magnetic strip cannot be read, decoded or duplicated. If numbers were used instead of magnetic strip cards, these could easily be obtained and used illegally.

Access systems of this kind can have features that are impossible in normal locking systems. If access is gained by punching code numbers (and this is one alternative) then a wrongly punched number can start an alarm.

It is possible to have systems which link several doors to one control panel and controller. These can allow new card holders into the system, change the status of other card holders, or discriminate amongst users – some can gain access to all secure areas, others to only one or two.

Another type of system is built around radio transmitters. Each person given authority to enter a secure areas receives a radio transmitter that emits a signal which automatically opens a door.

In spite of all these devices, brute force can usually break locks and even the most costly access system is still only a deterrent.

Security guard services and the receptionist still have a useful role to play. Vetting the use of outside services, especially outside cleaning contractors, is important.

7.4   General theft

Many companies tempt both their staff and outsiders, such as cleaners, by issuing and leaving valuable equipment unguarded. Calculators may have reduced in price considerably, but are still a worthwhile 'snatch', while typewriters are of major significance. All equipment should be numbered and a register kept. From time to time an audit should be carried out to determine the equipment availability and location. Theft by employees can only be kept under control by good records, key control, and the removal of undue temptations.

The perenniel problem in most offices is to prevent the abuse of telephones and copying machines. What is important is the degree of abuse. The odd photocopy may be acceptable, but numerous copies of the agenda for the local tennis club meeting is not. Local telephone calls are not untoward. An STD to the other end of the Kingdom certainly is.

Rank Xerox provides a small key counter which has to be used to unlock a copying machine and counts the copies taken. Small special dial locks can be fitted to telephone dials to prevent unauthorised use. PABX systems can have 'barring' and counting devices fitted that allow limited access to the system for certain extensions and a cost counter for those with unlimited access.

7.5   Industrial espionage and breaches of security

Industrial espionage is an emotive subject, with its overtones of James Bond and others of a similar nature. If 'breaches of security' were an alternative to 'industrial espionage' then the subject becomes a little less cloudy. Breaches of security can be accidental or malicious. The spy finding out boardroom secrets or the new technology being developed in R&D is still not in everybody's company, but knowledge about the general commercial activities being carried on could be vital to a competitor. For example:

- price lists
- special discounts offered to special customers
- lists of suppliers of special materials
- product range forecasts
- cash flow forecasts
- profitability of certain products

- plans of all kinds
- wage rates

could all be of help to a competitor in deciding his own strategy. Employees can be 'planted' and staff who know what is going on poached. Bribery might be tried. Measures to prevent breaches of security include:

1   Severely restricted access to key information – at a time when communication is all the rage and 'telling it like it is' the aim, this could be difficult.
2   Disaffected staff should be monitored and taken out of key jobs.
3   No security devices of any kind will be of value if complacency and indifference to security risks exist.
4   Security has to be in mind – an appropriate attitude can only be brought about by constant reminders of the need for security and training in security activities.
5   Desks are often left unguarded at lunchtimes with confidential papers not put away securely. Desk locks are often of the same type for all desks in an office and can be opened by a single key.
6   Filing cabinets can usually be opened easily, even when locked. The metal from which they are made is usually thin and can easily be forced.
7   Office staff must be aware not only of the security dangers of the equipment they use, but also of the security risks of the paper they handle. Documents should be classified where possible and access to them restricted.
8   All strangers who enter the office should be challenged. The person involved might be the managing director but equally he might be an industrial spy. Visitors should always be escorted and never allowed to ge freely from the reception desk to the office they want to visit. Offices should always be warned of visiting typewriter engineers or photocopying machine repair men.
9   All paper that is remotely important should be destroyed after use. A shredding machine could save the loss of valuable secrets to a competitor. Duplicating and photocopying are spots where potentially serious leaks can take place. All spoilt copies should be shredded even if they are only semi-legible.
10 Only regular employees should handle confidential information. The temporary typist may be brilliant at being a secretary to the chairman, but deadly in the knowledge which she quickly acquires.
11 The industrial spy with his 'bugs' and cameras should perhaps be combated by professional anti-spies, but normal everyday leaks can be avoided by common sense precautions and constant repetition of the need for security.

7.6   Cash office security

The cash office is one of the most tempting targets for any intruder. This office and the computer room should be in a security zone with strictly limited access. Access should be monitored and identification required before access is gained.

The cash office should be made secure. The door should be built to resist attack, probably with an air lock device that can act as a security screen. Ceilings, floors and windows should all be checked to discover possible illegal entry points. The door should be opened as infrequently as possible and a hatch provided for wages payment, etc. An adequate safe is obviously desirable – preferably one which is fireproof.

7.7   Attack

Some organisations, perhaps rightly, suggest that if their staff are attacked they should not resist – money is not worth a lost life. This seems too easy an answer for many, and various devices can be used that will either deter attack or frighten off the attacker once he has made a move, e.g. an anti-mugging smoke alarm that operates when a bag or satchel to which it is attached is grabbed, releasing clouds of coloured smoke. Signals that transmit an alarm can also be used. They can be as small as a wristwatch and fitted to something likely to be stolen. Push-button alarms may be suitable for use in cash offices or banks.

7.8   Fire

Fire is always the greatest risk to life and limb in most offices. It is a growing danger to every office worker. As prevention is better than cure, the office manager would be advised to first consider fire-detecting devices. Simple heat detectors that operate through a thermocouple and sound an alarm when the temperature goes beyond a preset figure are the simplest and cheapest.

Fire alarms should be considered next in priority. The 'break glass and sound alarm' system has much to recommend it, especially if it is linked to a voice intercommunication system, that can be used to report the position of the fire.

Using fire doors and furniture that is flameproof, if not totally fire-resistant, should be considered. Some fire-resistant doors, even when made of timber, can resist fire for an hour or more. Upholstery of office furniture can now be made from fire-resistant materials.

Paper starts to turn brown at temperatures of approximately 350°F (177°C). The computer and its associated data files need special protection. For magnetic tape and other data storage media, the harmful temperature is much lower than for paper – probably less than 100°C. Insulated safes and filing cabinets are required. As the majority of input records to a computer are still on paper, the danger of fire in storage must be considered. Various safes and storage units will resist fires of considerable intensity. All is not lost when a conflagration occurs.

Automatic fire-fighting systems usually dispense CO_2 or water when temperatures go beyond a critical limit. Portable extinguishers with approved CO_2 or foam should also be available to tackle localised outbreaks of fire.

7.9   Computer security

7.9.1   Introduction

The increasing use of computers and associated data files makes computer data processing exceedingly vulnerable to those who wish to tamper with or destroy it. It is foolish not to take account of the potential security risks that exist and for various social reasons are, in effect, increasing daily. Computer crimes will grow severely in the coming years. Analysis of crimes connected with computers suggests that comparatively simple audit or security procedures would have prevented most of them.

In an era which might see serious social disruption, the security of the computer could be one of the most vital activities in the company. Security can be breached both:

- *internally* - which can stem from criminal interest by computer or other personnel who can gain access to the computer. More usually 'performance security' can be breached by negligence or inefficiency;
- *externally* - which can be either criminal intent or natural hazards.

Privacy in computer activities has been, and will always be, a problem despite all methods of security. Access to the computer room may be restricted, but absolute loyalty of personnel will never be completely achieved. Many apparent breaches of security might be due to negligence rather than design. A payroll tabulation can be left on a desk to which many people have access. A stock print out can be placed in the warehouse where all personnel have access to it. Often no checks are made on the final destination of computer tabulations.

7.9.2   Criminal intent

Staff integrity is vital in considering the possibility of criminal intent which might spring from internal or external influences. Internally the maladjusted are a problem; personnel who have suffered either a real or imagined slight are always a potential danger.

Rigorous interviewing can, with a shortage of good computer personnel, be rather overdone. But loyalty must be gained from even the highest calibre systems-programming personnel. Loyalty tests may be difficult to administer, but a simple attitude survey might be considered. Everything possible in the way of merit and acceptable performance appraisal and salary adjustments should be done. Anyone who considers that they have been slighted in some way should be denied the opportunity for a criminal act against the computer.

Restricted access to the computer was at one time the rule rather than the exception. With greater familiarity, the computer room has often become a meeting place for anyone remotely connected with the computer either as a member of the department or as a user. Restricted access is still the best prevention of criminal intent. Only operating staff should actually go into the computer room. Even these should be vetted carefully and access only allowed during normal routine working.

The possibility of *social unrest* should be met by insisting on the computer room being bomb- and assault-proof as far as possible. Architects will need to be brought in to design a suitable building or framework to prevent interruption by outside attack. Steel doors, absence of windows and isolation of the computer room from other parts of the company, may all be necessary.

To prevent entry, security guards and door-opening identity discs may be needed. Closed circuit television is recommended for constant supervision of the computer area. Putting a computer into a glass box in the middle of a well used and open part of a building with good access from the street is asking for trouble.

It is also essential that files are regularly dumped in storage, some distance from the main computer activity, in case of trouble.

Computer misuse   It is comparatively easy for operating staff to duplicate a file and carry it out of the computer room, or patch a program to produce a result they require. Regular policing of the computer building, or even transmission devices on equipment that could be misused, may be necessary.

Programming techniques   Modular programming has many advantages as it allows full and exhaustive testing to be carried out. Large integrated programmes are difficult to test. High-level languages are usually considered to be safer than assembler or machine languages. Programs should always pass through the operating system to access files. Changes to operating programs should always be authorised and checked on a test harness.

Program and file safety   Duplicate programes and operating procedures should always be stored away from the computer. However, these would be useless if a computer of similar capacity and type was not available as a back-up facility if anything went wrong with the company computer. Instructions for the recovery of the program, etc., must be explicit. Appropriate maintenance should always be carried out.

Putting the duplicate files and programs in another location may in itself cause a security risk and regular auditing of duplicates needs to be made.

Operating procedures   The activities of the operating personnel should be divided and as far as possible kept within well defined limits. Job enrichment may not apply in a high-security activity. Development staff should have limited access to the computer room and, as far as possible, not be allowed to operate the computer. There should be limited access to the file library.

The staff on each computer shift should be changed at regular intervals to avoid collusion which might cause a security leak.

Secrecy   For high security in data transmission, the only real solution may be coding of all messages, which could be expensive, with error detection and recovery a problem.

Terminals should always be guarded – it may be very easy to use one to gain vital information. Similarly the use of VDUs should also be restricted, which may be much more difficult to enforce than the restriction of access to the computer room.

The use of VDUs, etc., spreads the risk of a security breach enormously – equally it enhances the possibility of error. Passwords and other security devices should be used. A pirate terminal between a legitimate one and the computer may be an effective way of criminals gaining information *(See* Auditing VDUs, page 82).

Cost or risk   Many of the recommendations made are expensive; some will be very irksome. A balance between cost and the possibility of security leakages has to be made. In the past too little attention has been paid to security aspects. A computer is extremely vulnerable to anyone who seriously wants it incapacitated and is prepared to act in a criminal way. Security needs to be tightened in many computer rooms – in some cases considerably.

7.9.3   Internal incompetence

The possibility of error or incompetence is always with systems management:

1   Corruption of files due to program errors – the answer to this problem is to keep several generations of file always available – the father-son technique.
2   Incorrect information on file – mispunching or wrong completion of a data sheet must always be guarded against. Rigorous input validation checks must be introduced.
3   Hardware faults can also cause incorrect data input and 'checksums' and parity bits are needed. 'Read protection' of the main memory ensures that a user can only access data that he is permitted to use. There are other hardware security facilities and these should be discussed with the computer supplier.
4   There is also a variety of software applications that will enhance security. These include:

   - *reprisals* - this is an action taken by the system when violation of security is attempted;
   - *security parameters* can be established so that only authorised users can use the computer;
   - *audit records* check on the use of files and terminals; they will mainly act as a deterrent.

   There are other software security applications,which, depending upon the degree of security required, can be used to detect and deter security lapses. Frequent checks on operational programs and the computer executive are essential.

7.9.4   Natural hazards

Largely these can be attributed to fire and flood. Physical detectors of heat and smoke are mandatory for a computer room. Non-inflammable materials should always be stipulated for walls, floors and ceilings. 'No smoking' should be a rule. The immediate removal of all potentially inflammable materials as soon as they can be removed, should be insisted upon.

Computer staff should have well developed contingency plans for combating possible natural hazards. They should practice fire-fighting and other appropriate activities regularly. Files should always be placed in fireproof safes or rooms when not in use.

Sluices or flood barriers should be installed wherever there is a risk of floods

7.9.5   Computer systems audit

Auditing computer systems needs the same skills as auditing manual systems, i.e. the systems are evaluated for soundness, adequacy, security loopholes, accountancy principles, compliance with policy decisions, and reliability. Safeguarding against potential losses is paramount.

However, the audit personnel need computer systems knowledge much enhanced from their colleagues carrying out manual systems audit. Because of the cost of developing such systems, an auditing method designed to check systems development from inception to application is desirable.

It may be necessary, indeed desirable, to develop computer audit specialists. Training computer specialists of various kinds to be auditors may be worthwhile. Such personnel will be auditors, but will be able to suggest corrective measures that can be introduced into computer systems activities. With increasing security risks, greater expenditure on audit could be worthwhile.

Various auditing or security principles might be considered at the systems design and programming stage. For example, systems development should be carried out to ensure that potential security leaks are identified and corrected before great expense has been incurred in design and programming. The early involvement of audit personnel should develop an exchange of skills essential in computer systems auditing.

Other systems design facets might be:

a   The system should enable the following checks to be carried out:

- the processing of transactions to confirm their accuracy;
- the authorisation of data transmitted or input;
- maintenance and control of computer files, particularly amendments;
- amendment to programs.

b   Control totals should always be designed into the system. Programs reconciling individual quantities with totals should be used.

c   Exception reporting should always be used to check on data in systems. For example, in the payroll suite the numbers of salaries above £X might always be printed or the number of invoices above £X00's might be given as exceptions.

d   The audit trail should follow:

- source documents
- input media - punch cards, paper tape, etc.
- programs/systems
- print-outs whether on paper tape, microfilm or microfiche
- interrogation routines are needed in each case

General auditing rules   A computer systems audit must determine whether:

- the system has security leaks
- company policy is being followed
- the specifications agreed with management are being followed

The various elements might include:

1   Checking the accuracy of data on file by constantly sampling items and comparing them with actual situations.
2   Creating data and, through 'test packs', inserting it on file for verification.
3   Ensuring that data files are so established that an audit trail can be followed.
4   Retrieving data from files by an enquiry program with an ability to select certain elements of the data.
5   Using live procedural testing in ledger-based systems to evaluate controls, allocations and analysis, etc., which has the advantage of being used with live data during the actual running of the jobs being audited.
6   Creating experimental test data, which is similar to live procedural testing. Audit test data is created and prepared. The results are predicted, the data input and actual results evaluated against the prediction.
7   Isolating the operation of one program, but also integrating it with a suite where this is in existence.

It seems necessary to develop program verification to establish the integrity of operational programs that might be used for criminal purposes. Payroll programs are an obvious target and should be checked ruthlessly. 'Surprise' checks of vulnerable programs seems essential.

Terminals/VDUs   Perhaps the most vulnerable part of a computer application is the terminals. These are usually manned by comparatively junior personnel in offices where access restrictions are few and the possibility of abuse or misuse quite high. The following checklist suggests how some of the security risks might be lessened:

a   How many terminals do we have, what type, where are they located?
b   What relationship has been established between terminals and the mainframe:

- enter command only
- conversational
- interterminal activity?

c   What linkage has been introduced to the mainframe and is there an alternative?

d   Systems design - comment on:

- systems in use
- on-line/batch mode
- data input for transactions
- data input for master file changes
- enquiry mode

e   What confidential information is obtainable via the terminal on:

- company performance
- price lists
- discounts
- sales to key customers, etc.?

f   What written instructions have been given on:

- use of the terminal
- confidentiality?

g   Who could have access to the office where terminals are used? What restrictions are placed on:

- visitors
- other company staff
- locking/unlocking office doors?

h   How is the terminal put into use:

- lock or badge – who holds these?
- passwords – who is aware of passwords? how often are they changed?
- sign-on routines?

i   What other systems could be accessed from the terminal if the appropriate passwords were known?

j   Has each user been provided with a user manual to help ensure data accuracy? If so does it cover:

- control of data being input: document numbering, authorisation, completion of batch slips, registration of batches and, data retention periods?
- process controls: corrective procedure for all errors indicated on VDU, verification procedures using a second terminal, and control totals?
- after process controls: manual check of printouts produced at the terminal (termiprinters) and tabulation agreed with register of terminal usage?

k   Check:

- who issues operating manual?

- who updates it?
- who records faulty input and output?

l Check: systems breakdown procedures: fall-back methods, computer and manual.
m Check service contracts against terminal breakdown.

Local data processing Like terminals, local data processing, especially through the use of minis and distributive processing, could be a major source of security leaks and data mishandling. While the staff of major computer installations are often well versed in security, local data processing people may lack the skill, training or attitude to prevent serious security problems occurring.

While giving local management data processing facilities is admirable in theory, a Pandora's box of trouble may result. An audit of local, even major, data processing might follow these lines:

1 Type of equipment, location, people involved, first-time users or not, staffing.
2 Software – in-house, computer supplier packages, languages.
3 Processing mode – interactive, on-line, file update, batch, transaction processing.
4 Responsibilities – are these clearly defined for the following?

   - initiation of data and later input
   - job scheduling
   - data control and accuracy and input
   - file structure
   - programming and systems analysis
   - total management

5 In-house programs – check following:

   - initiation and authorisation
   - support documentation
   - software and utility programs needed to support any changes made
   - passwords
   - test data use
   - compilers and compiled versions
   - read-only programs

   Bought-in programs - check:

   - source codes
   - object codes

6 Access – how far is access to data processing restricted?

   - equipment – locks and passwords
   - files

- program libraries and labels
- running logs
- systems documentation
- back-up systems
- terminals

7   Data accuracy – how is this verified?

- manual input controls
- data editing
- validation
- batch control
- controls totals:
  - counts of transaction types
  - values and quantities
  - summaries
  - recording on logs and master file

8   General control:

- opening balances
- summary transactions

Risk management   As security becomes a bigger and bigger problem, it may become economic for organisations to have a specialist whose job is to consider and, if possible, reduce the security risk to the computer installation. His role will be to:

a   Be aware of the risk to security.
b   Assess the possibilities of attack.
c   Be knowledgeable of all the mechanisms that limit risk.
d   Help apply such mechanisms where feasible.
e   Obtain economic insurance rates to cover security breaches.

Conclusion   The antipathy of people towards computers could largely be responsible for many computer crimes. The invasion of privacy, the threats to jobs and to peace of mind all have some impact on the psychology of people and how they view computers.

7.10   Where to go for help for security devices and advice

- Equipment supplies:
  - Locks – Chubbs, Ingersoll, Bramah, Copydex.
  - Electronic systems: Tann Synchrome, Card-key, Memory Lock, Securimaster, Data-lock.
  - Surveillance systems: Pye Business Communications, Phot-scan, Reliance Systems.
  - Security services: Securicor, AFA-Minerva, Reliance, Group 4.

■   General advice: local police station, British Security Industries Association, Home Office.

7.11   Further reading

1   D. Broadbent, *Contingency Planning,* NCC (1979).
2   K.K. Wong, *Risk Analysis and Control – a guide for DP managers,* NCC, (1977).
3   L.P. Waring, *Management Handbook of Computer Security,* NCC (1978).
4   C.R. Wagner, *The CPA and Computer Fraud,* Lexington Books (1979).
5   Peter Heims, *Countering Industrial Espionage,* Gower (1981).
6   J.R. Talbot, *Management Guide to Computer Security,* Gower (1981).
7   E. Oliver and J. Wilson, *Security Manual,* Gower (1979).
8   A. Bequai, *Computer Crime,* Lexington Books (1978).
9   A. Bequai, *White-collar Crime – a 20th century crisis,* Lexington Books (1978).
10   A. Fennelly, *Crime Prevention,* Butterworth (1982).
11   R.L. Barnard, *Intrusion Detection Systems,* Butterworth (1981).
12   E.D. Finneran, *Security Supervision,* Butterworth (1981).
13   D. Berger, *Security for Small Businesses,* Butterworth (1981).
14   L.E. Rockley and D. Hill, *Security – its management and control,* Business Books (1981).

Eight

Specialist Offices

8.1 Introduction

It would be wrong to assume that all offices need either the same planning, organisation, furniture, equipment or even environment. Function will largely determine office layout, ambience and, eventually, cost. What needs to apply in a general office may not be appropriate in, say, an office carrying out some technical functions.

Analysis of office environments, therefore, should be viewed against the functional activity of the office concerned. This chapter outlines only a few of the technical offices that might need to be evaluated.

8.2 Factory offices

The general problems of cost control are similar for staff in the accounts department as those in factory offices. They can be tackled by similar techniques – budgeting, standard costs, some form of clerical work measurement and performance monitoring – but the factory environment generally seems to have a deleterious effect on clerical efficiency. There is a distinct tendency for factory office staff to work at a lower productivity rate than general office personnel. The reasons seem to be:

a Small offices which usually proliferate around a factory are often subject to noise, fumes and dust which are not conducive to clerical efficiency.

b The small size of most offices prohibits the full utilisation of clerical staff. A manager, for example, may have demanded a clerical service for less than half a day's work, but is none the less allowed a clerk for it. These clerical 'half bodies' exist in most small factory offices.

c The small size of the offices does not, economically, justify introducing modern office equipment.

d   With a widespread clerical staff, supervision of any kind is very difficult. Most of the clerks involved will be reporting to supervisors or managers who will know very little about clerical work or systems.

e   Many of the factory office workers will be ex-shop floor personnel who have been given clerical jobs either because of some injury or because they happened to be available. They will usually have received little training and have small prospects of promotion. Their general ability and attitude to their jobs will, therefore, be inferior to that of staff in a well run medium-sized office.

8.2.1   Central factory office

General cost-control techniques will have little influence on the conditions described in the previous section, whereas they could be applied if a central clerical group or central administrative section were set up. The obvious benefits from such an arrangement are:

1   Staff can be supervised and adequate work output planned and controlled.
2   The office can be made environmentally superior to any of the smaller offices in the factory.
3   No clerical half-bodies need exist – everybody should be allocated a reasonable day's work.
4   An efficient secretarial service can be established – most typists would not work in an average factory office.
5   Full use can be made of all the modern office furniture and equipment, with economic justification.
6   Adequate training can be given.
7   Job flexibility is possible – staff can be trained to take over two or three other jobs apart from their own.

8.2.2   Factors to be taken into account

Various aspects need to be covered:

a   Communications between the central office and managers wanting its services should be excellent, otherwise there will be a constant demand for 'my own clerk'. If a centralised dictation unit is established, the return of letters and other typed data should be prompt.

b   Extra precautions for soundproofing, vetilation, lighting and heating should be taken. The central office should be equal, if not superior, to the environment of the main office block. If the factory office is seen to be superior in amenities and equipment to the general office, it is far more likely to attract and hold clerks of superior intelligence and ability.

c   The site of the office is very important. It should, if possible, be on the outside of the factory building, with access to natural lighting. Strategically, it should be situated so that there is the least possible travelling distance between the office and the personnel wanting to use its services. A string or movement diagram would assist in establishing the correct location. The junction of the two biggest manufacturing departments might be ideal, with the offices of the shop floor managers close by. The despatch area, too, may be a suitable location.

d   The functions that might be centralised are:

- production planning and control
- stock control
- despatch/consignment
- factory incentive and wages
- general factory administration
- secretarial services for the factory

e   Once a factory is built, the opportunities for establishing an optimum central office are limited. Many of the best sites will be taken up by machinery or other equipment. The problems of factory administrative and secretarial services should, therefore, be considered in the factory design stage.

8.2.3   Data processing and factory offices

Though slow to be introduced, shop floor data-collection terminals are becoming increasingly important for production control and wages payment purposes. They can be operated in two ways. Operatives can use a punched card, plus their own badge, and insert them into a data-collection unit set up by their machines. The second method, often to be preferred for industrial relations reasons, is to set up terminals in a factory office to which production documentation of all kinds can be directed and so input to the computer.

8.3   Outstation offices

Many organisations have problems establishing and maintaining outstation offices, perhaps at considerable distance from the main general office. Regional sales offices, warehouses and depot offices plus technical offices of some kind are all usual.

Once removed from the close supervision which is possible in a large general office, outstation staff will tend to build up their own methods and systems. Control in many instances will be lax. The possibility of peculation will grow. Yet many organisations need outstation offices; their businesses depend upon local sales contacts and order processing. The problem will be determining the degree of autonomy necessary, compared with the strict conformity necessary to ensure rigid cost control.

8.3.1   Factors to be considered

1   Is it possible – or necessary – to have organisation-wide systems and ensure that, through strict auditing procedures, they are maintained?

2   How much local autonomy is required to enable the outstation office to carry out its required function? Would having a standardised system restrict the speed of service that may be necessary?

3   What overall restrictions need to be imposed on the outstation office, e.g. on supplies purchasing, employing staff, obtaining office equipment, etc.?

4   What work can be done centrally that is normally done in the outstation office? Stock recording and sales invoicing could be done by a centrally located computer, for example, or by other data processing equipment.

5   Conversely, it may be worthwhile to set up a devolutionary activity in outstations, complete with minicomputers and other data processing equipment. It may be less costly to have fully staffed outstation units and minimum personnel at head office. This is an organisational problem that each company will treat differently, as costs and service requirements will differ in each case. Figure 8.1 shows most of the major factors to be considered in establishing resources at head office or the periphery of the organisation.

6   Cost control and budgeting will have to be strict for outstation offices. In a sales organisation, for example, it is likely that a comparison of contribution earned per £1 of outstation cost will be a very useful measurement of efficiency.

8.4   Specialist offices

Most organisations have one or even a number of offices occupied by specialists of various kinds. These people are often a 'law unto themselves' in the view of the general clerical workforce. These offices housing management services, draughtsmen, or technicians of some kind have a common thread of being different from general clerks.

8.4.1   Should they be treated differently?

a   Offices housing specialists need to be established in particular positions in an office building, e.g. drawing offices need north light to give, as far as possible, a shadowless environment. The position of the office must therefore be appropriate.

b   Equipment may require special one-off adaption – light fittings, windows, sound insulation, etc. In a drawing office, for example, the following equipment may now be necessary:
   • computer terminals for graphics display and computerised design
   • microfilm equipment with processing cameras and storage for drawings on aperture cards
   • dyeline printers

Figure 8.1 *Resource utilisation*

Head Office	Outstation
1 Standardisation of systems, probably with commensurate savings.	1 Flexibility and service likely to be enhanced.
2 Empire-building will be limited or at least under the control of main administrators.	2 Job satisfaction likely to be improved.
3 Cost control likely to be improved. Clerical work measurement possible.	3 Possibility of lower-cost order-processing due to lower overheads.
4 Use of expensive equipment probably better justified (computers, photocopiers, etc).	4 Senior personnel, if good, can probably provide a more efficient service than in head office.
5 Use of better-qualified personnel possible.	5 Speed of recording may be faster. Better chance of records being up to date.
6 Stock control easier if all depot stocks and sales can be amalgamated for forecasting purposes.	6 Visual impact of out-of-course events likely to be better than at head office. Less need for control over possible faults, delays, etc.
7 Less possiblity of collusion with local suppliers, customers, etc.	7 Knowledge of local customers and suppliers will avoid having to carry some records.
8 Specialisation possible.	8 Messages can be handled by telephone and personal contact. Communications will be much easier, saving paper work.

- drafting stands and posture chairs
- reference tables
- various storage units

c Normal staff control procedures may not apply, e.g. standard clerical work measurement is inappropriate for draughtsmen. However, some adapted form may suit them, but this will need to be a separate development, specially designed for the purposes. In the case of management services, project control may have to be rigorously applied and not day-by-day or hour-by-hour work measurement.

d Discipline may, of necessity, be less rigorous than in, for example, the accounts department. This may cause resentment among the general workforce. Despite their technical quality, management services or specialist personnel should not be seen to idle their time away, while others are working hard.

e It is often necessary for specialists to be slightly non-conformist in their approach to work. In a period of time when conventions of all kinds no longer apply, the unconventional specialist may go unnoticed. Specialists do occasionally work long and inconvenient hours (less so than at one time) and some relaxation in dress and even behaviour may be permissable in consequence.

8.4.2   Separate development – how far should it be taken?

1 Senior office administrators need to consider specialist offices carefully. Individualism can be taken too far, but without some individualists, expertise may be missing in the organisation.

2 Specialists, however, should still be expected to give an appropriate return to the company. Allowing non-conformity must not mean abrogation of work control, either in quality or quantity.

3 What rules should specialist personnel conform to?

  ● *Time-keeping* – within reason specialist personnel should report to work on time. Time off in lieu of overtime pay may be permissable.

  ● *Normal company rules* concerning holidays, absence and sick leave should be obeyed.

  ● *Status rules* – if these exist – should be followed. It may be comparatively easy to allocate a higher status than is warranted, purely to decrease the turnover of specialists. This should be restricted.

  ● *Salary, promotion and job evaluation* should all follow company practice. Payment for specialist knowledge should be given where necessary, if supply and demand dictate, but such payment should be known and separated from evaluated salary levels.

  ● *Use of company facilities,* such as cars, should not be abused.

  ● *Discipline* generally should be good.

8.4.3   Office design

Specialist offices will need equipment and fittings appropriate to their function, which should be provided with the specialists' guidance. Otherwise such offices should not have furniture and equipment not normally found in general offices, e.g. furniture should not be provided for personnel whose status does not allow it, and separate telephones should not be provided for those whose work does not require them.

The standard of a specialist office should be comparable with general offices in the organisation. The level of sevices should be comparable – lifts, lavatories, vending machines, etc. General office equipment – desks, chairs, filing equipment – should be of the same standard as that used elsewhere in the organisation.

Space usage should be the same. The standard floor area per person should be the same for all administrative personnel.

8.4.4   Conclusion

Employment of specialist personnel often causes resentment among general employees. The former's status is often higher, they are often paid more, their privileges seem to be greater. Offices for computer personnel, for example, have often been superior to those of general clerical personnel. There is no reason for this. One standard should prevail throughout the organisation.

Specialist offices should not arouse envy. They should be considered – by everyone in the organisation – as neither more nor less superior than any non-specialist office.

Part Two

People in Offices

Nine

The People Environment

9.1 Introduction

People are difficult. They tend not to behave like machines, which on the press of a button will perform repetitive and often boring tasks extremely accurately. Some managers still believe – secretly perhaps – that replacing people by machines is a good thing. A machine does not answer back. Certainly from experience, investment in machinery of some kind has often been seen by the decision-makers as a means of getting round the people problem.

Most managers, hopefully a large majority, identify with the organisation for which they work. They have status and what the sociologists call social honour – the prestige of carrying out a particular job. It is not just how much money people make, but what they have to do to make it and how confident they can be that their level of earnings will be maintained. For individuals at more lowly levels, the situation is different. Social honour may not be theirs. Yet they are individuals, concerned with their own lives.

There is a good deal of F.W. Taylor left in some managers. Workers are seen as individual machine-like units. If the methods of work can be improved, if payment can be directly related to reward and if the work environment can be made so that it distracts as little as possible from the tasks to be performed, then the worker will give as much as possible.

It seems curious therefore, that while we all view ourselves as being unique in some way, senior management can view their employees as belonging to a team. The members of the team all respond to the same stimuli and consequently appear to have the same psychological characteristics. Little wonder that many managers, especially those in industry, can recount numerous occasions when their employees have behaved in a way that seems illogical and occasionally obstructive to the organisation that has treated them well, paid them regularly at a rate as good as most companies or organisations in the area.

This chapter is concerned with analysing relationships and the conflict they can bring within an organisation between individuals and their peer groups, managers and their employees, the 'amorphous organisation' and those who work for it.

Conflict may not necessarily be harmful. Indeed there are some behavioural scientists who positively endorse it. It may help to keep organisations on their toes, and responsive to social and economic pressures, which organisations with less conflict may not discern and so consequently decline.

9.2 Why conflict arises

What is conflict? An obvious answer is that it is any situation where there is a struggle between two or more contending parties. It is often a trial of strength between groups using or wanting to use the same resources for different objectives. The conflict between increased pay and increases in profit (or lower rates in local government), is a good example. A strike is only one manifestation of conflict that could be going on all the time but only rarely erupts into a physical confrontation.

Discussion and argument are common in a conflict where people are in contention. Non-cooperation or a failure to 'do one's best' is often more difficult to discern. The local government employee who feels upset about his working conditions, and consequently fails to complete any task in a reasonable time, is in conflict not just with his senior management, but also the employer who ultimately pays his salary, i.e. the ratepayer.

What then are the main causes of conflict or poor relationships of this kind?

9.2.1 The outside world

It really needs little explaining that many of the problems which an office manager faces are none of his doing. If society as a whole generates views and opinions contrary to the good running and work disciplines required in an administrative activity, then the manager's task in achieving results is made many times more difficult than it needs to be.

If the nation has lost its 'work ethic', then it will be very difficult – but not impossible – for a manager to recreate it within his own organisation. If the people about to retire say that things are not what they were, that could be true. No organisation can remain isolated from the world outside the door, from the educational system from which new recruits are drawn, from the people who buy its products and, above all, the influences on the need for people to work.

9.2.2 People as machines

People can be seen as units of production, as a resource that can be manipulated to achieve an end that the company wants. This was the view of F.W. Taylor, the American founder of the time study method of motivation.

Taylor's work convinced him that people could be motivated in a machine-like way and be paid to behave in this way. How true is this? Is labour a 'commodity', as many economists suggest? When most senior managers believe that they work for 'self-fulfilment' and 'not for pay', why should their employees be different? Is there a dividing line between those who work because they like to and others who have to be dragooned into working at all?

The generalisation that people have to be made or perhaps bribed to work gains strength from the clamour for high wages, but is somewhat refuted by the consistently high number of people who, from opinion polls, think a national incomes policy is necessary.

If managers see their workforce as machine resource units while they themselves are somehow different, is it possible that the two sides will gradually assume these suppositions are true? The labels will stick. A gulf in attitudes will emerge.

9.2.3 The group view

The mechanistic view of people expressed in Section 9.2.2 seems likely to reduce the personal contact between employees and managers. As a result social relationships at work tend to be confined to the people who share the same economic and social values and who have probably had the same education. To speak of class may sound anachronistic, but where a body of people have similar interests, social experiences, traditions and value systems, almost inevitably it polarises views and opinions and hardens any putative 'them and us' attitudes.

As more and more of the senior positions in an organisation are taken up by those who have gone to university or business school or are a member of a profession, the promotion ladder for many relatively unqualified people has been kicked away, irrespective of innate ability. The days when a lab boy could work his way to the top of the company seem over for ever.

With avenues to promotion closed off, some employees are bound to feel frustrated, unrewarded, pushed aside, for some who have had better chances. The group will find a ready leader in the disillusioned and rejected. Blue-collar workers have rarely had the opportunity to climb to a manager's job. The same is now happening to white-collar personnel, the result being that militancy is no longer a blue-collar preserve.

9.2.4 Status

There is much evidence to show that, while many people in industry or elsewhere earn high wages, often much higher than managers, they still resent their occupation and the way they earn their pay. Status is something that is accorded to a job that has prestige in the eyes of others. A degree of deference is also involved. The people who do jobs with status – airline pilots, doctors (though possibly becoming less so), scientists, senior lawyers – have 'social honour', which is more often than not denied to many people who work in 'lesser' occupations. Increased earnings, more liberal employment policies, better working conditions, have not fundamentally improved the status, say, of office workers, how they see themselves and how others regard them.

Hence the apparent need to flex industrial muscle to ensure that management does notice them and take heed of what they say. Most people want to be considered when actions or decisions affecting their lives are being taken.

9.2.5　Relative deprivation

It seems curious, but in practice true, that wage rates or status or even working conditions to some extent only appear to be inferior when compared with something better. Trade unions have definite views about comparability and during the wage round the 'going rate' is frequently used as the basis for pay claims, irrespective of all other considerations, including the organisation's ability to pay.

Whenever people feel that, compared with others, especially one group with another, they are relatively worse off, they will feel ill-disposed, irrespective of the overall standard of living or working conditions. It is the comparison with others that causes dissension and conflict.

9.2.6　Objectives

The company and employees may in practice have only one objective in common – that the company survives and if possible prospers. For employees, the key objective (as determined by many surveys) is, first and foremost, job security, then secondly steady if not high wages.

For the company profit is always high on the list, perhaps overtaken on occasions by a positive cash flow. Efficiency and productivity are stepping-stone objectives so that profit or cash can be generated. Making profit may not be anathema to employees – how it is shared out certainly could be. The dichotomy in objectives, therefore, is often a major cause of conflict.

9.2.7　The division of labour and the nature of work

Modern industrial society, through its need to be efficient, has established methods of production, administration and distribution where there is intense division of labour. This seems to push individuals inexorably into patterns of relationships with supervisors and managers that must produce some alienation, antagonism and a feeling of solidarity with fellow-workers.

What is alienation? Karl Marx suggested that capitalism has forced workers to become separated or estranged from work, their colleagues and their true selves. A worker is no longer in control of his own life as he was before capitalism emerged. This may be political nonsense, but there is truth in the assumption that for many work is monotonous and unrewarding.

9.3   Lessening conflict

With society generally having an all-pervading influence, how can conflict be lessened? It is doubtful if it can be eliminated completely. What solutions then can be offered to solve the 'people problem'? Many other parts of this book will provide some solutions, e.g. job study is likely to help with relative deprivation; communications and industrial relations may help with morale and objectives problems.

The behavourist's approach is often quoted as one solution to conflict containment. Industrial psychologists have been keen to propogate the theories of Herzberg, Maslow and McGregor. The phase seems to be dying somewhat but still seems important. For many office managers the problem can be partly solved by structuring the relationship between management and employees. It seems possible to set out the relationship in an employee's handbook, where the 'rules of the game' are firmly stated. Sticking to these rules may only delay conflict, but at least people will see what is expected of them and what can be anticipated from management. This must be an improvement on the unknown.

9.4   Legislation and the employees' handbook

The flood of legislation in the last decade or so has given employees many more rights than they have previously had, and employers the headache of many more duties than they have ever had to carry out.

It is strongly recommended that the various pieces of legislation and how they affect duties and responsibilities are set out in a 'staff handbook', which should have four purposes:

1   To define employees' rights under the legislation and other aspects covering their employment.
2   To establish, in part, the responsibilities of local supervision and management and how they can handle local working conditions.
3   To help eliminate the need for a major personnel function in the organisation, thus allowing local management to carry out joint consultation.
4   To help eliminate the various niggling disputes that lower morale, cause dissension and perhaps a major industrial relations crisis.

In an increasingly complicated world, made no easier by the Government defining rights and responsibilities, a structure or policy framework within which industrial relations and manager-worker relationships can be fostered is needed. A 'policy document' should become a means for avoiding conflict. It should embody a 'code of practice' for industrial relations.

9.5   A staff-employees' handbook – general contents

Section 1 – Preamble

The organistional viewpoint on industrial relations and employment should be expressed in general terms along with perhaps a brief history of the company.

Section 2 – General working conditions

Under this heading the normal or even prosaic employment conditions might be recorded:

- Training, internal and out-of-company possibilities, including day-release for approved courses.
- Staff grading and whether grades have any effect on how salaries are paid, and other conditions.
- Parking of cars – often a bone of contention.
- Time recording – time clocks are still in vogue.
- Private telephone calls.
- Confidential information – signing a secrecy agreement is often useful, but it will not stop some people from betraying company secrets.
- Company's property – permission to search employees is a safeguard that should be recorded.
- Sports and social clubs – who can join and what happens when they do.
- Suggestion schemes and payment for suggestions, with a statement that suggestions should have some real benefit to the company.
- Change of address – the need to report if this has taken place.
- Leaving – employment contracts or merely periods of notice might apply.

Section 3 – Health and safety

Many of the policies, procedures, rules and general statements made in Chapter 3 should be recorded.

Section 4 – Conditions of employment

Some personnel, especially management-grade employees, may need to have 'personalised' contracts of employment, but for the majority a standard contract will suffice. This should include the following:

- Hours of work – lateness and its consequences might be stressed.
- Payment, especially payment or non-payment for overtime or shift premium.
- Holiday entitlement, including public holidays and what extra payment or time off in lieu is possible if public holidays are worked.

- Staff pension scheme if one exists.
- Time off for public duties.
- Sickness and entitlement to sick pay and for how long – the importance of doctor's certificates and when these are needed, if at all (self-certification has now been introduced), should be recorded.
- Absence from work – when permission is required for specific reasons.

Section 5 – Industrial relations and security of employment

This section plus the next two should set the minimum legal rights of employees, and the circumstances in which local agreements might have improved on legislation.

Sex Discrimination Act 1975   An affirmation that no one will be treated either favourably or unfavourably on grounds of sex or marital status, except where sex is a genuine occupational qualification. Favourable treatment to pregnant women might be stated.

Equal Pay Act 1970   Men and women employed on like employment or work rated in some way as equal shall be treated equally in terms of conditions of service and pay.

Employment Protection (Consolidation) Act 1978   The minimum rights under this Act should be stressed for all employees, including those working part-time.

Guaranteed pay   If an employee is not provided with work for the whole of the normal day he will be entitled to pay not exceeding five days in any calendar quarter at a rate laid down in the Employment Protection (Consolidation) Act, providing the person concerned is available and willing to work at any tasks provided. A refusal to do alternative work will result in no payment being made.

Maternity   A person shall not be dismissed for reasons of pregnancy unless she cannot do her normal work. She will be given six weeks' maternity pay if she continues to be employed until 11 weeks before the expected confinement, and has two years' continuous service. If she complies with these conditions she will have a right to return to her job within 29 weeks of her confinement.

Trade union membership and activities   Employees have a right to join a trade union and take part in union activities.

Time off   Employees are allowed reasonable time off with pay during normal working hours for trade union duties – either as an official or lay member, but not for carrying out industrial action. Time off is also allowed for employees to carry out public duties and to look for work when made redundant.

Dismissals Employees are entitled to a written statement setting out the reasons for a dismissal.

Section 6 – A disciplinary code of practice

The Advisory, Conciliation and Arbitration Service (ACAS) was empowered by the Employment Protection Act to issue codes of practice containing guidelines to both employers and trade unions for the purpose of improving industrial relations. A draft code of practice resulted which gives a very good indication of how employers might draw up disciplinary procedures within their organisation.

The *Contracts of Employment Act 1972,* as amended by the *Employment Protection (Consolidation) Act 1975,* requires employers to provide written information about certain aspects of disciplinary procedures. This is particularly important as the way discipline is enforced or how a dismissal has been carried out can be brought before an industrial tribunal by the aggrieved employee. Where it is found that a dismissal is unfair, the employee must either be reinstated or compensation (often considerable) has to be paid.

The disciplinary procedures, therefore, need to be specific and agreed with the local trade union. They must obviously be in writing and directed towards achieving a speedy resolution of any breach of discipline. The steps in carrying out the procedure should be clear-cut.

Which levels of management have authority to take disciplinary action should be stated, e.g. it is not normal practice for supervisor-grade personnel to be able to dismiss an employee for whatever reason, without reference to senior management.

Normally an employee who is subject to a disciplinary procedure will be allowed to hear the evidence against him and to state his own position. The employee's trade union representative will usually be present at such hearings. Except for gross misconduct, it is not normal practice for an employee to be dismissed for a first offence. A 'warning', perhaps verbal, initially, or written in moderately important cases, will be required. Once a written warning has been issued dismissal can follow. A written warning in the guise of a re-issued general instruction has been proved to be sufficient.

Rights of appeal are normal in severe disciplinary cases when local permanent trade union officials may be present. The case should be carefully investigated and sustainable proof of guilt is essential. Explanation of penalties is proper.

As in road accidents, management must acquire as much irrefutable evidence as possible. Industrial tribunals are usually impressed with documentation that seems to prove conclusively that discipline has been breached. Copies of written warnings containing a statement that recurrence will lead to suspension, if not dismissal, are necessary.

An industrial tribunal will usually look for 'reasonableness' in any case brought before it. For example, the employee's past record should be taken into account and whether it appears that there is any chance of victimisation.

Disciplinary proceedings involving trade union officials, e.g. shop stewards, can be dangerous. If the local trade union considers the case to be an attack on the union in general, a dispute may arise. Beyond a verbal warning, no disciplinary action should be taken without a senior trade union representative or full-time official being present.

Records of all verbal and written warnings should be made. Details of the offence, whether an appeal was lodged and subsequent developments are required, if only to present evidence at an industrial tribunal.

Occasionally, when gross misconduct has taken place, it is prudent to suspend an employee provisionally, with the understanding that the suspension period will be paid for if the subsequent investigation proves that the person suspended was penalised unjustly. Gross misconduct is normally construed as theft, assault, wilful damage or, in some circumstances, refusal to obey a legitimate request.

The penalty for offences that have been proved to the satisfaction of management and trade unions should vary with the evidence available, the past record of the person involved and the nature of the breach of discipline.

Any action taken outside the company which will be the subject of police proceedings, such as theft or unprovoked assault, deserves dismissal. Other actions, such as failure to carry out agreed and well known business procedures, or to do a job 'properly', might be treated more leniently if the offender is not persistent.

Section 7 – Grievance procedures

It seems important that employees have, and fully support, a grievance procedure through which they can approach senior management with problems that they believe cannot be handled by their local supervisors. The various stages that could be accepted are:

- *Stage 1* Employee should discuss his problem with his local supervisor. If the problem is not resolved, employee contacts his union representative.
- *Stages 2 and 3* Union representative and employee discuss problem with local supervisor. If no resolution is found within, say, two working days the local supervisor contacts the employee relations manager and the employee the union branch office.
- *Stage 4* Further meeting between management and union, but this time the employee relations manager and the union branch official will attend.
- *Stage 5* If the problem cannot be resolved within ten days, the union side should contact their district officer, or permanent official, and a further meeting called.

If the problem has not been solved, the grievance procedure will have been exhausted. No industrial action should take place until the full grievance procedure has been exhausted.

9.6   Further reading

1   K. Hawkins, *Conflict and Change – aspects of industrial relations*, Holt, Rinehart and Winston (1974).
2   R.L. Kahan and E. Boulding (Editors), *Power and Conflict in Organisations*, Tavistock (1972).
3   R. Schacht, *Alienation*, Allen & Unwin (1971).
4   S. Terkel, *Working*, Wildwood (1975).
5   Aims of Industry, *Reds Under the Bed* (1974).
6   R. Hyman, *Strikes*, Fontana (1972).
7   A. Kakabadse, *Alienation at Work*, Gower (1981).
8   K. Davis, *Human Behaviour at Work*, McGraw-Hill (Sixth edition, 1981).
9   E.M. Wilson, O.D. Jones and D. Golding, *People and Employment*, Butterworth (1981).
10   'On human relations', *Havard Business Review*, Heinemann (1979).
11   M. Taylor Coverdale, *On Management*, Heinemann (1979).
12   D. Biddle and R. Evenden, *Human Aspects of Management*, IPM (1980).
13   G. Thomason, *A Textbook of Personnel Management*, IPM (1978).

Ten

The Role of the Office Manager and Supervisor

10.1 Introduction

What a manager and his function is has been the subject of management textbooks since 'scientific management' was first recorded. I have written previously that the role of a manager is to measure, plan, motivate and control the resources he has in order to achieve whatever corporate goals he has been given or at least agreed to.

This might seem an over-simplification, especially in these difficult times. It is necessary to introduce another concept to explore the matter further – that of 'authority, responsibility and power'.

10.2 The basic principles

10.2.1 Measurement

Any manager should measure the actions, activities, functions and departments for which he has responsibility. In a sales order processing activity he should be aware of:

- numbers of orders handled per day
- numbers of orders not completed within one/two/three days
- the value of orders
- number of people
- number of orders handled by each person
- cost of handling

These are fairly basic measurements by which the manager should be able to judge the effectiveness/value of the sales order processing activity.

10.2.2 Plan

Planning either on a short-, medium- or long-term basis is an essential element in the manager's role. In the short term he may be concerned with organising his available labour force to achieve the daily order flow. In the medium and long term he could be concerned with training or succession plans, or the use of data processing equipment of some kind.

A plan assumes that objectives will be set as a precursor to the planning process.

10.2.3   Motivate

Either in his role as leader, through cooperation, or by his authority, a manager must be able to motivate his workforce to achieve the plans he has set them. (Motivation is discussed in Chapter 12.)

10.2.4   Control

Once plans have been made, they need to be monitored. 'Control' envisages that a comparison of actual performance with the original plan will be carried out, and corrective action instituted if the plan is not being achieved.

10.3   Management's role

The four basic principles in Section 10.2 are by far the most important parts of the manager's role. Any other activity he is asked to carry out should be judged against these principles:

- Do they aid them?
- Could the manager spend his time in a better way?
- Is value being obtained from time spent?
- Could the manager's work routine be altered so the principles could be followed more closely?

Too often, in practice, a manager will take on duties that are in no way connected with his role. Opening the post, or serving on a committee that helps some other function, is common in many organisations. These activities should be stopped or at least delegated.

10.4   Power, authority and responsibility

It would be wrong not to highlight the most important element in the manager's role and why this could, and in practice often does, lead to frustration, disillusionment and eventually conflict. Three words sum up the situation:

- *Power* – defined as the means of ensuring that people do what is required whether they want to or not.
- *Authority* – the legislation of certain rights or roles, especially in the use of 'power'.

■ *Responsibility* – accountability – answerable for the achievement of certain actions and goals.

These three words seem to encapsulate the dilemma in which many managers find themselves. Power, as defined, is practically non-existent in some areas or activities. Trade unions are too strong. People need to be consulted before actions are taken. Orders have been changed to requests.

In these circumstances, 'authority' may have a hollow ring. The responsibility or accountability for achieving certain goals may not carry the requisite power or need the necessary authority. Managers should analyse their position and determine what responsibilities they have been given and accepted and how far their power and authority allow them to achieve their responsibilities. This should provide a fruitful basis for establishing the limits of their role.

10.5   The supervisor's role

The position of the office supervisor, like his counterpart on the shop floor, is often an invidious one. For example, he will usually have a clash of loyalties.

Loyalty to management   The supervisor will have to:

a   Understand local objectives and how they affect his group. While appreciating the constraints implicit in the objectives, they need to be achieved as far as possible.
b   Allow full and complete discussion of any new objectives proposed.
c   Ensure that the personnel he supervises are loyal and efficient.
d   Maintain cooperation between himself and his staff so as to institute change at any time.
e   Keep management informed at all times of his group's views and opinions if they impinge on either the short- or long-term achievement of corporate objectives.

Loyalty to the group   In having loyalty to the group, the supervisor:

1   Organises and plans the group's work so that it is a cohesive and efficient whole that operates with the minimum of disruption and friction.
2   Ensures that his group is recognised and give status appropriate to the tasks is performs.
3   Establishes, if necessary, an organisational structure which ensures that the group has status and job opportunities equal to other groups.
4   Ensures that the objectives which the group is asked to achieve are fair and reasonable.
5   Tries to establish the best pay and environmental conditions for the group which the total organisation can provide.

6   Includes the group – as far as he can – in decision-making that affects them.
7   Establishes a group-discipline which ensures that group backing will be readily obtained for disciplinary procedures. Similarly, he must have group support for merit rewards and promotion.
8   Assumes that he is a member of the group – but with special duties. He must not consider that he is outside the group.
9   Always gives time for the group to express grievances about company policy, ensuring that a two-way exchange of views, opinions and ideas operates.

Loyalty to individuals   The supervisor should:

a   Ensure that the objectives which individuals are asked to achieve are reasonable, fair and within their competence.
b   Be aware of each individual's strengths and weaknesses, utilising such knowledge to build on strengths and eliminate weaknesses.
c   Develop individuals to their maximum potential. To do this their potential should be assessed and a development programme, especially training, be devised to suit each individual.
d   Ensure that merit rewards are seen to be fairly given.
e   Make sure that each individual always knows what to do. The supervisor must indicate the work which is expected (both volume and quantity) and explain, as far as possible, how the job should be carried out.
f   Rotate individual's tasks so that they obtain maximum experience and training.
g   Handle disciplinary matters promptly, giving the individual every opportunity to make his case and proceeding only when there is irrefutable evidence.

Managers should realise that supervisors are not managers – their situations are often very different. The supervisor:

1   Has minute-by-minute contact with the workforce. He is the first to feel its resentment when things go wrong and is not cushioned by a private office or some other status barrier.
2   Needs to reconcile his loyalties between management, individuals and the group he controls. A supervisor needs the group's trust and loyalty, far more than a manager does, if he is to fulfil his functions properly.
2   Makes few, if any, major policy decisions. He tends to interpret policy not make it.
4   Has pay and conditions often dissimilar to that of a manager.

10.6   Further reading

1   J. Adair, *Training for Leadership,* Gower (1978).

2 J. Adair, *Training for Decisions,* Gower (1978).
3 A. Adamson, *The Effective Leader,* Pitman (1971).
4 R.L. Bentin, *Supervision and Management,* McGraw-Hill (1972).
5 J. Adair, *Action-centred Leadership,* Gower (1979).
6 T. Boydell and M. Pedlar, *Management Self-developer,* Gower (1980).
7 R.E. Tannehill, *Motivation and Management Development,* Butterworth (1978).
8 G. Hinrichs, *Motivation – winding down and turning off,* AMA (1978).
9 P. Drucker, *Management – tasks, responsibilities and practices, Heinemann (1976).*
10 J.R. White, *Successful Supervision,* McGraw-Hill (1975).
11 A. Sartain and A.W. Baker, *The Supervisor and the Job,* McGraw-Hill (Third edition, 1978).
12 H. Koontz, C. O'Donnell and H. Weihrich, *Essentials of Management,* McGraw-Hill (1981).

Eleven

Work Organisation

11.1 Introduction

The neat little boxes and lines of command shown on many organisation charts seldom reflect the truth as it is at ground level. Status is rarely equal. One person has a greater say in what decisions are made, on the committees which are formed and on attitudes that permeate the organisation. The rest – apparent equals – accept leadership.

Organisation is the formal way a company projects job responsibilities and the interrelationship and communication between the members of the company having the job responsibilities.

Organisation is the arrangement that should secure the participation and cooperation of all members of a company so that corporate objectives are achieved. It should have a linking effect on everyone's efforts to secure corporate objectives.

The basis of organisational planning is matching the company's organisation, competence and capacity to the environment in which it has to operate in order to survive. This indicates, rightly, that an organisation must be constantly changing in order to meet the challenge of technological, competitive and general environmental change. But first of all some fallacies and comments.

11.1.1 Line and staff organisation

Various organisational maxims have become enshrined in the theory of the subject. One of these is the line and staff organisation. Line organisations, it was said, were based on military precepts with separate departments commanded by line managers. Managers would be non-specialist and support was to be provided by staff personnel, each of whom would be a specialist in some field. Figure 11.1 shows such an organisation. The advantages of such divisions of responsibility were that strict ranking was

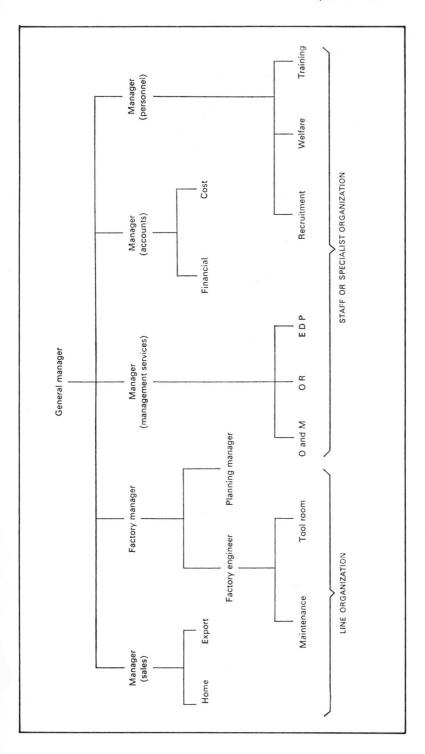

Figure 11.1 *Line and staff organisation chart*

possible, delegating authority was easy and the chain of command usually clear and well established.

With rapid technological and managerial changes – techniques for example – this kind of organisational division is quickly becoming obsolete. The line managers – if that is what they are still to be called – need the assistance of specialist staff almost constantly. The interchange between 'line' and 'staff' is taking place more often. No longer can a line manager claim that he has no specialist knowledge and still hope to retain his job. The terms line and staff are, therefore, an anachronism and the sooner they are dropped the better.

11.1.2 Functionally based units

The functionally based unit of management is rapidly gaining favour. In this type of organisation managers control a particular function in the company which is usually largely autonomous. The advantages of functionally based units are that line and staff are integrated into one unit where the specialists are constantly available to support the non-specialists. However, responsibility is often diffused and indeterminate lines of command may cause frustration. Figure 11.2 shows such an organisation.

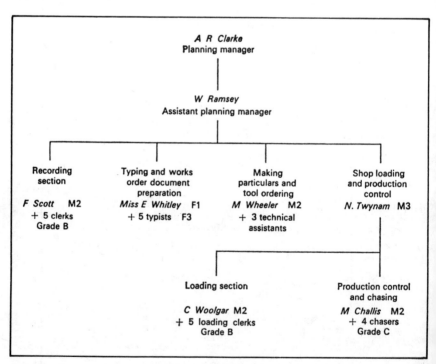

Figure 11.2 *Functional organisation chart for a profit-planning and control office*

11.1.3 Span of control

This concept was a favourite of early organisation theorists who suggested variously that 5 to 10 or, perhaps, 15 subordinates were the maximum that should report to a supervisor or manager. The duties or responsibilities that were being carried apparently had no influence on the decision. But, of course, this is the crucial factor in span-of-control considerations – a senior manager may be overburdened with 4 junior managers reporting to him; but a supervisor in charge of a football-pool vetting operation may find 40 clerks reporting to him are too few.

11.1.4 Centralisation and decentralisation

This subject too has caused considerable anguish to organisational theorists. The trend in the last decade has been towards decentralised units, but now seems to be somewhat the reverse. Decentralisation was thought to improve local decision-making – as the manager on the spot knew best. As a result morale was supposed to be higher, span-of-control and communications problems were minimal.

In an age of increasing specialisation, local autonomy has often failed to produce reasonable results. When no specialist assistance is available local decision-making is probably no better than can be achieved centrally. Now that increasingly difficult decisions have to be made, autonomy of the kind that complete decentralisation has engendered is often wrong.

11.1.5 Committee organisation

This has long been an anathema to many theorists. It chokes decision-making, managers can hide their responsibilities behind its cloak and it produces anonymity and time-wasting, or so it is said. It is only now being realised that committees play a vital role in establishing a battleground on which managers can fight out their prejudices. If managers must play behavioural games, then a committee is as good a place as any in which to do so. Problems arise when one or two strong personalities combine to dominate the committee and decision-making becomes warped in consequence.

These dangers are real, but not to have a battlefield is probably just as dangerous.

11.1.6 Our organisation is right because it is our organisation

This perhaps is the greatest fallacy of all. It infers that the present organisational methods have grown with the company, personnel are used to them, they have been adapted over the years and seem to suit the situation, therefore the current organisation must be right.

It is not surprising that many companies are warped in favour of strong managers or because someone once had an idea which, at the time, was appropriate, but is no longer. A company's appropriateness is constantly being eroded by new managers of different calibre to the old, by new technological factors and by market and product changes.

11.2   Hierarchies

Traditionally most, if not all, organisations have operated on a hierarchical basis. The organisation has steps with increased status and, perhaps, authority at each. In reality the power of trade unions and the workforce generally has proved that the hierarchy is often a sham, with its members having only a moderate amount of power

11.3   Managers and the organisation

With the passing of the cruder forms of motivation, such as the threat of dismissal, the manager, to be effective, has been forced back onto his own ability as a leader and motivator. His ability in ensuring that his staff perform well and appropriately is often of much greater importance than his knowledge of a specialist activity.

There is a distinct interrelationship between the performance required by the organisation, the needs of the group, and of the individual within the group. The first-line supervisor often has difficulty in discerning his loyalty to each party to the relationship.

The interaction between group, individual and performance demands leadership which ensures that performance is achieved, while the group and individual achieve in a large part their own objectives. A manager therefore must be able to:

a   Clarify objective and performance requirements in such a way that his subordinates may relate to them.
b   Plan to achieve a good performance with the resources he either has or can justify.
c   Keep within the company style and management methods which are implicit in his organisation and also his authority.
d   Ensure that he has sufficient monitoring procedures to know whether he is achieving an appropriate performance or not.
e   Organise his workforce and their job responsibilities to ensure his objectives are achieved.
f   Establish key results so as to concentrate primarily on those things that really matter.
g   Eschew technical considerations as far as possible, and concentrate on his leadership role.

11.4   Groups

The term group is used where a number of people have either voluntarily or involuntarily come together to achieve a common goal. Membership of the group is usually dependent upon the individual accepting the group's norms or standards. People join groups for several reasons – to provide security being one of the main ones (witness the rush of junior managers to join a trade union when redundancy threatens). Others include dependency, reinforcement of prejudice and self-identity.

Decisions made by groups do not always reflect the common views of all the group. 'Group think' can suppress dissent. One or two articulate people can become group leaders. Groups are not always good at solving problems. Personal doubts of knowledgeable individuals are often suppressed to achieve group loyalty. Discussion is limited to the knowledge of the individuals comprising the group. Opinion leaders often dominate discussion to the group's detriment

11.4.1 Group jobs

The term 'group dynamics' is widely used to describe behaviour and how it might be influenced. A major part of a manager's job in the future might be considering the group or groups he leads and determining how 'group dynamics' can be used to improve group performance. One important aspect in considering groups is the design of 'group jobs'. One way in which effectiveness might be increased is by creating group jobs with more rather than less autonomy.

The job design might begin with job allocation and job rotation, both of which could be put into the hands of the group. Output levels are often already in the hands of the group who restrict them to achieve a group norm. Perhaps allowing groups to set these norms openly might be beneficial.

Establishing manning levels and related pay could be another role which the group rather than the manager might undertake. The group's composition might also be agreed by the group. Hours of work is another subject over which the group might have jurisdiction. Work allocation and how it can be carried out could be the ultimate in local group autonomy.

11.4.2 Manager's and group's role

It is perhaps the role of first-line supervision that will change most if more autonomy is given to working groups. Some, if not most, of the traditional roles that the supervisor has played could be taken away. This is the problem of giving job enrichment to one group and not to another.

It is likely, therefore, that managers will need to become supportive rather than issuing commands as in a conventional hierarchy. The supervisor might become an elected team leader. The manager must still manage the group, however. He should be aware of the group's:

- personality – its standards of behaviour, attitude towards perform-ance and the wider organisation

- morale
- efficiency
- needs
- size and effectiveness

Even with the autonomy that might be given to a group, the manager should consider the individuals concerned and:

- tell them how they are performing
- treat them as human beings and be sympathetic towards their personal objectives and problems
- reward them fairly
- explain what is going on in the company to the best of his ability
- attempt to know as much as possible about the work being performed by his group
- accept ideas and listen to suggestions
- give out as much responsibility as possible
- defend his group against the criticism of others
- try to obtain resources for his group
- always praise success

11.5   Further reading

1   A. Adamson, *The Effective Leader,* Pitman (1971).
2   J. Childs (Editor), *Man and Organisation,* Allen & Unwin (1973).
3   L. Davies and J. Taylor, *The Design of Jobs,* Penguin (1972).
4   D. Katz and R.L. Kahn, *The Social Psychology of Organisation,* Wiley (1966).
5   M.J. Leavitt, W.R. Drill and H.B. Eyring, *The Organisation World,* Harcourt, Bruce and Jovanovich (1973).
6   K. Legge and E. Mumford (Editors), *Designing Organisations for Satisfaction and Efficiency,* Gower (1978).
7   R. Stewart, *Choices for the Manager – a guide to managerial work and behaviour,* McGraw-Hill (1982).
8   *Humanisation of Work in Western Europe,* IPM (1979).

Twelve

Motivation

12.1 Introduction

There must be few office managers in recent years who have not bemoaned the fact that their employees no longer seem to be motivated. Perhaps the threat of dismissal might have greater potency now we are in more straightened economic times, but to be able to dismiss without passing through a rigorous sieving process is now nearly impossible. Conversely higher salaries, better working conditions and shorter hours rarely seem to motivate either.

'People are lazy', say the office managers with many years' service. But what is laziness? Slow processing of orders received by the company or failure to take corrective action when something appears to be going wrong? Is there a difference between the quantity and quality of work performed or are both equally disregarded by a 'lazy person'?

There seems to be truth in the contention that many managers tend to look for ways and means of improving output rather than understanding the more fundamental reasons why people work and at what pace. Motivational theory appears to be easy but obviously very difficult to apply, otherwise there would be many more successful examples to discuss.

12.2 Why people work

There seems to be four reasons why people work:

1 Economic necessity If they do not work then their house and car and good life could be forfeited. They might not starve if they do not work, but most of the good things that a capitalist society sees as being necessary – washing machines, colour television sets, central heating – may disappear. It is when these 'necessities' no longer appear to be attractive or the social pressures to buy them diminish that economic necessity to work could wain.

2 Social need There must be many thousands, perhaps millions, of people in the UK who have no real economic need to work. To be slightly chauvanistic, working wives whose husbands already earn enough for economic necessity are one example. Many people past retiring age miss the social relationships that work gave them.

3 *Psychological need*   Work, it has been said, structures the passing of time. For many, it provides the focus for living. Marxists might say that this is merely a capitalist view of work, where work is seen to be a social necessity. Pressure on non-workers is huge. Most unemployed people would appear to want to work rather than sit at home and do nothing with their lives. For many work is its own reward, which is particularly true for scientists or others who gain self-fulfilment from what they do. Writing a book can often bring its own satisfaction as well as the small amount of royalties that occasionally accrue. Work itself can be deeply satisfying psychologically. For many work is a career – witness the dedication of nurses.

4 *Ethical reasons*   What Weber describes as the 'protestant work ethic' is still with us, though it appears to be dying on its feet. Max Weber, a sociologist of course, suggested that capitalism was characterised by the devotion to earning wealth, together with avoidance of the use of it when earned for personal enjoyment. Inflation, a welfare state, and the conspicuous consumption of the latter half of the 20th Century, may have eroded the spirit of capitalism, but not completely.

If any or all these reasons why people work are true, what does it tell the hard-pressed office manager trying to get a little more production from his people? Perhaps the following:

1 *Is money the only motivator?*   The first reason given for people working would indicate that this was true. The young married man, with a house on mortgage, a car on hire purchase and a wife who would like a new freezer, is obviously someone who would like more money and would perhaps work harder to get more. What then of his elder colleague who has paid off his mortgage, has already got two Datsuns in the garage and the biggest colour television now made? Money is obviously not a problem. How is he to be motivated?

Various experiments have been done – the classic being that at the Hawthorne works of the General Electric Company in the USA carried out by Elton Mayo – that tend to prove that money is not the only motivator. Consider some other factors:

■ Most managers would say that an extra £10 or so a week would not get them to work harder – they already work as hard as they can (if the £10 was taken away or if it was given to someone else then the story might be different). So money as such does not motivate.

■ Many people who have won or inherited a lot of money still want to work. Again money seems secondary to some other reason for working.

- There are a whole range of jobs that people will do despite the low wages. Various 'caring' professions, such as social work, tend to attract people who, until recently, had no great wish for a large salary. The nature of the job was sufficient. There are those who have set up self-sufficiency units who will accept few of the benefits of the 20th Century. What little they earn gives a way of life that fully compensates them.
- Anyone who has worked in industry knows well that many British workers do not maximise their earnings. In many, perhaps most, incentive schemes in British factories, the workforce limit the output they are prepared to achieve. There is an accepted pay norm, which few will be prepared to break. Work, often, is a group activity and the group, or group leader, sets the pay limits.
- Overtime, although apparently a British way of life, is often ignored by many people even when it is offered. They are not prepared to trade leisure for the rates of pay being offered.

In many job situations money, therefore, may not be the main motivator in doing a job as well and as quickly as possible. For some people it could be important, often very important, but for others it may only impinge on motivation if they suffer monetary loss compared with others.

2   Social motivation   If people work for reasons other than money (though it may still have some importance) the company will obviously have greater difficulty in motivating them. Despite the immense literature on the subject, designing an incentive scheme based purely on reward for effort is comparatively easy. What happens when, say, middle-aged ladies whose children have grown up and left home decide to go back to work, purely for the social relationships which work brings? Getting them to come to work may be easy – getting them to work effectively is a good deal more difficult. The group obviously has to be called in as a motivational organisation.

3   Hierarchy of needs   It might be useful at this stage to introduce the concept of a hierarchy of needs first formulated as long ago as 1943. Maslow suggested that people's needs change as one need is achieved. For example:

Level 1   At the lowest level people want to survive physically – they need air, water and food. Once these basic requirements have been met, the hierarchy gets a lot more complex.
Level 2   Safety needs predominate. In any organisation this might relate to job security or freedom from job pain.
Level 3   The need to belong. People at this level need affection, praise and friendship.
Level 4   The need for status, prestige, or social honour – to be considered worthy.
Level 5   The need for self-actualisation – the ability to use all their talents and abilities in a creative way.

Money seems to be strangely lacking from the hierarchy. (It is perhaps incidental that a sufficiency of money may allow the satisfaction of all the needs including self-actualisation, if this requires to be divorced from work altogether.)

While a hierarchy of needs, like many psychological assumptions, appears to be crude and theoretical, it does point to the possibility that even if a manager satisfies one need, such as job security, he will be faced in a short time with 'belonging requirements'.

12.3 Motivating people to work

Those who ask, 'How can we get people to work harder?', might start by considering what makes them work as hard as they do. Then ask – what would happen if the well trained, highly educated, highly motivated person who has a job with considerable flexibility and decision-making was suddenly transferred to one which was boringly monotonous with little scope for self-expression or individuality? How long would motivation last?

Herzberg suggests that there are six aspects of work which might improve motivation:

- achievement
- recognition
- advancement
- work itself
- possibility of growth
- responsibility

While many managers will regard 'motivational theory' with considerable scepticism, they may still regard (and perhaps rightly) that laying down precise job duties, agreeing objectives and monitoring results and taking action when achieved, is still the best way. The design of jobs may be important and to motivate they must include, if possible, all the following factors:

a   From beginning to end, a job must have a visable end-result.
b   The job should be completed with as little supervision as possible, preferably none.
c   There should be a performance appraisal that will enable the job holder to match his performance against that required and to know why he failed – if he does.
d   The job should, if possible, be changeable – the same routine should not be followed day after day.
e   The implication of the job and general duties should not be so fully defined as to prevent improvement by the job holder.
f   The job description should be so established that it will be easy to see how it links with everyone else's job in the department, etc.

g   The worker must be given responsibility for a well defined job, tools, equipment, raw materials, etc.

h   He must be given an opportunity to look after and develop other people.

i   If possible, he should be given responsibility to carry out research and development into his job and the wider aspects of the activities he is performing.

j   He should be asked to contribute ideas and thoughts about his job.

k   Pay and other rewards should be related to the results achieved, which should be quantifiable if possible.

l   Promotion should be made on the same basis.

m   Success should always be recognised, never ignored.

12.4   Further reading

1   D.R. Davies and V.J. Shakleton, *Psychology and Work,* Methuen (1975).

2   S.W. Gellerman, *Management and Motivation,* AMA (1968).

3   F. Herzberg, *Work and the Nature of Man,* World Publishing Co. (1966).

4   F. Herzberg, 'One more time – how do you motivate employees?', *Harvard Business Review* (Jan/Feb 1968).

5   F. Herzberg, B. Mausret and B.B. Synderman, *The Motivation to Work,* Wiley (1959).

6   Linda King-Taylor, *Not for Bread Alone,* Business Books (Third edition, 1973).

7   W.J. Paul and K.B. Robertson, *Job Enrichment and Employee Motivation,* Gower (1970).

8   R. Cooper, *Job Motivation and Job Design,* IPM/Prentice Hall (1974).

9   A. Lawler, *Motivation in Work Organisation,* Brooks Cole (1978).

10   W.F. Dowling and L.R. Sayles, *How Managers Motivate,* McGraw-Hill (Second edition, 1978).

Thirteen

Clerical Work Measurement

13.1 Introduction

It is still comparatively rare to find measurement applied as rigorously in an office as it is on the shop floor. In the last 10 years many organisations have attempted serious work measurement, but for various reasons the application has often failed.

The reasons for the lack of clerical output standards seem to be:

1 Most clerical jobs are thought to include too many non-routine elements to justify work measurement of any kind.
2 Office workers are somehow different from shop floor personnel and can be trusted to turn out a reasonable work output without incentives or work controls.
3 The proportion of clerical costs to total factory costs is not high enough to warrant introducing work standards and incentive schemes.
4 The absence of simple and acceptable work measurement techniques that take account of non-routine work has been an excuse for avoiding any of the accepted work measurement methods used on the shop floor.

In many ways these arguments are invalid:

a There are now several techniques that can take account of the non-routine elements in clerical activities. They are usually simple and can be applied by practitioners after a comparatively short training.
b The gap in status and income between factory and office personnel is now all but closed; indeed in many cases the shop floor people are now ahead. Loyalty and good output can no longer be accepted as normal in any office.
c The increasing use of machinery in the office has also created 'factory conditions' where none previously existed. For example, the output from a system copier is as measurable as the production from a lathe.

13.2 Benefits from work measurement

Work measurement can fulfil many useful functions in the office, the following being amongst the most important:

1 It can be used as a control factor to establish manning standards.
2 Once established and accepted, output standards provide data on which to base the need for overtime, or more staff, to handle extra work. Peaks and troughs in the workload can also be highlighted.
3 Workload between clerks can be distributed more equitably.
4 Time-saving by doing jobs in different ways can be assessed. Staff savings can be calculated after certain jobs or job elements have been eliminated.
5 Where realistic output standards are in use it is possible to compare the efficiency of one section or department with another.
6 The need for training and retraining of staff may become apparent when work measurement is applied.
7 Incentives, though they have fallen into some disrepute, can only be applied following work measurement.
8 Budgets of manpower and cost are unlikely to be realistic unless work measurement of some kind has been applied.

13.3 Choice of work measurement technique

Work measurement is 'the systematic determination of the proper time for the effective accomplishment of a defined task carried out by a specified method'. There are numerous techniques that help to achieve this objective. Many are simple but some need extensive training and experience before they can be applied appropriately. Most work measurement techniques have been developed on the shop floor and it can be dangerous to transfer them directly to the office. The choice will depend upon several factors:

a   The confidence of staff in the proposed technique and whether they are being given reasonable output targets.
b   The complexity of the technique and whether the investigator will be capable of applying it efficiently.
c   Whether the technique will provide the information required – whether, in fact, manning standards and output targets can be derived from the data produced.
d   Whether the jobs being investigated lend themselves to strict time study or involve so much non-routine work as to make it invalid.
e   Cost and time of the investigation are pertinent. How long will the study take and how effective will it be when it has been carried out?
f   Many jobs vary in work content and the work measurement technique used should take this into account.
g   The work to be measured has to be in controllable quantities or countable units.

The full range of measurement techniques is given in Figure 13.1. Further descriptions of the techniques are embodied in the text of this chapter.

Type	Self-recording	Activity sampling	Direct time study	Pre-determined motion time studies	Analytical estimating	Corporate estimating	Work scheduling
1 Brief description	Records of output maintained by staff showing total tasks performed and time taken to perform them	Technique of work measurement that uses a large number of observations taken over a long period essentially at random intervals. Each observation records what is happening at precise moment in time it occurs. System operates on the basis of law of probability	A method whereby the rate of work and actual time spent carrying out work is recorded. Actual time usually determined using a stop-watch	A method in which pre-determined times are used to build-up total time for carrying out job elements	A method of work measurement based on the use of knowledge of past practical experience	A method in which required times are found by comparing work content of a job being timed with others which have been previously carefully determined	Method of work control based on issuing work to staff in controlled batches. Records of average product times are taken and used for control purposes
2 Applicability	Clerical activities generally	Any area of job activity which needs broad time study, machine usage, job activity, etc.	Either clerical or manual operations; but particularly where elements can be devised and where there is a large amount of repetition	Both manual and clerical activities where a sound definition and description of work methods is possible			General clerical activities
3 Advantages	Useful at beginning of a clerical measurement assignment when an assessment of work loading and bottlenecks is required. Useful also in confirming job duties and responsibilities	Can quickly give an indication of the effectiveness of work distributed and incidence of idle time, etc. Does not need trained observers	Simple and easy to teach operatives to carry out the study. Can be understood clearly by job operatives. Maximum tion.	Low cost of application, reliable and accurate Consistency between analysts and areas of applica- ability to transfer data between job areas.			Provides a valuable method of control for supervision

but over a period
the situation
tends to average
out.

5 Types - use

union
representatives
nearly inevitable

1 Rated activity
sampling uses
technique set
out above but
a rating factor
is applied to
observations to
enable times at
a defined rate
to be calculated

both limited
and well defined

1 Simplified
predetermined
motion time
studies. A
simplified
version of
PMTS achieved
by reducing
many of the
variables in
original method

2 Basic work data
– a development
of PMTS which
uses minor
elements of
work to build up
times for major
elements. Used
mainly for
maintenance
operations

3 Master clerical
duties – a
method based
on the Birn
Organisation

4 Clerical
milliminute
Data (Clerical
MMI). Devised
by PA
Consultants

5 Clerical work
data. Developed
by BR

1 Universal
maintenance
standards
(Maynards) are
similar

Figure 13.1   *Types of work measurement system*

13.4   Types of work measurement system

13.4.1   The use of past data

Often certain historical records are available that indicate past work performance, e.g. a manager who has kept a record of the daily number of orders his department has handled over the past 10 years. It seems comparatively easy to suggest what productivity the 10 people he employs have achieved. However, each order may have a different work content.

Historical data has doubtful value. If a department has operated at 50 per cent efficiency in the past, using historical data may ensure that it will operate at 50 per cent efficiency in the future.

13.4.2   Simulation

This technique is preferable to using past data. The usual procedure is for the investigator and supervisor together to simulate each of the job elements being investigated. If recording stock transfers is being investigated, for example, the simulation of perhaps 100 or more entries is made and the length of time taken to carry them out recorded. Once a sufficient number of simulations have been undertaken and allowances made for queries and rests, a realistic time/output standard is obtained. But there are weaknesses in this method:

1   Bias by the supervisor may make assessments less than objective – the investigator may be misled.
2   Efficiency which a clerk acquires over the years may improve output standards by 30 to 40 per cent. Simulation may, therefore, tend to overrate the activity being investigated.
3   Many jobs cannot be simulated; the investigator and the supervisor will not have the necessary experience and skill.
4   Staff are usually highly suspicious of output data derived from simulation, especially if the supervisor is not particularly popular. Setting output standards would, therefore, be difficult.

Simulation has often been associated with 'analytical estimating', a technique in which the time required to carry out elements of work is estimated from knowledge and practical experience.

13.4.3   Activity or work sampling

This technique is also referred to as a 'random observation study' or just 'observation study'. Sampling has long been one of the major tools of statisticians and is covered by the law of statistical regularity; a sample taken from a large number will tend to reflect the composition of the larger number. The degree of similarity between the small and large number will depend upon the size and make-up of the sample. It is usually expressed in terms of confidence limits.

The statistical law embodied in activity sampling is used to provide a measurement of activity instead of undertaking long and involved time-study measurements. It is usually applied to departmental or group activity, rarely to an individual or a single machine.

Advantages It can be used comparatively unobtrusively, without the observer having to sit with the group and take continual time-study measurements. It is a useful short-cut in gaining supporting data for detailed study, or as an initial study to see if there is need for a detailed investigation. It quickly and cheaply helps to determine where there is trouble, such as under-employment or machine down time.

Disadvantages If the sample size is inadequate or has been taken at non-random intervals, the data collected can be invalid. In the hands of inexperienced observers the data could then form the basis of completely erroneous conclusions.

The fact that a clerk is at his desk and apparently working could have no bearing on whether his productivity is high or low. Activity sampling in this context cannot prove whether the clerk is working effectively or just coasting.

Factors to be taken into account In taking samples, the following formula can be used to determine the number of samples which need to be taken to conform to specified confidence limits or the theorectical accuracy of the results which will be obtained:

$$L = \sqrt{[P(100 - P)/N]}$$

where P is the percentage of the time observed being taken up in a particular activity, N the total number of random observations on all activities and L the percentage of accuracy of P, plus or minus.

This formula will give 95 per cent confidence limits if applied to a homogeneous population. However, various rule-of-thumb tables have been devised which will help determine the size of the sample needed. The following table appears in *Work Sampling* by R.M. Bàrnes.

Type of work sampling	*Approximate number of observations*
Help determine general objectives (general trouble spots)	100
Help determine specific management objectives (causes of down-time, idle time, etc.)	600
Appraise specific conditions (set-ups, delays)	2,000
Appraise machine utilisation	4,000
Set time standards, determine allowances – up to	10,000

ACTIVITY SAMPLING SHEET

Department ....

Study no.	Study no.	Study no. ....
Study by	Study by	Study by ....
Date	Date	Date ....

Op. no.	I	2	3	4	5	I	2	3	4	5	I	2	3	4	5
I															
2															
3															
4															
5															
38															
39															
40															

RECORD AS FOLLOWS
A—Clerk at desk and working.
B—Clerk at desk and not working.
C—Clerk at desk and discussing.
D—Clerk at desk and on telephone.
E—Clerk not at desk.
F—Clerk not at desk but working.
G—Clerk not at desk and not working.

Figure 13.2 *Activity sampling sheet. Various derivatives of activity sampling have been formulated: sequential activity sampling, non-random sampling, etc.*

A sheet similar to the one shown in Figure 13.2 should be used where all the activities being sampled have been coded so that the observer has only to write a code letter against each of the clerks (who have been numbered 1 to 5).

Observations should be random. This is very important. If the observations are made at regular intervals, the activity in the office will not be a fair sample of the total. The route taken by the observer should also vary, otherwise he will get biased results – staff will know when he is coming, for instance.

13.4.4   Self-recording

Employees are asked to complete activity log sheets so that some assessment of their workload can be gauged. Normally each activity and the time taken to carry it out is recorded. The disadvantages of this method are that employees can misreport their functions so much that erroneous conclusions can be drawn. The work procedure may be inadequate, but this will not be shown on the records. Unless precise instructions have been issued, it is unlikely that uniformity of recording will result. Sometimes this is deliberate, but more often it will be due to operatives not having the experience or perhaps ability to complete the job logs appropriately.

Where there is considerable lack of uniformity, consolidation and presentation of factors will be a problem. When office morale is low, participation in completing log sheets could produce irrelevant data.

However, when used with activity sampling and simulation, self-recording can often prove valuable in allowing broad assumptions to be made about workloads and work allocation.

13.4.5   Time study

Time study can be both the most and least accurate of all work measurement techniques. The shop floor has often been a battleground where operatives attempt to outwit the time-study man during the work measurement–followed by long and tedious debate between unions and management when the rating is argued endlessly.

The operation of time study is as follows:

1   Jobs being timed are broken down into elements. An element is defined as the part of a job that can be isolated from other parts and timed. Making entries on visible card index records, for instance, could comprise many elements, perhaps as follows:

- search for tray, hand on tray handle, pull out tray
- search for card, flip over other cards ready for recording
- enter date, amount received, calculate balance
- flip down other cards, close tray
- stamp 'recorded' on goods received note and put into out tray

2   On the shop floor, therbligs or basic motions such as search, find, select, grasp, hold, etc., are used. These can constitute the basis for predetermined time study where a predetermined time has been calculated for each motion. A total of these times can therefore be built up without the actual job being timed.

3   Once the elements have been decided, the operation cycle can also be determined.

4   Times can now be taken for each element and for the cycle as a whole. A sufficient number of timings should be taken to ensure that, when a weighted average is applied, a sufficiently accurate result is achieved. An assessment of the rating of the speed of carrying out the operation should also be made. Basic, as opposed to actual, minutes can then be calculated.

5   The information is then collated to find the weighted cycle times and the collated element times.

6   The need to put down rated standard times may puzzle the inexperienced observer. Normal rates have been expressed as the equivalent of dealing a pack of cards into four piles in half a minute, or a man walking 4 km over flat ground without a load in an hour. There is a British Standard defining standard performance as: 'The rate of output which qualified workers will naturally achieve without over-exertion as an average over the working day or shift provided they know and adhere to the specified method and provided they are motivated to apply themselves to their work'.

Adhering to the specified method is important and making sure that the operative is using the best method is a prerequisite of time study. In the office, systems study should be carried out prior to time study. The priority in office efficiency should be eliminating or streamlining an operation before time study is applied, but long-term method study may be avoided.

7   The two rating systems used in Britain are either the 60/80 system or the British Standard scale which uses 100 as a normal output figure. Normal output can, therefore, be expressed as 60 in the 60/80 system or as 100 in the British Standard, with 80 as standard in the 60/80 system and 133 in the British Standard system. This implies that though normal output is either 60 or 80, a standard performance, as defined previously, should result in staff working a third more, so that wages plus bonus will be on a time (normal) plus a third basis.

Both scales have their advantages. The 60/80 system can be related to standard minutes, while the British Standard 100 system can usefully be seen in terms of percentages.

8   The rating factor system is customarily used in Britain to help determine the rate of work. In this system, various factors such as effort, skill, environment, consistency, are used by the observer to judge or rate the operative.

Allowances   As it is usually impossible to adhere to the standards throughout the whole day at work, various allowances are added, including:

1   Contingency allowances covering all the factors that cannot be timed: answering telephone calls at random intervals, being consulted and consulting other people, and various non-routine factors such as being unable to find a record when it is needed and the searching that follows.

2   Relaxation allowances made on the basis that full activity is not possible or desirable throughout the day and that some time must be allowed for rest and recuperation. The period allowed will vary according to the job being done. Heavy labouring jobs on the shop floor will have large relaxation allowances, clerical jobs will need less. In total, it is rare to give less than 10 per cent of total time to contingency and relaxation allowances on any kind of clerical job.

3 Other allowances Various other types of allowance should be considered when applying work measurement. These include training allowances while the operative is still learning his job, and job cycle allowances when, because of the stage of the cycle, there is no work for the operative.

13.4.6 Predetermined motion time systems (PMTS)

PMTS is a 'technique in which predetermined times for basic human body motions are used to build up times for elements of work' (BS3138, 1959). To establish a time for carrying out an operation it is first necessary to break the operation down into job elements as in time study. A table or catalogue of predetermined times is then perused and the appropriate time assigned to the job element.

This method of achieving clerical work measurement has many advantages, not least that the application – if well taught and applied appropriately – gives a standard time no matter what the job or the time of application. The rating element so much abused and misused in normal time study is eliminated.

Synthetics can be used on a job which has never been previously performed. The use of a stop watch is not obligatory. Incentive schemes can be discussed fairly and openly.

Method study or work simplification is an integral part of the application so that full benefits can be obtained from work elimination and systems improvement as well as from work measurement and labour control. The major types of PMTS are:

1 MTM or methods time measurement This was first designed for use on the shop floor and it has needed considerable adaption to make it suitable for use on clerical activities. The system was formulated by Maynard Stegemerten and Swab of the Methods Engineering Council (a consultancy organisation). The definition of this system as given by the Methods, Time Measurement Association is: 'A procedure for improving methods and establishing production standards as a result of recognising, describing and classifying the motions used or required to perform a given operation and assigning predetermined time standards'.

The initial MTM procedures have been simplified and many systems are now offered that are less difficult to apply than the original system.

2 Master clerical data (MCD) was developed by another consultancy organisation in the USA – Serge A. Birn Co. The system has 12 basic pretimed clerical activities ranging from calculating activities to writing operations. Time values are expressed as TMUs (time measurement units), one unit being 100,000th part of an hour. The data used is said to correspond to a rating of 83 on a British Standard Scale of 0 to 100

3 Clerical milliminute data (clerical MMD) This system was developed in

Britain by PA Consultants. It is a derivative of MTM and covers a series of activities from body motions to typewriting. It is said that through the use of programmed learning texts and loop films, training of analysts can be carried out in a matter of days.

A derivative of milliminute data is clerical basic minute data, which uses standard times for many similar operations that occur in an office – such as using a particular office machine.

An MMD card has been prepared that lists the job elements and standards, e.g. 'move chair' has a code of SCM and a time of 86 milliminutes; 'open and close drawer' has a code of ODF and a time of 35 milliminutes (one milliminute in this system is equal to 0.001 min at standard performance).

4   Basic work data and clerical work data   ICI and British Rail have devised their own comprehensive work measurement techniques known as Basic Work Data (BWD) and Clerical Work Data (CWD). Details of these systems will be made available by the organisations concerned and clients can take part in courses and exercises organised for them.

5   Clerical standard data (CSD)   Universal Office Controls (UOC) and Office Staffing Standards (OSS) are also based on either PMTS or simplified PMTS.

6   Clerical work improvement programme (CWIP)   The CWIP system as used by W.D. Scott and Co. Ltd uses a predetermined time standard developed by Paul B. Mulligan in the USA. Like variable factor programming (which is discussed next) W.D. Scott emphasises: participation by line managers, self-control (line managers run their own schemes) and security – job security is usually guaranteed.

The Mulligan standards are derived from micromotion films taken in typical office conditions. Element times range from hundredths of a second to minutes, where this is necessary.

7   Work measurement/batch control/VFP (variable factor programming)   Like CWIP, VFP claims to be more than a work measurement technique. It is said to be a complete procedure to improve clerical performance. The initial task of VFP, as with method study and work simplification, is to find out what is being done. To this end clerks are asked to fill in activity or task sheets, giving a description of each activity being carried out, the quantity of documents handled and the time taken. As soon as possible, task descriptions are standardised between clerks – often descriptions of the same activity suggest that two different ones are being performed.

Unlike methods time measurement (MTM) or any conventional work measurement techniques, the work standards evolved in VFP are not exact. They are basic standards that can be assessed from the work activity sheets and agreed with supervisors. They are what the supervisor feels are reasonable targets to aim for. In any case, the accepted time standards should not be in any way exceptional. A fair hour's standard output should eventually be agreed, calling for no excessive pace or need for anyone to feel hard-driven. The standard time should take account of queries, telephone calls, or anything else likely to detract from achieving the major activity under consideration.

13.4.7 Control

Once standards of output and manning have been established, control can be exercised by the supervisor and staff undertaking several simple control techniques. All work coming into the department should go to the supervisor. None should be issued to staff without the supervisor being aware of it. Work is split into batches of approximately one hour's duration by the supervisor and then issued accordingly.

The work is 'signed out', i.e. a record made of when the work was issued and when it was completed. Because only an hour's work is issued, it is possible to maintain a very tight control over output. If, for example, an hour's standard work takes an hour and a quarter, this is immediately noticed by the supervisor. The reason for the delay can be investigated and any snags or queries tackled by the supervisor.

Daily performance reports from each department are an important factor in maintaining departmental and company clerical cost control. The completed employee control sheet should be consolidated into a departmental operating sheet which should show the total work processed in terms of standard hours and the total number of 'clock hours' available.

13.4.8 Conclusion

The potency of clerical work measurement as a cost reduction and control weapon is considerable. It makes the hard slog of method study to achieve probably smaller savings seem unrewarding by itself. Application ought to be the final part of every method study to assess manning standards for the new systems.

Many companies that have based the economic justification of a computer on a reduction in clerical costs would surely have had to revise their ideas if detailed work measurement had been carried out prior to the computer feasibility study. If a computer was still found to be economically justifiable, its scope would probably have had to be extended to the vital parts of the company – stock control, production planning and control areas – rather than be used, say, on wages and invoicing alone.

13.5 Other techniques

Other important techniques used in clerical work measurement and control are:

1 Group capacity assessment (GCA) As its name implies, this method has been devised to measure and control work of groups rather than individuals. The need for detailed standards is therefore reduced. Any of the following techniques can be used to determine standards:

- multiminute measurement (no stopwatch)
- time study
- standard data (predetermined from departments or activities previously studied)
- work sampling (for long cycle times) – continuous reporting is established to ensure that groups are operating efficiently and that personnel are equated to work to be performed

2 Short interval sceduling is a technique which is used in other techniques (VFP for example). It needs a control manager or supervisor through which all work entering the department or section is channelled. Work is then issued in regular and controlled batches. No actual work measurement is needed, or necessary – close control is enough to ensure that work and clerks are equated and an appropriate performance achieved.

13.6 Techniques to use

One could begin by pleading for the introduction of any form of clerical cost control and standards of work output, the actual technique used appearing to be of less importance than its implementation. In practice, however, the chosen scheme will be dictated by the analyst or investigator who is available to carry out the assignment. Real knowledge of time study can only be gained by actually carrying out time-study exercises – the problem of rating has already been emphasised and MTM is a technique which needs careful tuition.

The degree of accuracy required will also dictate which technique to use. Work estimation in this context will come out worse than PMTS, but it will still give some control and this is the main point. The kind of work, its frequency, the percentage of proved non-routine work, the results which are required, will all suggest the technique to be used.

It will be likely that two or more techniques should be used together – activity sampling and time study for example

13.7 Further reading

1 'An introduction to clerical work measurement', *BIM* (1979).
2 R.M. Barnes, *Work Sampling,* Wiley (1957).
3 L.H. Bunker, *Measuring Office Work,* Pitman (1964).
4 E.V. Grillo and C.J. Berg, *Work Measurement in the Office,* McGraw-Hill (1959).
5 J. Constable and D. Smith, *Group Assessment Programmes – the measurement of indirect work,* Business Publications (1966).

6 H.P. Cemachz, *Work Study in the Office,* Maclaren (1965).
7 M. Smith, *Short-interval Scheduling – a systematic approach to cost-reduction,* McGraw-Hill (1968).
8 D.A. Whitmore, *Work Measurement,* Heinemann (1976).
9 Purcell and Smith (Editors), *Control of Work,* Macmillan (1980).

Fourteen

Industrial Democracy

14.1 Introduction

Industrial democracy has been given many wide-ranging definitions, but all seem concerned with the probability of trade unions and individuals having some influence over the way an organisation is run. Even in these straightened economic times the possibilities of a manager having complete authority over his people is increasingly remote.

With more difficult economic times, talk about 'participation' and 'industrial democracy' is more muted than it was two or three years ago, but industrial democracy is slowly and surely making ground. Whether managers like it or not the day of industrial democracy will surely dawn. Amongst the welter of debate, what is industrial democracy or participation? Well it seems it can be any one of these:

1   Joint consultation with management on working conditions, job opportunities, welfare facilities and local conditions of employment.
2   Participation in management's tactical decision-making role – manning levels and performance achievements and how to change if not improve work organisations and control. This might be called office or shop floor democracy.
3   Participation at the highest level in the company, i.e. the board, on strategic decision-making. The decisions will be concerned with capital investment, plant closures, new products, distribution of profit, etc. This might be called company democracy.
4   Ownership of the company either jointly with shareholders or government or entirely by the workforce. This might be called economic democracy.

Eyebrows might be raised about these four types, but before dissension begins, it might be useful for readers to consider how in each of the cases quoted non-management pressure is already in evidence. What organisation ever makes major redundancies without consulting the unions? What unit can be closed down without the understanding if not agreement of the local labour force? To some small degree, we already have the four types of industrial democracy quoted.

14.2 Joint consultation and participation

Joint consultation was conceived as a way in which employees could express opinions and make complaints and suggestions to their employers. The employers would find it convenient to use joint consultation procedures to inform employees of changes in their work situation. In some form or another, joint consultation has been used by most British companies. Most available evidence suggests that it has had little impact on solving many of the problems of employee and management relationships. It is now certain that the next decade will see a steady rise in the importance and use of joint consultative procedures and also participation. Definitions will show the basic difference between the two.

Joint consultation is a procedure whereby employees and employers can get together, either formally or informally, to discuss matters of common interest and perhaps determine action to further their common interests. Participation is a formal procedure whereby employers and employees unite to discuss and make decisions upon an agreed range of topics.

Both the TUC and the CBI have given joint consultation their blessing. Both believe that joint consultation will provide the means whereby greater common understanding between employers and employees will result in greater cooperation and the rapid implementation of decisions that enhance the survival and prosperity of their organisations.

Joint consultation should not be confused with collective bargaining, which is a process whereby trade unions and employers (or employers' associations) negotiate so as to reach an agreement usually about wages and fringe benefits.

14.2.1 Failure in joint consultation

Reasons for the failure of joint consultative committees have been widely sought and all the evidence suggests that the following are amongst the major causes:

1 Many companies have set up joint consultative machinery without any real knowledge of its underlying concepts or philosophy. Formal consultative machinery has been set up in the nationalised industries yet there is no evidence that communications or morale are any better on the railways or in the electricity industry than in most of private enterprise. A formal approach to consultation will rarely work if informal consultation is not functioning well already.

2 The design and make-up of joint consultation committees has also been

found to present many problems. Rigid adherence to one delegate per x number of people has meant that many departments in a company have been without representation, the delegate being elected from the biggest department. This disenfranchisement has resulted in lack of interest among a large minority.

3   Supervisors and middle-ranking managers have often felt left out of the joint consultative machinery. A direct link between desk worker and the chief executive has often bypassed the local manager. The local shop steward has often known more about company affairs than his supervisor.

4   How far should trade unions be linked with joint consultations? The fear in the hearts of trade unions is that they will be frozen out of negotiating procedures if they are not allowed formal representation. There is always a fear of company unionism.

5   Subject matter for discussion has often been a bone of contention. Management, in practice, has often used joint consultation to get across company policy. Employees on the other hand often set out with the idea of sniping at management. No wonder, on occasions, so little is achieved.

From a management viewpoint, there is no reason why company profit and loss statements should not be analysed and discussed and the committee told of steps being taken to improve profitability. If, however, productivity is the most important discussion point, formal joint consultation will inevitably be dismissed by the employees as a management gimmick to make them work harder. Reciprocal topics of discussion from the employee viewpoint might include:

- adequacy of heating, lighting, ventilation, fume-extraction
- overcrowding in sections of the factory or offices
- questions of noise
- office furniture
- hours of duty – how these are split
- canteen – a perennial problem, probably best dealt with by a special canteen committee
- safety – here again a special safety committee might be preferable
- first-aid equipment
- complaints about supervision and allocation of duties
- all matters coming under the heading of welfare

It should be the responsibility of management to try to ensure that committees do not become complaints sessions, with the company forever on the defensive. But once a complaint has been make it should be investigated and a report submitted to the next committee meeting.

6   Company personnel departments should be closely involved with the joint

consultation procedures. It should be their active function to take up any complaints made, and provide a secretary to take minutes and organise election procedures. Voluntary effort of this kind should not really be expected from employees.

7 Most companies consider the reporting-back procedure adequate if a notice of the proceedings of the various committees is pinned up on the noticeboard. As statistical samples have shown that only three to five out of every 10 people ever bother to read noticeboards, this is surely inadequate.

Where a point is raised and the decision taken is such that it will affect most of the staff in the company, a direct statement should be given to all staff, either in a letter from the chairman or branch manager, or as a note in everyone's pay packet. A loudspeaker announcement in the canteen at lunchtime might not be out of place. The action taken should be dictated by the degree of importance attached to the decision made.

8 The most fundamental reason why joint consultation has failed is the attitude of unions and employers. It is difficult to divorce a total industrial or social atmosphere from a single point. Local attitudes often reflect a national outlook. If worker management alienation is to be avoided locally, very special care must be made to ensure that management and unions have absolute faith in joint consultation.

14.3   The situation in the 1980s

The need to reconsider and perhaps rewrite joint consultation and participation procedures is becoming more plain as the following factors suggest.

14.3.1   Social and political pressures

In a free society with well educated citizens, there seems no reason why the democratic principle cannot be extended to all spheres of life. Allied with a change of attitudes to authority, which denies authoritarianism of any kind, the desire for democratic decision-making in business life is totally understandable.

14.3.2   Economic pressures

The modern industrial organisation is one where capital investment is constantly increasing. Most activities are machine-dominated. Strikes that cause machine stoppages are more important now from an economic point of view than, say, 25 years ago, when less was at stake. The corresponding importance of maximising machine usage through good behavioural relations is stressed.

14.3.3   Need to change

The need to change and especially to adapt to changing technological and economic environments is growing year-by-year. Once it seemed only technological change was important. Now social and economic changes could be more important still. Adaptation and change was never more essential than now. Speedy and effective change can only be brought about by cooperative efforts – not just by management alone.

Participation is very much concerned with establishing a bridge between employers and employees, and covers the joining together of emplyer and employee on an equal basis to discuss and decide upon a predetermined range of activities. This definition is reasonably anodyne until the 'range of activities' is discussed.

For office management the following should be determined:

- What is participation? How is it to be achieved?
- What can be conceded to employees who demand participation? What new elements can be introduced?
- Participation is not a disaster. It could have very definite, positive advantages. What can these be? How can they be achieved?
- How can responsibilities be given to employees as well as rights?

Given that participation will face most office managers more and more, what strategies can be adopted to ensure that management still manages? This certainly seems to be the crux in the 'participation activities' which might be tried. The need to forestall and not be forced to follow demands for participation is strongly stressed.

The aspirations of employees are rising. The days when autocratic control was acceptable are numbered, if not already over for ever. Participation could give a real opportunity for advancing the organisation's efficiency.

14.4   Structures for participation

Setting up a structure where participation takes place seems a particularly trade union response to a situation. In the early days of joint consultation it was said that if informal procedures for problem-solving did not exist, then formal procedures would not work. Attitudes, then, are important.

Following are some structures which have been recommended for participation:

1   *Two-tier boards*   These seem a favourite with the rest of the EEC, particularly as they are applied in West Germany. Trade unions are represented on the senior board, but not necessarily on the operational executive that actually runs the company.

2   *Works councils* are established to carry out local or factory participation.

3   Departmental participation groups are normally the lowest level of the participation activity and handle office or departmental affairs.

4   Problem-solving seems, in practice, to be the most helpful structure (to management that is). Employees and managers are brought together to solve one or more problems. Once a solution has been agreed the group is abandoned.

The type of industrial democracy that might be introduced in the UK can be foreseen in the White Paper, *Industrial Democracy,* published in 1978.

14.5   Further reading

1   J. Bink and K. Jones, *Worker-directors Speak,* Gower (1977).
2   W. Brown, *Employee Participation in Management,* Knight, Wegenstein Consultants (1973).
3   W. W. Daniels and N. McIntosh, *The Right to Manage,* MacDonald (1972).
4   D. Guest and K. Knight (Editors), *Putting Participation into Practice,* Gower (1979).
5   M. M. Scott, *Every Employee a Manager,* McGraw-Hill (1970).
6   Lynda King-Taylor, *A Fairer Slice of the Cake,* Business Books (1976).
7   'Participation, democracy and control', *BIM* (1979).
8   P. Anthony, *The Conduct of Industrial Relations,* IPM (1977).
9   D. Quinn Mills, *Labour–Management Relations,* McGraw-Hill (1981).

Fifteen

Job Study

15.1 Introduction

Job study is a conglomerate term given to all the factors which determine job descriptions and definitions, job evaluation (and, hence, wages payment) and job performance. This latter factor has been superseded somewhat by the various performance analyses introduced by 'management by objectives', but it is still valid as an integral part of performance assessment.

15.1.1 Job descriptions

Job descriptions are the cornerstone of any performance analysis, merit rating, or more basically still, profit planning. Unless managers and other personnel are aware of their total responsibilities, their key results and major objectives, the constraints inherent in their job and the factors on which their performance will be appraised, it is unlikely that they will perform appropriately, and they will certainly suffer from frustration and lack of direction. Without adequate job descriptions, recruitment, salary/wages payment and promotion will be haphazard at best. If personnel are absent, or leave, job descriptions give some guidance to others of the work which is not being performed.

The job description is a formal mechanism for translating the essential features of a job into a factual and concise format so the key job areas can be recognised and objectives set for the job holder. The job description should show:

- what is done – the key areas of the job
- how it is done – what methods, skills, expertise are required
- why it is done – what the job is about

The record should then describe the job under the following main headings.

Purpose Why does the job exist? For what is the job holder paid ? What company objectives must the job holder help to achieve?

Dimensions   The pertinent dimensions of money, capital and manpower considerations should be listed.

Nature and scope   The various headings which ought to be considered in this section are:

a   What organisational position has the employee? To whom does he report? Which other job holders report to the same person? Does the job holder have a seat on a committee or planning group?

b   What supporting staff respond to the job holder? Have they any grades? If so quote them. What experience have they generally?

c   What technical, managerial, behavioural and organisational skills are apparently needed to carry out the job successfully? What qualifications are needed? What experience (quote type and length of time) is desirable? How does this compare with other jobs of apparently equal status in the company?

d   What problem-solving is carried out? Are intricate and intellectually demanding problems solved frequently? What creativity is necessary?

e   What is the greatest challenge in the job? What appears to be the most rewarding element?

f   What freedom of action is given to the job occupant? Is he, for example, responsible for:

- recruitment, selection, dismissal
- capital expenditure
- setting prices
- changing production methods
- changing design and quality
- changing salaries?

g   What are the principal constraints in the job?

h   What are the inherent difficulties in carrying out the job?

Key accountabilities   What key accountabilities are inherent in the job, for example:

1   In setting objectives, planning, determining company policy?

2   Directing the attainment of objectives – directing, organising, staffing, communicating, motivating?

3   Measuring results?

4   Promoting innovation?

5   Developing people?

15.2   Job grading

Job grading, as used in the armed forces or the Civil Service, strikes terror into many hearts. It suggests inflexibility, a firm edge round every job and the introduction of hard, unbreakable lines of command. In smaller offices job grading is obviously unnecessary and would also be unwise. It can, however, have very positive merits. It defines areas of responsiblity, provides a logical promotion ladder and, if associated with job evaluation and merit rating, provides an equitable basis for wages payment.

Where job grading does not exist, salary and responsibility anomalies will certainly be present. As part of their challenge on wages payment, trade unions are suggesting that a logical job grading scheme is most important.

Flexibility can be ensured by limiting the number of grades. Few grades, with a broad range of wages payment in each grade, should be the general aim. The more that are introduced, the finer will have to be the definitions of grade responsibility.

The Institute of Administration has a grading system which suggests six grades of clerical labour. For most small companies, however, it seems that five grades might suffice. These could be:

Grade 1 Clerical and administrative jobs of the simplest kind which call for no previous experience, but are of a higher grade than a junior who would be outside the grading category. The jobs covered would demand some training – perhaps two or three weeks – and would be under constant supervision. Jobs covered would include simple record-keeping; document sorting; simple filing.

Grade 2 would cover the jobs that demand a minimum amount of training but at least four months' experience before an acceptable standard of efficiency is reached. Some initiative would be involved, though supervision is still close and fairly continuous. Jobs would include superior recordkeeping where action would follow recording, e.g. stock records and creating replacement requisitions; purchase order chasers and ledger entry clerks keeping pay records in the wages department.

Grade 3 Fairly senior clerks, probably with some years' service in the company, carrying out jobs involving a fair amount of initiative and responsibility, probably in charge of a small section of staff of a lower grade. Jobs covered would include production-planning clerks issuing planning programmes for the factory; clerks controlling limits of credit in a credit control department; purchase clerks responsible for negotiating small purchases with a strict financial limit.

Grade 4 Senior clerks in charge of a section of a department with considerable service in the company and perhaps consolidating the work of subsidiary clerks. This grade would also act as assistants and deputies to the Grade 5 clerk. In many offices, this grade is described as 'section supervisor'. Jobs included are senior cost and accounts clerks; deputy purchasing officers; senior cost-estimating clerks; deputy production controllers.

Grade 5   This grade will normally be in charge of a small department – credit control, internal audit, sales ledger or wages department. In some companies he will be called 'junior manager' or 'assistant manager'. The major departments will be managed by a senior manager nominally outside the clerical grading system.

15.2.1   How to grade

Grading, job responsibility and equitable rates of pay should all be regarded as flowing from the same initial investigation. To grade jobs fairly, therefore, it is necessary to carry out a job description and job evaluation process. If, for example, the points system of job evaluation is undertaken it is comparatively simple to apportion a range of job evaluation points for each grade and fit in jobs as they are evaluated. This process seems the fairest way of carrying out what can often turn into a bitter wrangle between staff and management.

Several factors can produce anomalies in any job-grading scheme. The company may employ specialists of various kinds – computer programmers, organisation and methods men, or systems analysts – whose rates of pay (because of the going rates) do not allow their jobs to be fitted into a logical job-grading scheme. Many companies have overcome this by creating a technical grade additional to the general clerical grade. The junior technical staff are given the title of 'technical assistants', the seniors are designated 'technical officers'. 'Specialist assistants' and 'specialist officers' are other names given to similar personnel. Rates of pay, conditions of service and job requisites can all be tailored to fit existing conditions.

15.3   Job evaluation

Job evaluation is the systematic comparison of the value of a range of jobs, so that, ultimately, an equitable wages or salary payment scale is produced for them. In the past, it has been used largely for manual workers and the various schemes which will be discussed later have all been developed with manual worker job evaluation in mind. Schemes, however, have been successfully adapted to take in clerical and administrative staff, and job evaluation is now widely employed in the administrative field.

Job evaluation is not concerned with the actual person or people employed. It does not take into account attitudes, sex or the speed at which the job is done. It is concerned with determining the mental and physical characteristics, qualifications and experience that a person should have in order to carry out a particular job successfully. It also prescribes the area of responsibility implicit in the job.

The importance of using the joint consultative machinery to advertise the fairness and equity of job evaluation should never be overlooked. It is not enough to put in a fair scheme – it should be recognised as such. Job evaluation is not an easy technique to implement. It usually uncovers many anomalies in the company wage and salary structure. Jobs which, for decades, have been thought to be important, and consequently well paid, are suddenly demoted in the pay scale. This could bring about resentment.

15.3.1   Job-evaluation procedure

1   The usual procedure is to form a job-evaluation committee – an impartial and technically competent body, capable of analysing and evaluating all the jobs that will come under its jurisdiction.

In administrative and clerical jobs, a representative committee might be the personnel manager, the company accountant, the office manager, a senior departmental manager of known fairness and technical ability, plus an employees' representative. Where technical ability or job knowledge is absent, the services of the manager or supervisor controlling the job being evaluated should be enlisted. The testimony of the person doing the job should be treated with reserve.

2   The description of the physical and mental characteristics required should be deduced by the committee from job-description sheets. A visit by the committee to see the job being done can be used to support the job-description sheet. The supervisor will be able to supply additional information.

3   Having discovered all the relevant details on which to base objective assessments, it is necessary to decide which types of job evaluation suit the situation.

15.3.2   Types of job-evaluation schemes: the points system

This system is the most popular on the shop floor and can well be adapted to office conditions. The committee lists, under main headings, the job factors it considers important and then attributes to each of them a number of points reflecting their importance. For example, the following fairly stereotype table will indicate the type of job factors involved and the weighted points rating that might be given:

Education and training

Qualifications needed for the job	30
Mental development and maturity	15
Experience in the job	20
Previous experience necessary	20
Training and experience – time necessary	15
Total	100

Job skill

Job knowledge	15

Accuracy	12
Ingenuity	7
Initiative	12
Judgement	10
Intelligence	15
Resourcefulness	9
Ability to do detailed work	10
Social acceptability	10
Total	100

Effort

Mental effort	8
Mental application	8
Concentration	8
Visual application	8
Fatigue due to mental effort	12
Fatigue due to visual effort	12
Nervous strain	12
Monotony of work	12
Total	80

Responsibility

Responsible for equipment	15
Responsible for work of others	25
General supervision	15
Accuracy in counting or weighing	6
Spoilage of materials	15
Protection of materials	12
Cooperation with others	12
Total	100

Work conditions

Hazards	7
Exposure to health hazards	8
Dirty work conditions	10
Disagreeable environment	10
Total	35

The range of factors is reasonably wide and, in practice, some might be eliminated. Not every committee will agree with the values the weighted points have been given, e.g. in a company that does not pay great heed to qualifications, experience and job knowledge will be rated far higher than academic qualifications; in other companies the reverse may happen.

The points given to individuals should, as far as possible, reflect a quantitative assessment of the job factor being considered, e.g. for 'qualifications needed', top points should be based on a degree or professional qualification. In the case of responsibility, quantitative assessments of the number of staff controlled, or the possible value of material that could be spoiled, are the criteria.

Some of the office factors will have to be subjectively assessed, and many committees fall into the trap of trying to average up or allocate some points even when the job does not warrant them. Points are allocated by judging the job against the whole spectrum of all job activities. Many committees produce a high, low and mean job for each job element and then compare the job under discussion with these jobs. This helps to avoid any serious over- or under-allocation of points.

Once the points have been allocated and jobs evaluated, a scale of jobs arranged in job points importance can be drawn up by the office manager. These can be agreed with his departmental managers and employees through the joint consultative machinery. Current rates of pay can then be set against each job and any anomalies will become apparent. How, then, should the equitable wage rate be set? The following factors should be considered:

1 Set a base rate for the lowest-rated job sufficient to attract both a reasonable amount and a reasonable standard of labour from the local labour market.
2 Assess every other job by adding a relative money percentage for each 10 points over the base job that has been evaluated. Compare this calculated rate with the current rate being paid.
3 Establish grades that will cover a range of jobs within a reasonable points range. No one should actually lose money following job evaluation, but anyone found to be overpaid in a lowly rated job should be promoted as soon as possible – if he deserves it.
4 Compare the graded job scales with outside rates and assess the possibility of attracting and holding a sufficient number of people to fill the jobs. If the graded job rate is obviously too low it should be increased, even though this is not in line with the points scheme. Job rates above this graded level should be reconsidered. Grades and pay rates should overlap so as to give flexibility in making merit and long-service rewards.

15.3.3 Factor comparison method

The factor comparison method is another job evaluation scheme which is widely used on the shop floor. In this method, main job factors similar to the ones quoted in the points system are chosen. These would be:

- education and training
- job skill
- effort

- responsibility
- working conditions

Each committee member should compare and rank each job by these factors. The jobs most demanding of the factor concerned will be listed first, the least demanding job will be placed last.

The committee decides how to allocate the actual salaries of each key job

FACTOR COMPARISON EVALUATION SCALE

Date 1/1/82

Pence	Education and training	Job skill	Mental effort	Responsibility	Working conditions
1850	Financial accountant	Financial accountant	Financial accountant	Financial accountant	
1800	Senior cost clerk	Senior cost clerk	Senior cost clerk	Senior cost clerk	
1750	Draughts-man	Draughtsman			
1700			Draughtsman	Draughtsman	
			Forms controller		
1650			Planning clerk	Planning clerk	
1600			Purchasing clerk	Purchasing clerk	
				Forms controller	
1550	Planning· clerk	Planning clerk			Office cleaner
	Purchasing clerk			Sales record clerk	
1500	Forms controller			Stock records clerk	Draughtsman / Planning clerk
	Sales record clerk				Stock Records clerk
1450	Stock records clerk	Purchasing clerk	Sales Record clerk		Financial accountant
		Forms controller	Stock records clerk		Senior cost clerk
1400	Office cleaner	Sales record clerk			Purchasing clerk
		Stock records clerk			Sales record clerk
1350		Office cleaner	Office cleaner	Office cleaner	Forms controller

Figure 15.1   *Factor comparison evaluation scale sheet*

over the chosen factors. The allocation is usually in the form of numbers of pence of the total pay that each factor is worth. The jobs are then ranked in factors according to their penny-values.

The penny-value ranking and the original job factor ranking can then be compared and any anomalies eliminated either be reranking or taking out the job involved. A scale similar to the one shown in Figure 15.1 can be made. Once this has been done, all other jobs that need to be evaluated can be inserted on the ranking list – following the ranking methods already discussed – and a final total of salary values calculated.

15.3.4   Ranking methods (matched pairs)

This is the simplest job evaluation commonly used. From job descriptions, each member of a job-evaluation committee ranks the range of jobs done in one department in order of importance. It is usual to rank pairs of jobs, matching and rematching pairs until the whole of the department has been ranked. Jobs in different departments are then considered and integrated by 'matching pairs'.

This is a simple and useful way of establishing job grades or groups of jobs which appear to have the same importance. The allocation of pay is not as easy as with the points and job factor schemes and it is not, therefore, so valuable a method of job evaluation.

15.4   Performance appraisal

Performance appraisal or merit rating is a formalised way of determining how well an individual has carried out a job and whether a merit increase is deserved. Formalising the procedure should eliminate much of the favouritism or bias that often exists. It should provide the basis for constructively discussing performance, strengths and weaknesses with job holders.

Merit rating or performance appraisal schemes start by establishing the key factors that will be used in the appraisal, e.g. job knowledge, all-round ability, dependability, initiative, cooperation, enthusiasm, etc. Often a form similar to Figure 15.2 can be introduced for the purpose. As a result of such an appraisal, recommended action should follow on:

- training or retraining
- promotion
- demotion

In many instances management-grade personnel will have been allocated targets of various kinds (most likely after a suitable period of discussion). The achievement of the targets will be the basis of the performance appraisal. This process is to be strongly recommended as it tends to create a 'performance improvement ethos' if applied appropriately. However, things can go wrong:

a   The targets set have to be realistic. In some budgetary control systems, for example, there are many ways in which a manager can decide on his own targets. Where 10 per cent is habitually knocked off a proposed budget by the general manager, 10 per cent too much is often added before the budget is inspected.

b   Sometimes impossibly tight targets are fixed, simply to meet a predetermined profit estimate. Although the target might act as a spur, it can also affect morale and discourage any positive drive to try to achieve it.

c   A change in market conditions or the action of competitors can nullify targets. For example, if the company's products become non-competitive, why penalise the sales manager when factory costs or the design department are really to blame?

d   Targets can be achieved in one department at the expense of other departments in the same company. For example, the labour-cost target in one department can be controlled at a predetermined level by making more work for another department

Chapter 22 carries the debate further.

15.5   Salary administration and job study

This chapter has outlined various procedures that should be included in any discussions on salary administration. One or other of the various means of carrying out job evaluation should be introduced if, for example, any pretence at equity in salary payment is desired. Other factors that need to be considered are:

1   It is important that job study and salary administration are a planned activity, not a hasty response to legislation or pressure from local trade unions.

2   Formal assessments seem vital in any salary administration. Evaluating jobs and appraising job holders seem easy in theory. In practice they are extremely difficult to carry out fairly.

3   The fringe benefits that go with a job might also be evaluated in a salary administration scheme. Often such benefits form a considerable proportion of total remuneration, and should be seen as such.

4   The usual method of salary apportionment is to provide salary bands for each grade or evaluated position in the organisation, based on its points rating, cost of living and the salaries other organisations are prepared to pay for such grades of staff. To meet cost-of-living rises, the salary bands are raised when necessary. This is usually done separately from merit rises given for performance achieved.

5   Communications are vital in overcoming difficulties concerning job study and salary administration. It is no use having a good and equitable system

STRICTLY CONFIDENTIAL

Location	Date of birth	Date of starting	Name and initials	Grade
Department			Position	

JOB KNOWLEDGE

A	Exceptional range and depth of knowledge
B	Sound knowledge of function
C	Good knowledge. Needs occasional help
D	Fair knowledge. Still some gaps
E	Has a lot to learn about the job

EFFECTIVE OUTPUT

A	Outstanding in the amount of work he does
B	Gets through a great deal of work
C	Output satisfactory
D	Does rather less than expected
E	Output regularly insufficient

ACCEPTANCE OF RESPONSIBILITY

A	Seeks additional responsibility. No supervision required
B	Accepts obligations. Minimum supervision required
C	Requires only general supervision
D	Unsure of himself. Needs frequent supervision
E	Avoids responsibility. Needs constant supervision

ANALYTICAL ABILITY

A	Can solve original problems. Keeps to essentials
B	Picks out relevant details. Reaches correct solution
C	Generally sound. Sometimes led astray
D	Adequate analysis of simple problems only
E	Tends to make unwise decisions

CO-OPERATION

A	Goes out of his way to be helpful
B	Fits in well with group
C	Generally works well with group
D	Co-operates if given a lead. Sometimes awkward
E	Prefers to get through single handed

RELIABILITY AND ACCURACY

A	Very accurate and completely reliable
B	Makes few mistakes and seldom forgets
C	As accurate as most. Reliable on the whole
D	Makes a few mistakes. Requires supervision
E	Tends to be inaccurate. Needs frequent attention

INITIATIVE

A	Quick to seize opportunities and develop them
B	Resourceful in most situations
C	Generally decisive. Sometimes needs guidance
D	Slow to act without conformation
E	Routine minded. Will not act on own initiative

ORGANISING ABILITY

A	An extremely able organiser
B	Good organising ability. Can plan ahead well
C	Efficient in normal circumstances
D	Not a very good organiser on the whole
E	Sometimes gets in a muddle. Hold-ups occur

OVERALL RATING OF EFFECTIVENESS IN PRESENT JOB

To be completed by departmental manager

Barely adequate	Adequate	Average	Very good	Outstanding

... taken during year, new qualifications and anything of significance not mentioned overleaf. Highlight strength(s) and weakness(es)

Action taken

RECOMMENDED ACTION – What action is proposed in view of strength(s) and weakness(es) disclosed above? Consider training, transfer and promotion

POTENTIAL – How do you rate the employee's future potential?

Code		POTENTIAL CODE
FP	Has now reached full potential	
P1	Could do a job one grade higher than his present one	
P2	Could do a job two grades higher than his present one	
CP	Considerable potential. Should eventually reach senior management level	
NP	Has not the capacity to do his present job adequately	

First assessor	Second assessor	Interviewed by	Date of interview
Date	Date		

Figure 15.2   Staff appraisal

unless it is well known and understood. Disclosure of salary policy is essential.

6   Responsibility for the salary administration programme will usually lie in the hands of the personnel department, though other management staff must also be involved.

7   Salary administration policy has tended to give greater central control, but also to allow individual managers to decide on merit increases for their own staff.

8   High-fliers in the organisation need to be handled carefully, and it may be necessary to build 'overtaking lanes' into the system to accommodate them.

9   Market information concerning the competitiveness of the company's salary structure is constantly required. Informal contact, using external salary surveys and government reports, are the usual methods of gaining the information.

10   Most organisations carry out salary reviews, depending upon the salary and status of the individuals concerned. Juniors may be assessed twice a year, while middle-management appraisal is done annually. Senior personnel may only be checked every 18 months.

11   Pay scales need to be flexible and also comparable with outside wage rates. Because a job-evaluation scheme suggests that $£X$ a month should be paid, it should not be rigorously applied, if $£X + 10$ per cent is the going rate outside the company.

12   Job grading suggests inflexibility; a firm edge around every job; the introduction of hard, unbreakable status positions. Obviously this should only be accepted if there are considerable advantages.

15.6   Further reading

1   A. Bowey (Editor), *Handbook of Salary and Wage Systems,* Gower (1975).
2   T.L. Whistler and D.E. McFarland, *Performance Appraisal,* Holt, Rinehart, Winston (1962).
3   A.E. Roff and T.E. Watson, *Job Analysis,* Institute of Personnel Management (1961).
4   T.T. Paterson, *Job Evaluation.* Business Books (1971).
5   G. McBeath and N. Rands, *Salary Administration,* Business Books (1976).
6   M.S. Kelly, *What to Do About Performance Appraisal,* AMA (1966).
7   T.H. Boydell, *A Guide to Job Analysis,* BACIE (1969).
8   F.D. Blau, *Equal Pay in the Office,* Lexington (1977).
9   *Job Evaluation,* BIM (1970).
10   *Job Evaluation – theory and practice,* BIM (1979).
11   G. Thomason, *Job Evaluation – objectives and methods,* IPM (1980).
12   P. Genders, *Wages and Salaries,* IPM (1981).
13   E. Keyney, *How to Write a Job Description,* IPM (1981).

Sixteen

Manpower Planning, Recruitment, Training, Discipline and Redundancy

16.1 Introduction

The idea that it is possible to plan an organisation's manpower requirements for a year, or perhaps two or three years, ahead is hard to accept. The imponderables, the changing economic conditions, death and resignations, decline of facilities, the new recruit who turned out to be better or worse than anticipated, will all throw any manpower planning awry. Yet not to attempt it is to admit that it is impossible to match manpower with profit-planning requirements. Surely the one vital element in any organisation – its human resources – must be planned like all lesser elements in the plan.

Most pundits consider that manpower planning should ensure that the right number of personnel of the correct competence will be available to an organisation in desired locations, so that corporate objectives are achieved. The operation of manpower planning – in theory – seems perfectly straightforward. A situation and skills audit should indicate the basic weaknesses in management numbers – age, technical expertise, experience, etc. The audit should indicate current skill levels, efficiency performances, training requirements for management and overall manpower requirements.

The initial analysis is concerned with the calculation of either the gap or redundancy situation which the organisation will have at a point in the future if current trends continue. It is possible that the company may have an excess in some grades/types of manpower and a deficit in others.

Training and recruitment requirements need to be assessed carefully and the possibility of retraining semi-redundant personnel should be probed. It is possible that personnel employed by the company will be unable to carry out new jobs because they are inherently of low calibre. Recruitment, at some time, must have gone wrong.

From an analysis of current personnel and future requirements, a clear picture of the numbers, type, calibre and skills of personnel required at various times in the future should emerge. Once a dated manpower schedule has been drawn up, a training programme, a recruitment plan and a redundancy plan will be required. The manpower plan should aim to match manpower to company requirements, avoid panic redundancies and recruitment and ensure that manpower levels will always be pretty near optimum.

16.2   The procedure

There are a variety of behavioural/personnel/organisational techniques that should be brought under the manpower-planning umbrella. Each one will demand its own specialism and can be applied in its own right. In total, however, they can add up to a formidable, powerful operation if they are successfully carried out.

16.2.1   Organisation planning

The company organisation has to match its strategy and objectives. This could mean, for example, low-level decision-making, speedy communications and close financial control of all activities. The organisational plan may have to provide for the development of each or all of these activities.

16.2.2   Job evaluation, merit rating, performance measurement

These factors have already been considered in the previous chapter. They are a necessary part of manpower planning.

16.2.3   Succession planning

Organisations that have attempted to carry out succession planning have found it extremely difficult. Key people have a tendency to resign unexpectedly or someone does not live up to expectations and so the plan becomes invalid.

Integral with succession planning is career-path planning (discussed next) and the ability to quantify in some way a manager's attributes, potential and current job performance so that a choice can be made between candidates competing for promotion.

Usually the organisation is analysed function-by-function, department-by-department, and management assessed in terms of job attributes, skills and performance rating. Current job holders are then matched against the job they hold and their potential. The following are usually considered the key factors:

- age
- length of years in current job
- current job performance
- future potential (which could be broken down into potential ability to do

his superior's job or to be promoted elsewhere outside the job holder's current function)

Some methods grade job holders from 1 (good) to 6 (bad). Once this has been done a senior manager can take a coherent and objective view of the whole organisation. He can compare rival candidates for promotion, consider personnel for transfer from one function to another, see which manager is apparently getting stale and needs retraining or, if necessary, demotion.

A succession chart can then be worked out. X will take Y's job in Z years and needs training in A, B and C subjects before becoming established in the new job. A chart of this kind should give a clear indication of the potential promotion patterns by showing weaknesses and strengths, as set out in Figure 16.1.

16.2.4 Career planning

Career planning should be a concomittant of succession planning, though in this field a manager's as opposed to the organisation's desires are taken into account. Each manager or potential manager has a career path mapped out for him based on his aims, ambitions, desires, qualifications and attributes.

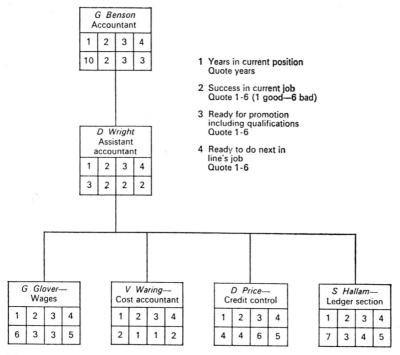

Figure 16.1 *Organisation promotion key*

Both current job performance and the job holder's potential are discussed formally.

It is obvious that the organisation's requirements must still be paramount, but within the broad organisation strategy and manpower plan, an attempt should be made to ensure that as far as possible appropriate individual career paths are suggested.

16.2.5   Potential analysis

If career planning is to be successful potential analysis is required. In an era when graduates are accepted to have all the managerial talents that are apparently necessary to be successful in industry and commerce, it is becoming increasingly difficult for non-graduates or professionally qualified people to gain promotion. Despite current educational opportunities it is still possible to find managerial talent at many junior levels in an organisation. Potential analysis should unearth any unused talent that the organisation possesses.

16.2.6   Training

Training, though accepted as a vital part of any administrative function, is still often carried out in an unplanned *ad hoc* way, which must surely waste a considerable proportion of the money spent upon it.

The needs for training are well recognised. These are largely to:

- Perform a job as efficiently as possible.
- Reduce the time a person might take in learning a job by actually carrying it out.
- Develop job skills and prepare for promotion.
- Ensure that maximum use is made of intellect, character and dexterity.
- Avoid recruiting personnel who have some desired skill.
- Reduce turnover and low morale by giving job satisfaction through enhanced skills.

All these needs should, if appropriately diagnosed, help to reduce administrative costs.

Who needs to be trained?   Identifying training requirements is the essential precursor of setting up a training programme. Who, in fact, needs to be trained?

New recruits   Apart from the induction course that should take place immediately after recruitment, recruits may need immediate job and business training.

Promotion candidates   After identifying possible candidates for promotion, training appropriate to the possible position should be given.

Ongoing training The need to keep up-to-date is a constant battle, which training should help to win. It will be necessary to identify new techniques or procedures that staff should be concerned with and then ascertain new developments taking place with such techniques.

Training needs which become evident when performance appraisal has been carried out. These mostly concern enhanced job skills that should improve performance. Training needs largely stem from performance evaluation and manpower planning. The training programme needs to be integrated with job study and overall resource utilisation. It should not have a separate existence of its own.

Training to be done The training officer should prepare details of the likely skills and knowledge required by each job holder in the organisation. Largely, this should follow employees' job descriptions, but it may be necessary to record the techniques, knowledge and skills required more fully. The training needs revealed, plus those derived in studying job descriptions, should help to formulate corporate training requirements. The training officer should be aware of the changing environments which necessitate further training.

Normally, a training budget will have been established and, within this financial framework, training needs can be reviewed. The training officer will be concerned with evaluating the cost/benefit of the various types of training which could be introduced, weighing need against cost, training value against type of training, speed of skill acquisition against the effort of obtaining such skills.

Types of training should be suited to the skill enhancements required. As the subsequent examples of training methods show, the formal lecture is perhaps one of the least useful. The type of training should be chosen to:

- Suit the capabilities of the personnel needing training.
- Fit in with the organisation's economy.
- Obtain the highest value and quantity per £1 spent.
- Provide continuous skill acquisition so that the overall capability of personnel is constantly rising.
- Avoid, as far as possible, individual and non-continuous training.

The training programme should be adapted to suit personnel's training needs, age, experience and past training. An assessment of this type should determine:

- The mix of training types to be used.
- Who should be trained and for how long.
- Who should do the training.
- Where it should be done.
- What evaluation of the success of the training programme should be established.

In-company training   The benefits of in-company training could be:

- The interaction between participants can help to strengthen organisational team spirit.
- Time is not wasted in travelling to conference or training centres. Hotel bills are avoided.
- Training can be orientated towards the organisation and specific company problems can be raised.
- Training can be specifically directed towards the participants.
- The language of the course can be common for the organisation.

In-company training can be recommended, therefore, where a number of personnel need to be trained. It is usually cheaper and often more effective than training undertaken outside the organisation.

External courses may often be the only way in which appropriate skills can be gained. They are useful in meeting the specialist needs of one or very few of the organisation's personnel. Their use should be limited.

Non-specific training   There are numerous methods whereby personnel can gain experience without actually undertaking formal training, e.g.

- *Job rotation* is a valuable method of enhancing job skills. It tends to cause some disruption unless it is very well planned and there is some spare capacity in the department or section where rotation is practised.
- *Group discussion* is a comparatively simple method – personnel interested in a particular subject get together to discuss experiences and problems. It is usually unstructured.
- *Special assignments*   From time to time key personnel might be relieved of their routine duties and directed to carry out a special non-routine activity which should enhance their knowledge.
- *Job instruction* is particularly suitable for new recruits. Well written job instructions can be a powerful training aid. Learning from another employee or machine operator may not be very useful as it normally perpetuates errors and lack of skills.

All these 'non-training' situations have some danger. They tend to allow parochialism and lack of internal skills to be reborn in each person joining the organisation. Though this can be guarded against, it could have a very debilitating influence on job performance.

Programmed learning has been used very successfully in many organisations. It requires a degree of self-discipline, which is lacking in many people. The trainee reads an instruction text in a manual, carries out an example to prove that the instruction has been understood, checks the answer and, if it is wrong, rereads the instructions, until the example can be worked successfully. This method has been used to teach computer programming and accountancy. Lack of discussion with trainees, and a tutor, is an obvious drawback.

Business games hope to simulate real-life situations and, by demanding that decisions are made concerning the game, it is hoped that decision-making and thus management can be taught. Most games are computer-based. There are many limitations to such games – simulating a real-life situation with all its nuances is not easy. Most games have simple rules that can be easily understood, but which participants can manipulate to their advantage. It is doubtful, therefore, if skill in decision-making is always enhanced.

Case studies Most business schools pay great attention to the use of case studies. By analysis and evaluation of real-life situations, it is hoped that students will gain an insight into how organisations succeed or fail and what, in each case, a potential manager might do. The case study method has probably more relevance than business games but, even so, the activity can be artificial.

Role playing has been developed as a means of training. A simulated situation is posed to students who are requested to act out the roles of the personnel concerned. It has been useful in aiding job selection and general interviewing skills, selling and general counselling activities.

Extending this method to cover 'T' Group or Coverdale training should help to improve social skills. ('T' group and Coverdale training both emphasise the interactive commitment of people in working groups and how they relate to each other. See also Section 16.3 – Further reading.) Much of a manager's job skill must lie in the ability to communicate effectively, to weld his team together, and to create social relationships between his peers, supervisors and subordinates, which enable work to be carried out effectively. Regretfully, social skills training rarely seems to be undertaken even in the most progressive of organisations.

Action learning is a term used by training specialists to denote any situation where real-life problems are being tackled either by one person or a group of people. With groups, a 'chairman' and 'trainees' establish procedures to analyse a problem, solve it, and implement their solution.

16.2.7 Recruitment

If training and manpower planning fail to provide the requisite number of people of the right calibre, then recruitment is the last answer. Following are the steps that should be taken when recruiting:

Job descriptions These are an essential prerequisite to any form of recruitment. They should list the job in detail, recording the skills required and the responsibilities and activities they embody. They should be so recorded that a match between a potential recruit and a vacancy can be quickly established as follows:

- preferred age
- preferred education
- preferred experience
- personal attributes required
- special skills needed
- future prospects
- salary offered
- facilities and fringe benefits offered
- the job itself

Set out in this way potential recruits can be evaluated quickly, probably using a weighting scale.

Where to recruit   Recruitment can be internal or external. Internally, noticeboards or circulated vacancy lists are the usual methods used to notify vacancies. Externally the local Department of Employment's Professional and Executive Recruitment service may be helpful. For fairly senior positions, recourse to the national Press or professional journals may be necessary.

Application forms should be designed to produce the maximum amount of verifiable information which will be of use in considering candidates. The form should be set out so as to facilitate interviewing. Most people would like to hide something; the form should be designed to prevent them doing so.

The shortlist   Any comparatively important job should have a shortlist drawn up for it. Who should be on it should be decided by weighting desired attributes. It is unfortunate that some people of high potential will be missed out in consequence and some non-starters included.

Checking references   References should always be checked. It is unlikely that a potential recruit will give the name of anyone who will give a bad reference, but some useful inferences usually emerge. Equally it is not always wise to pay complete attention to a previous employer's opinions. Clash of personalities or vindictiveness can spoil the apparent objectivity.

Choice of candidate   Rather than recruit someone who is only just acceptable, it may be wise not to recruit at all. The expense of readvertising may be less than having a substandard recruit.

Success of the company's recruitment activities   It is always wise to look at recruitment and ask if it is being done successfully. Many interviewers have ideas about the kind of person they think will suit the organisation. Often they are not true. Recruits have to have the necessary job qualifications but also they need to fit in with organisational style and ethos. To discover whether a man has an appropriate personality that will fit in with his potential colleagues is extremely difficult.

Induction courses should be established for all recruits, irrespective of their eventual employment. Even a new gatekeeper should be aware of all the products the company makes. When several recruits start on the same day, an elaborate induction course is possible. Where a single recruit is involved, the course will be more difficult to arrange.

Employees' handbook   Most of the subject matter contained in the induction course should be put on permanent record in an employees' handbook, which should be a ready reference to the recruit's position in the company, what is expected of him and what, in return, the company offers. (See also Section 9.5.)

16.2.8   Disciplinary procedures and redundancy

Redundancy, sadly, is now more prevalent than at any time since the Second World War. It is something which most office administrators have either come to face with already or will in the future. Of all administrative situations it is probably the most painful, not least for the manager making the decision and telling the staff involved – anyone who has done it will never forget.

Redundancy is a state of being made jobless, through no fault of the redundant person. This is a definition that puts the onus for redundancy firmly on the shoulders of senior managers in the organisation.

The problem of discipline and activities leading up to a person being dismissed are part of the same broad procedures. It is commonplace for senior managers to bemoan the fact that they cannot enforce discipline. This is nonsense. Management is responsible for maintaining discipline within an organisation and for ensuring that there are well understood rules and procedures covering working practices and discipline.

16.2.9   Carrying out a redundancy programme

It is assumed that the organisation will have established a redundancy policy of some kind, which will be followed through, and that local trade union and Department of Employment requirements will be met. It is further assumed that it has been decided whether redundancies will be voluntary or non-voluntary.

It seems that a warning ought to be given so as to stifle rumours about redundancies which will debilitate company affairs, lowering morale and efficiency. Some extremely good personnel who are not being made redundant may resign.

After consulting the personnel department, a decision should be made on who is to be made redundant, and also the amount of severance pay and any other 'easing the pain' activities. Decide how affected employees are to be told of their position and issue a statement concerning the redundancies. A statement should also be prepared for the Press.

Speed is essential once a decision has made if rumour is not to take over completely.

Perhaps groups of all the company's employees should be told of the situation, starting early one morning and finishing, if possible, before lunchtime. One senior person might be given responsibility to handle the whole programme. He might like to nominate assistants from key departments to help him. His responsibilities should include the following:

- Ensuring that the redundancies are seen to be fair by everyone affected.
- Making sure that the reasons for redundancies and the fact that redundancies could not be avoided are well known.
- Carrying out negotiations with trade unions, either through the normal joint consultation arrangements, or as special procedures. He will have to take into account national agreements, number of trade unions and redundancies from each union, local community feeling and size of the redundancy programme. He must be seen to be fair and to be giving equal treatment to all the groups affected. The limits of negotiations will have to be known before the meetings begin.
- Ensuring that all senior managers cooperate fully in informing people of redundancies.
- Carrying out individual counselling where this is considered necessary.
- Preparing contingency plans for any likely backlash which redundancy may produce – unfair dismissals accusations, race relations problems, sit-in or other disturbances, or false stories to the Press, etc.
- Planning a new job provision programme, if this seems possible; helping those redundant to find new employment.
- When the redundancy programme is over, introducing a morale-building plan to ensure that those who remain see opportunities for future security and growth inside the organisation.

Redundancies have to be seen to be absolutely necessary and they have to be carried out fairly. The trade unions must be involved at a very early date. Naturally, trade unionists have job security uppermost in their minds and redundancy must be handled honestly and deftly. If redundancies occur in an *ad hoc* and apparently unsatisfactory way, it is natural for the unions to demand greater knowledge of company plans and business activities in order to ensure that redundancy only occurs after the most rigorous assessment of the company's position.

Organisations have a social and moral responsibility to retain people who have worked for them long enough to have economic ties – such as mortgages children at school, etc. – if at all possible. Redundancy is mainly caused by poor business planning and employees have some right to compensation for lack of management skills.

16.3   Further reading

1   A.R. Smith (Editor), *Corporate Manpower Planning,* Gower (1980).

2 D.H. Gray, *Manpower Planning,* IPM (1972).
3 M.M. Mandell, *The Employment Interview,* Bailey Brothers and Swinfen (1965).
4 G. McBeath, *Organisation and Manpower Planning,* Business Books (1968).
5 P.C. Morea, *Guidance, Selection and Training,* Routledge (1970).
6 T.H. Patten, *Manpower Planning and the Development of Human Resources,* Wiley (1971).
7 R. Stammers and J. Patrick, *The Psychology of Training,* Menthuen (1975).
8 D.H. Sweet, *Recruitment – a guide for managers,* Addison-Wesley (1975).
9 D. MacKenzie Davey and P. McDonnell, *How to interview,* BIM (1975).
10 J. Angel, *How to Prepare Yourself for an Industrial Tribunal,* IPM (1980).
11 J. Bramham, *Practical Manpower Planning,* IPM (Second edition, 1978).
12 W. Marks, *Preparing an Employee Handbook,* IPM (1975).
13 M. Taylor, *Coverdale on Management,* Heinemann (1981).
14 'Company redundancy policies', *BIM Information Summary 137* (1969).
15 *Redundancy Act,* HMSO (1965).
16 D. Wedderburn, *White-collar Redundancy,* University Press (1964).
17 Greville Janner, *Janner's Consolidated Compendium of Employment Law,* Business Books (1982).

Seventeen

People and Change

17.1 Introduction

The last decade has seen considerable, nearly overwhelming, changes in the social, economic and cultural situation.

1 There have been changes in the balance of power between employees and management. Trade unions have proved that their power in some situations is nearly absolute. Management often feels bewildered and baffled that their age-old managerial authority no longer seems to exist.

2 The changes in the balance of power have not brought responsibility along with the rights that unions now believe are part and parcel of their activities. Managers, again, are often faced with a situation where contracts seem to be wilfully broken; solemn and binding agreements are suddenly no longer solemn and binding. Management has often delivered; employees have not often given a corresponding response.

3 Economic and political failures have undoubtedly brought about resentment and a lack of faith in 'leadership'. As managers have wrestled – unsuccessfully sometimes – with problems beyond their experience, employees have become increasingly sceptical of the skill of management and in consequence its right to manage.

4 The same failures to improve the standard of living have lead in part to social unrest and general disillusionment with traditional values. If society cannot deliver material requirements, then society must be changed – so goes the theory of the new radicals.

5 Improved education has automatically motivated a more discerning and demanding workforce. All organisations ultimately depend upon the willingness of the organisation's members to forego some freedoms in order

to gain personal objectives. Where it seems that the benefits to be gained are not matched by the freedoms given up, then the organisation is no longer a viable unit.

6   Economic changes are occurring much faster than ever before. Inflation is now a threat to total economic stability. Shortages of power, raw materials, labour, skills, all have an effect on a manager's ability to manage in the traditional way.

7   The whole problem of social, economic and cultural change has possibly squeezed middle and lower management most. Their authority has been undermined. Often their position is intolerable with the people they normally control being paid only slightly less than they are, but not encumbered with the same responsibilities. The prerequisities which mostly went with middle-management jobs have either been taken away or had to be shared with employees. So without doubt loyalty at first-line supervisor or junior-management level has suffered and will go on suffering until a satisfactory job and authority structure has been determined.

Technical skills were at one time a predominating need in being a manager. Now behavioural ability is a requirement that every manager needs to the full. He needs technical skills as well, but if he allows these to overshadow all his actions, then his success must be limited.

17.2   Change – why it is opposed

Why should people want to hinder, restrict or even prevent change occurring? The fact that change is presented in a logical and understandable way, and in a form which proves that overall benefit will accrue, is no guarantee whatsoever that it will be acceptable.

1   It is logical to assume that as change usually challenges the *status quo* and tends to undermine the security of some people to some extent, it will be resented unless it provides greater rewards and benefits than are gained from security.

2   Each person has his own personal objectives. These may be strongly orientated towards his job or conversely his social life. If change tends to undermine personal objectives, therefore, it is likely that it will be opposed. The degree of opposition will depend upon the character of the individual concerned, but will also stem from his perception of the change.

3   To have change imposed arbitrarily is usually resented – it attacks all employees' egos; it denies them the possibility of helping to formulate the change; it infers that the people who will undergo change have nothing to

offer in its formulation. It seems essential that if change is to be accepted with only minor qualms, it has to be worked through and agreed with the people it will affect. They should, if at all possible, be given an opportunity to have some impact on the change taking place.

4   It is possible that people with specific values, training, culture, class, age, sex, will accept change more readily than others.

5   If, in the past, change has been handled badly, ignoring people's views and opinions and so building a climate of hostility, it is not likely that change will be accepted even if it is being handled as well as possible. People in organisations have long memories.

6   If the company is doing well and is obviously well managed, it is possible that change will be accepted better than if the converse is true.

These statements, if true, indicate that those who would like to bring change about must direct their energies to ensuring that the change will appeal to those whom it will affect. They must assure themselves (if necessary carry out detailed analysis) that their proposals can be projected in such a way that the recipients will believe that the change will be to their benefit. The positive side of the change must be stated. Somehow a match between the aspirations and objectives of those affected and those proposing the change must be determined.

17.3   Aspects of change

The problem, therefore, for anyone involved in creating change is not producing ideas and better ways of doing things, but to get them accepted, implemented and running well. The precepts that change-makers might follow are given below.

17.3.1   Change as seen by the people affected

Director level   At this level in the company hierarchy, efficiency is often either pressed too vigorously or, for various reasons, not at all. In the former case, there are irrational impulses to be overcome, such as buying a computer without real justification. In the latter, the search for new ideas is regarded with suspicion, and no guidance is given on the way in which clerical routines can be improved, nor are the departments or areas which need to be investigated suggested. Line managers are not prodded into accepting changes in their systems.

Departmental manager or supervisor level   A request at this level for some change to be made is often looked upon as an unwarranted interference with the managerial function. Many recommendations to improve office efficiency founder because they either run counter to the local manager's preconceived ideas or are regarded as a threat to his ability or status.

Desk level At this level, more than any other in the organisation, reluctance to accept change is often indicative of deep-seated psychological fears. The main cause is lack of security. Systems changes and methods improvements are, it is often considered, a weapon of management, designed to create redundancy and to frighten staff into higher efficiency.

At each level it is important to ask:

- How will the person/people be affected?
  considerably
  moderately
- What kind of people will be affected?
  numbers
  sex
  age
  training
  company loyalty
  temperament
  trade union
  social values/culture
- What is the likely response to the change proposed?
  outright opposition
  general mistrust
  lack of cooperation
  strike
- What are the likely reasons for rejecting the change?
  redundancy
  lower status
  more work for the same pay
  habit
  culture
  alliances
  distrust of management

Answers to the questions posed will provide some excellent suggestions as to how the change might be carried out.

17.3.2 What does change offer?

Change, if possible, has to be seen to offer something of value to the people affected. What can be done to improve:

- status

- job security
- pay
- general working conditions
- promotion prospects

of people affected by change? What are the personal objectives of the people being affected?

- more social contact
- greater ego satisfaction
- to have superior fringe benefits
- to belong to a successful team

If possible, a match between these personal wishes and the change taking place has to be achieved.

17.3.3   People will want to influence change

Self-generating change groups are one means of making changes that will be acceptable to the group taking part. Unfortunately the group has rarely the knowledge, ability or conceptual vision to be able to play a leading role in creating change.

Whether an operative is afraid of redundancy or just working harder, the situation will only be aggravated by rumour. Good communications are, therefore, vital. The clerks being affected and the manager introducing the change must have a continuous dialogue.

17.4   Vehicles for change

The constraints on creating change – tradition, history, management competence, organisational rigidity, even the will to do so – need to be challenged by introducing procedures that will help change to occur. What are these?

1   A management services function. Despite the prevailing scepticism about management services personnel, they are change agents. They can help line managers to bring about change. Their skills should be largely orientated towards profitable change.
2   Consultants are in the same field as management services.
3   Changes in company style. The chief executive often has a major influence on the style the company adopts. He can create a conservative, no-change ethos, or provide the drive for major change.
4   Project teams, problem-solving task committees, and profit-improvement teams are all variations on the same theme. Various types of people – managers, management services specialists, trade unionists – are brought together to help create profitable change.
5   Organisational development is often used to help introduce change. OD is a participative process which is established to solve specific problems.

6 Work organisation and associated payment systems can be useful.

17.5 Change despite opposition

States of absolute cooperation in change situations are largely mythical. Few, if any, changes have 100 per cent backing from everyone involved. Some, however, face outright opposition, where it is impossible to reconcile individual desires with organisational goals. If cooperation cannot be gained it is often desirable to go ahead without it. What are these occasions?

a Where the board of directors or senior management are absolutely convinced that a course of action is really necessary and not only wholeheartedly support it, but openly show that they do. For example, where the organisation's future is at risk and some people must be sacrificed for the good of the whole.
b Where recalcitrants are few in number and known to be averse to giving a fair day's work for a fair day's pay.
c Where hostility is of a carping nature, without any justifiable foundation.
d Where it is thought that the opposition is purely temporary and that, once the scheme is in operation, it will disappear completely. This is perhaps the most common form of opposition. Some people's fear of change will not be allayed by words, only by action. Often the man most opposed to a new system is eventually its greatest advocate.

The greatest danger for anyone contemplating the installation of a new system in the face of opposition is to consider that he is a one-man commando battling against opposition, when it is neither in the company's interest nor his own to fight.

17.6 Further reading

1 D. Newman, *Organisation Change,* Arnold (1972).
2 K.D. Walters, 'Your employees' right to blow the whistle', *Harvard Business Review* (July/Aug 1975).
3 T. Burns and G.M. Stalker, *The Management of Innovation,* Tavistock (1961).
4 S.A. Judson, *A Manager's Guide to Making Changes,* Wiley (1966).
5 G.H. Varney, *An Organisation Development Approach to Management Development,* Addison-Wesley (1976).
6 W.G. Bennis, *Planning of Change,* Holt, Rinehart and Winston (1970).
7 C. Rallings, *White-collar Workers,* Gower (1981).
8 D. Birchall and V. Hammond, *Tomorrow's Office Today – managing technological change,* Business Books (1981).
9 H. Marlow, *Managing Change – a strategy for our time,* IPM (1975).
10 C. Margerison, *Influencing Organisational Change,* IPM (1978).

Eighteen

Work Patterns

18.1 Introduction

Work pattern is a term which covers the hours of work and general working conditions of people in offices. The foundation stone of establishing a good administrative service has been the rigorous application of single shift, 5- or $5\frac{1}{2}$-day, working with everyone working the same hours. This is changing in some areas and activities very quickly. This chapter indicates some of the changing work patterns that are being successfully applied.

18.2 Flexible working hours

With the relaxation in discipline in offices and a greater awareness of differences in individual psychology, the apparent need to work a rigid 9 a.m. to 5 p.m. pattern is being superseded by flexibility in working. Experiments have been made (and in some instances formal change has followed) in allowing flexibility in attendance at the office.

18.2.1 Systems adopted

Most systems that have been introduced have a core-time element. This is a time when everyone has to be at work, perhaps 10 a.m. to 3 p.m., so that customers can be dealt with, discussions held, workload planned and results discussed.

Outside core-time, participants are allowed to opt for an extension or reduction in hours at either end of the normal working day. They can also take a shorter or longer lunch break. Many organisations allow participants to take time off for extra hours worked. Two or three days of overwork fulfillment can be accumulated and taken as part of a holiday.

Most organisations impose restrictions on the degree of flexibility allowed. A starting time of no earlier than 7.30 a.m., for example, or no more than two days' holiday to be accumulated per month (which must be taken within a month of being earned) is fairly standard practice.

Normally a time-recording unit is used to ensure that participants do not abuse the system. The methods of time-recording used include:

Manual recording   This is often a reversion to the use of attendance books which were a part of many offices not so long ago. So long as staff are trusted, manual records can give information that only sophisticated data-collection or even computers could equal.

Time clocks   Clocking-in machines have been used in factories for many years and similar machines have been introduced by some organisations for their administrative personnel.

Meter time-recording   This form of recording mechanism merely records hours worked, not when they are worked. Employees are given a personal key (usually made of plastic) which fits into the mechanism. The key is inserted on arrival, and recording is continued until it is removed. (Employees often, apparently, forget to take out the key at the end of the day.) Some equipment necessitates only the input of the key and its immediate withdrawal to activate recording.

Computer-linked systems   Some computer systems are used to record time attendance. Employees use a badge which is inserted into a terminal near their place of work. Others are used to process data provided by a simple clocking system, the data being prepared on punched cards.

Most flexible-working-hour systems have a settlement or accounting period covering a period of time at the end of which personnel must settle their account, either by taking time off or working longer hours to ensure that full working hours have been recorded. Normally the settlement period is a month, though some organisations operate on two-weekly account periods.

18.2.2   Impact on the organisation

a   By permitting individuals to exercise freedom in the choice of working hours, the authority and discipline once considered so essential in running offices is diluted. A change in management behaviour and style is often necessary when flexible working hours are introduced.

b   Delegation has to be improved. If supervisors and their staff have opted for different hours, then it is necessary to establish work patterns and delegation which will cope with the change.

c   The delegation suggested in *(b)* might show a new need for training supervisors – especially in participation.

d   Some individuals who have been given the freedom to choose their working hours will find that they are unable to plan their work appropriately. They need the discipline that rigid hours provide if they are to be effective. Special training is required for these individuals and perhaps less flexibility in working hours.

e   Certain employees in the organisation will not be able to participate fully in the scheme. Wages must be prepared, for example. Receptionists are needed for the full working day, as are telephonists. Friction may occur if those thus affected are not allowed some extra fringe benefit to compensate for their job.

18.2.3   Benefits

1   Flexible working hours provide a positive contribution towards job enrichment and self-respect by helping participants to meet their social ambitions. This in turn, it is hoped, will provide a powerful motivator in achieving organisational as well as personal objectives.

2   To accommodate the idea of flexible working hours, team work has to improve considerably. A freer and more open relationship between managers and their staff often emerges. This in time could lead to improved performance, which is beneficial to the organisation.

3   By extending flexible hours, it is likely that staff who would not otherwise work at all will be attracted to administrative work. Women with young children, for example, want to be at home when their children arrive back from school.

4   Flexible working hours are often seen as a valuable fringe benefit and in many organisations it has been used to recruit a variety of scarce personnel – secretaries, computer programmers, etc. Absenteeism is lessened.

5   In an era when flexibility is a growing and essential part of the success of any organisation, the use of flexible working hours aids the generation of a flexible approach to work, job design, work teams and even work location.

6   Rush-hour travelling can be avoided by many staff.

7   Many organisations which have a flexible workload would be better served by having flexible working hours.

8   Metabolism of people tends to differ. Some are brighter and more active in the morning; others later in the day. Flexible working hours provide a situation where people can work at the time of day that suits them.

9   Many people prefer to have a part of the day when they can sit quietly and carry out 'quiet work'. Flexible working hours provide the opportunity.

10   Women, who often need to be able to alter the length of their working day to suit their personal situation, are usually more in favour of flexible working hours than men. Consequently organisations with a high proportion of women in their workforce might best be suited to flexible working arrangements.

18.2.4   Disadvantages

a   Increased costs will be incurred. There will be the cost of using the recording mechanisms (if these are installed), plus the cost of administering the scheme. If the day is lengthened, then increased lighting and heating will be required.
b   Where the company provides transport or has arrangements with local transport authorities to have transport for its staff, the problem of rearrangement could be considerable and might inhibit the scheme totally.
c   People may forget to take out their recording key at the end of their work period. Abuses may develop.
d   Where the organisation has commitments to outsiders, e.g. giving a service to the public, the service may be guaranteed only by providing extra staff.
e   In the event of failure, it may be difficult to revert back to a normal hours system.

18.2.5   Checklist to introduce flexible work hours

1   Why introduce FWH? What benefits could be gained? Does it suit us? What will it cost?
2   What core-time is needed?
3   What flex-bands could be allowed?
4   How is the flex-time to be recorded? What attendance equipment or system do we need?
5   Should anyone be excluded from the scheme?
6   What settlement period should we introduce?
7   Who will be responsible for administering the scheme?
8   How do we get general agreement and understanding from the staff?
9   What arrangements outside the organisation do we need to make?

18.3   Shiftwork in offices

Justification for the very heavy capital expenditure or rental involved in a computer installation must often lie in intensive machine utilisation. This, in many instances, must result in shiftworking, particularly where the normal eight-hour day proves insufficient to allow the equipment to cope with all the work required of it.

For example, in a medium-sized computer installation, the bottleneck in increasing throughput may be one particular machine. If extra capacity is needed and normal office hours are already being worked, two courses of action are open; either another machine is bought or rented, or some form of shiftworking is adopted. This section describes the difficulties and principles that are generally applicable to shiftworking in offices.

18.3.1   Difficulties

The greatest difficulty in introducing any kind of shift system lies in the psychological barriers that have to be broken down. Inevitably there will be strong resistance to the introduction of factory-type conditions into the office. Yet the office has already had to accept many factory conditions, not the least in the use of a wide range of machinery. The extended use of overtime, too, has introduced factory conditions into the normal lives of many office workers.

But even when psychological barriers to shift working have been breached, it will strain staff loyalty to work shifts without any extra pay when other work is available in the same area in normal working hours. Thus a company that introduces shiftworking into its offices must be prepared to pay higher salaries. This is common in most shift systems in industry. The added attraction of a bonus system might also have to be considered. If such financial inducements are insufficient for young females in, say, a computer installation, males may have to be considered, at least on any equipment likely to produce bottlenecks.

Shifts can vary in duration as well as starting and finishing times, but unless there are well defined periods, say 6 a.m. to 2 p.m. or 2 p.m. to 10 p.m., there will inevitably be an overlap of labour, i.e. shiftworking and normal office hours working should not be mixed indiscriminately.

18.3.2   Cost factors

The cost of shiftworking will not only be reflected in extra shift payments to operatives. Other costs may include:

a   Extra rental, if equipment is rented. The amount will depend on several factors: the extra running time needed; the size of the installation; the possibility of conversion at a later date to equipment with a higher capacity, etc.

b   The probable need to employ an extra service engineer.

c   Cost of ancillary services: gatemen, canteen staff, etc. Other costs, such as heating, lighting, ventilation and power for equipment, will have to be included.

d   Possibly late-night transport to take staff home after the local bus or train service has ceased to run.

e   Supervision, unless the operators themselves are sufficiently senior and responsible.

There are also reasons why the total throughput of equipment will not increase in direct ratio with the extra hours scheduled, which will affect the cost of the installation. For example, the following may happen:

f   The machines will be under greater strain and so breakdowns may occur more frequently.

g   With extra hours worked on only one section of an installation, it may be more difficult to schedule the workload and some delays may occur.

h When shiftworkers only are on duty, there can be no appeal to a departmental manager for clarification of problems, and it is seldom possible to give precise instructions to cover every eventuality.

18.4   Four-day week

The four-day week is a more radical time shift than either flexible working hours or shiftworking. It does not involve a reduction in hours but the working of a normal week (say 38 hours) in four days. Usually various bonus schemes and incentives need to be applied to ensure that the four-day week is effective.

The four-day week is an obvious step for any organisation that needs to keep capital equipment fully utilised. Whether it is required for administrative personnel is still to be truly tested.

18.5   Autonomous workgroups

Chapter 11 suggested how workgroups might be given more autonomy and flexibility. The changing working patterns of flexi-hours and shiftworking might make autonomy more and more important. If this is true, due regard must be paid to the ways and means by which autonomy is introduced and controlled, and the work for it planned. Autonomy might quickly lead to anarchy in some situations.

18.6   New payment systems

Along with new or revised work patterns, there is an obvious need to consider new payment systems. For some time now, some office functions have been 'paid by results', notably typists, photocopying activities and punched-card operatives, but generally there does not seem to be any great development of this method. The need for job flexibility has held back smaller concerns and most, if not all, successful incentive applications have been in medium- to large-sized organisations. Lack of an appropriate work organisation and work patterns has prevented the wide use of new payments systems. Those that have been tried have followed these trends:

a *Normal payment by results*   Typists have been paid for lines of type produced; punched-card operatives for the number of cards processed.
b *Departmental performance based on overall achievements*   For example, a sales office, where customer contact is important and some telephone selling has taken place, could receive a proportion of the sales made.
c *Overall company performance*   Some years ago various schemes were introduced including a bonus based on sales revenue/profit/added value. The latter seems a more realistic basis for wage incentive payment than many. A formula based on the ratio of added value to wages/salaries paid is determined, whereby a split of the gains beyond a specified base level is

made. These 'second-generation incentives' have been much in vogue in the last three to five years, but with a declining economic/sales picture, their advantages to clerks and shop-floor workers seem a little distant. With improving economic times, the use of added value should again be appreciated.

Salaries should still be based on job evaluation data, even with autonomous work groups. Job flexibility and autonomy need to be considered within the group. Stressful working environments and jobs must still be seen as essential parts of the reward system. This can best be done by a separate wage supplement.

Knowledge needs to be a key factor in job evaluation and its related payment, if knowledgeable people are to be retained. Wage payment schemes should be applied equally to blue- or white-collar workers.

It must be remembered that payment schemes on the shop floor have often been a direct (if not total) cause of poor industrial relations. Any payment system, work organisation or work pattern should be designed to help improve industrial relations, not bring about their decline. Loss of earnings due to influences and activities outside the control of the workforce are often a bone of contention.

Any new work patterns and payment systems should be designed to engender cooperation and a feeling that the success of the company is of equal importance to workers and managers alike. Any system of wage payment based on added value or any other overall performance measurement needs a considerable educational campaign before it is accepted by most of the workforce.

18.7   Conclusion

Office managers in a fast-changing world should be concerned with the kind of work patterns, work organisations and payment system that will help them foster and achieve change and yet, at the same time, cope with often dismal economic conditions. This is not easy. This chapter and previous ones pose alternatives that could be useful. Retaining the *status quo* obviously has little to recommend it.

18.8   Further reading

1   J.G. March and H.A. Simon, *Organisation,* Wiley (1958).
2   D. Birchall, *Job Design,* Gower (1975).
3   M. Woodcock, *Team Development Manual,* Gower (1979).
4   A. Hepworth and M. Osbaldiston, *The Way We Work,* Gower (1979).
5   W.R. Bion, *Experiences in Groups,* Tavistock (1961).
6   P.B. Smith, *Groups with Organisations,* Harper & Row (1973).
7   R. Wild, *Work Organisations,* Wiley (1975).

Part Three

Planning and Control of Office Administration

Nineteen

Planning the Administration Function

19.1 Introduction

It is not intended that a detailed record is made of profit-planning procedures. This is beyond the scope of this book and readers might refer to my *Profit Planning Handbook* (Business Books, 1978).

It seems important, however, to record how planning generally affects the administrative function. Like every other function it needs to be planned and controlled so that it plays its part in achieving organisational objectives. For some offices, administration may be the only function carried on, e.g. local government. The need to relate mainly clerical resources to required results is the same as for a production unit.

Administration managers should be concerned with the two normal levels of planning – operational and long term. Operational planning covers a short time span, usually a year, and is often covered by a budgetary control system. The long-term plan is frequently concerned with the use of resources in the next three to five years. There is nothing sacrosanct about five years and the long term should last only as long as major changes in resources can be achieved.

19.2 Planning activities

Planning usually follows well defined steps. In some organisations one or other of the steps may be more important than the rest. In any situation, planning must be considered to be a disciplined approach to achieving corporate objectives. Unlike many management techniques, planning needs a specific psychological and philosophical approach by the management team. They must feel that planning works. They must believe that the plans they make can and must be achieved. Planning must be a part (and an important part) of their life.

The steps in making a plan are clear-cut and should be followed no matter what is being planned. These are:

Definition of job responsibilities   Job responsibilities should provide the means of allocating and achieving planned results. They should be set out in such a way that performance standards can be quickly established.

Control systems   These need to be in existence to monitor results. Budgetary control systems, for example, are required as well as detailed cost control mechanisms.

Environmental audit which covers both the internal and external environment of an organisation. Past performance will be known, for example, but it should be qualfied by environmental factors that have contributed to the results. Environmental analysis needs to be rigorously carried out in order to ensure that full consideration is given to any factor that will influence the plan.

Desired results   Any organisation should have one or more desired results to which it aspires. For many commercial organisations these have to be established as 'trade offs' – profit and growth, for example, or market share and profit. For many companies, return on investment or net worth is a valid basis for determining a result. For others, earnings per share may be the key performance necessary. These corporate results will then have to be broken down into management objectives, e.g. production performance at x cost and y machine utilisation.

Gap analysis   The production of corporate objectives will usually show a gap between what is required and what seems feasible, when viewed against current internal and external environments.

The dialogue   As part of the gap analysis, therefore, it will be necessary to institute a dialogue that eventually determines what are realistic and achievable objectives. From this, strategies and tactics will emerge which, it is hoped, will help to achieve objectives.

Control mechanisms are then needed to ensure that plans are being achieved. While the act of planning infers that the plan will be achieved, monitoring of some kind is still necessary.

The steps often run into each other, especially where planning has been in operation for some years. For example, realistic objectives will have been determined for each year. The analysis of environments may be going on all the time and objectives setting may not be the independent step outlined.

Planning systems infer that a hierarchy of plans must exist. There will be an overall business or profit plan that will broadly give the direction in which the total organisation is going. Sub-plans of varying importance will then be made, although usually they will have no separate existence of their own. They will indicate how production, marketing, research and development resources will be utilised in order to ensure that the overall business plan is achieved.

For the office administrator in a manufacturing company, planning will largely be concerned with administrative resource utilisation to achieve corporate objectives. Normally this will be the service that administrative units will give in order that marketing and production personnel can achieve their objectives. The kind of plans needed, therefore, have to be concerned with such resources as:

- administration manpower
- the computer and data processing equipment generally
- systems development
- use of accounting resources, etc.

Many administrative resources will need no detailed plan. Accounting personnel, for example, may from one year to another carry out the same function – preparation of trading accounts, profit and loss statements, balance-sheets, etc. Others, such as systems development personnel and computer activities, where resources can be redirected comparatively easily, will need an appropriate plan. The process and plans involved are set out in Figure 19.1.

19.3 Administrative plans

As Figure 19.2 shows, the administration plan should have a direct relationship with other functions in the organisation. That said, what plans should the office administration manager consider? Normally these are as follows.

19.3.1 Cost and numbers plan

This should show the relationship between the cost and number of administrative staff and those in other functions and activities. The three measurements that might be used are:

- Current cost of each administrative function, i.e.:
    accounting
    cost accounting
    sales order processing
    management services
    credit control
    purchasing, etc.
- current personnel employed
- administration cost as a ratio of:
    total costs
    added value
    profit

This plan should show current and future cost, numbers and ratios which will be achieved one, two or three years ahead.

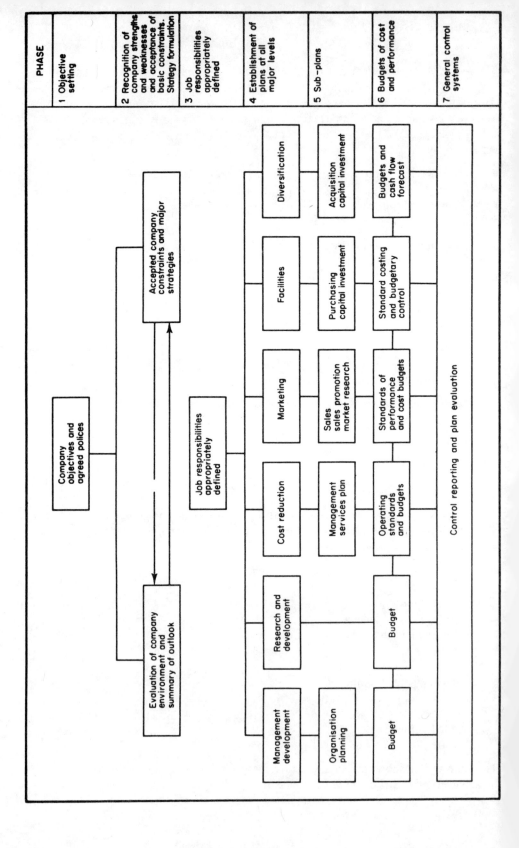

PHASE		
1 Objective setting		
2 Recognition of company strengths and weaknesses and acceptance of basic constraints. Strategy formulation		
3 Job responsibilities appropriately defined		
4 Establishment of plans at all major levels		
5 Sub-plans		
6 Budgets of cost and performance		
7 General control systems		

Company objectives and agreed polices

Accepted company constraints and major strategies

Evaluation of company environment and summary of outlook

Job responsibilities appropriately defined

Management development

Research and development

Cost reduction

Marketing

Facilities

Diversification

Organisation planning

Management services plan

Sales sales promotion market research

Purchasing capital investment

Acquisition capital investment

Budget

Budget

Operating standards and budgets

Standards of performance and cost budgets

Standard costing and budgetary control

Budgets and cash flow forecast

Control reporting and plan evaluation

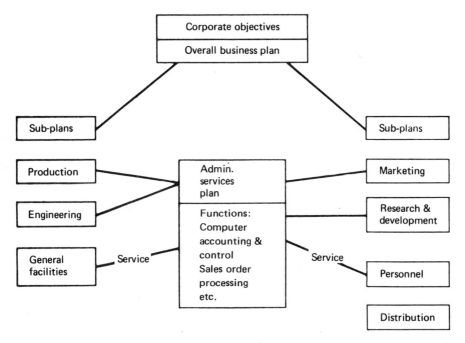

Figure 19.2 *Administrative services plan and its relationship with other plans*

19.3.2 Organisation planning

The basis of the organisation plan is to match the company's organisation, competence and capacity so as to adapt to the environment in which it has to operate to survive. This indicates, rightly, that an organisation must be constantly changing in order to meet the challenge of technological, competitive and general environmental change. Some factors embodied in this plan will be:

- a situation audit
- job analysis and design
- training, succession and management development plans
- work organisation development
- solutions to authority, power and responsibility problems

19.3.3 Cost-reduction planning

Five approaches need to be considered:

- systems analysis or method study
- value administration
- clerical work measurement

- organisational changes of various kinds
- the use of equipment of various kinds

19.3.4   Service plans

Services in this respect refer to the personnel who provide a service to line managers, e.g. organisation and methods, operations research, computer people, etc. When service departments are mostly engaged in 'fire fighting', planning on any long-term basis is irrelevant. Planning will be concerned with using resources in order to achieve desired objectives. Plans such as those in Figures 19.3 and 19.4 are needed. Figure 19.3 sets out a plan for business consultants for a year. Figure 19.4 shows a stategic plan for computer system usage. The computer plan should:

a   Indicate the resources being deployed, e.g. hardware, personnel, money.
b   Show how these resources are being utilised.
c   Give the likely cash flows.

In the case of the installation shown in Figure 19.4, for example, the two major systems that will be computerised are stock control and production planning and control. These two systems must have been determined as the key ones in improving company efficiency.

Once the two key systems have been established, the allocation of hardware and personnel resources will follow nearly automatically. The difference between the cost and the saving that each system's application provides should help to determine its priority in the overall plan.   The plan shown in Figure 19.4 is an example of a document likely to be included in the overall business plan. The savings and costs will have been added to the organisation's cash flow forecast and the staff involvement will have been embodied in the manpower plan.

The overview will be used to support the total strategy being followed by the organisation. As such it should be achieved and appropriate control systems to monitor its progress should be introduced. There will be a need for a series of sub-plans covering:

- each year (mainly for budgeting purposes)
- each system or application
- each major manpower resource

Each sub-plan should be in sufficient detail to facilitate weekly/monthly monitoring, e.g. for each application it will be necessary to have a man/week forecast of involvement, calculated for each systems analyst and programmer. Timesheets and work logs can then be used to judge whether the sub-plan will be achieved in the time and at the cost calculated.

19.4   Why plans and planning fail

1   *Plan linking*   Because it is linked closely with the business plan, the EDP

Practitioner	Skills	Allocated assignment	Jan	Feb	Mar	Apr	May	June	July	Aug	Sept	Oct	Nov	Dec	Comment
1) R Capper	Major business skills	1) Profit improvement program and I/C systems 3 installation 2) Management development program													Working on key result area. Appropriate assignments
2) G Taylor	Systems analyst major business skills	1) Profit improvement program and systems 3 installation 2) Management development program													Key result area
3) G Simpson	OR specialist	1) Stock control													Further assignment/s required
4) M Glover	OR specialist	1) Stock control													Further assignment/s required
6) G Procter	Time study method study	1) Time study													Time method study element missing

Figure 19.3 Management services department plan: resource utilisation

Years from acquisition	Planned applications	Planned hardware	Staff involvement		Planned current		Planned cumulative	
			Type	Man/years	Cost	Savings	Cost	Savings
−1	Invoicing sales ledger	Site preparation	Management Operational DP Systems analysts Programmers Other	2 — 3 1 2	£40 000	—		
0	Stock recording labour control & wages payment	Computer & associated peripherals	Management Operational DP Systems analysts Programmers Other	3 14 5 5 2	£70 000	—	£110 000	—
+1	Stock control sales analysis	Two shift working	Management Operational DP Systems analysts Programmers Other	4 19 6 7 2	£84 000	£30 000	£94 000	£30 000
+2	Production planning & control. Control of WIP	More disk storage required	Management Operational DP Systems analysts Programmers Other	4 19 6 7 2	£84 000	£150 000	£178 000	£180 000
+3	Despatch & warehousing control	Line printer of increased speed	Management Operational DP Systems analysts Programmers Other	4 19 5 6 2	£96 000	£130 000	£274 000	£310 000
+4	Order entry – on line	VDUs & terminals required	Management Operational DP Systems analysts Programmers Other	4 19 4 6 2	£95 000	£120 000	£369 000	£430 000

Figure 19.4 *Computer development program*

plan's success depends upon the accuracy of the business plan and its chances of success. All plans in an organisation are interdependent to some degree. If one goes wrong in some way, it has wide-ranging repercussions on nearly every other plan. A failure to recruit a systems analyst, for example, could delay the introduction of computerised stock control which could impact on marketing strategy and pull down forecast sales revenue. Eventually production facilities may be affected.

2 Planning is not taken seriously   The plan shown in Figure 19.4 is a key document in achieving good computer usage. If there is a significant divergence from the work set out, it is unlikely that the costs and savings will be correct. It is likely that using the discounted cash flow method, the computer application shown is scarcely breaking even, and any serious decline in achieving the systems development planned could result in a loss.

Administrative managers who complete a plan format and then forget all about it destroy their own credibility and the possiblility of the whole organisation moving steadily to the achievement of corporate objectives. Commitment to a plan, once it has been made and accepted, must be total.

3 Inaccurate forecasts   Forecasts are never accurate, but the limits of their accuracy are important. Over-pessimism can be as important as undue optimism. Personnel can be underutilised, systems delayed unnecessarily, profits not achieved.

4 Lack of flexibility   Plans cannot be totally rigid; some flexibility must exist. Spare resources, if at all possible, should be available to ensure that the plan is achieved.

5 Action from monitoring plans   There has to be a response to an out-of-course action – even minor delays in gaining savings may make the whole project uneconomic. Delay in replacing staff who have left is often a major cause for delayed computer projects. Potential staff turnover should be included in the manpower plan and the computer overview.

6 Inadequately defined responsibilities   Responsibility for achieving the results anticipated within planned timescales should be allocated for all projects, no matter how insignificant. The project leaders can then discuss timescales and resources with the manager to ensure that they are reasonable. Where no clear-cut responsibilities are recognised, delay and inadequate work will often result.

19.5 Further reading

1   B.H. Walley, *Profit Planning Handbook,* Business Books (1978).
2   L.A. Allen, *Making Managerial Planning More Effective,* McGraw-Hill (1982).

Twenty

Cost Control of Office Activities

20.1 Introduction

Various reports and calculations breaking down office-running costs have been carried out. The ones that seem to be most realistic give the following averages:

People of all kinds	70%
Furniture and office equipment	22%
Space and building/environmental costs	8%

Cost-control of office activities might, therefore, yield most benefit from keeping people-costs to a minimum. This, in practice, may not be true, as environmental costs could be easier to control, or furniture and equipment costs could be readily assessed to give an appropriate return on investment. However, by any calculations, people are important and control over their cost must be given priority. The general view that office workers only work effectively for up to half their time in the office adds urgency to cost-control of office activities.

20.2 Budgets

The Institute of Cost and Management Accountants defines a budget as: 'A financial or quantitative interpretation, prior to a defined period of time, of a policy to be pursued for that period to attain a given objective'. Budgetary control is determined as: 'The establishment of departmental budgets relating the responsibility of executives to the requirements of a policy, and the continuous comparison of actual with budgeted results, either to secure by individual action the objectives of that policy or to provide a firm base for its revision'.

A budget, therefore, is a standard by which the cost performance of a department, section or activity can be predetermined. During and at the end of a time period a comparison can be made between the budget or standard and the actual results achieved. This is the basis of most cost-control.

20.3   Establishing budgets

A budget should be prepared for all activities that incur cost. In administration budgets, forecast costs should be established for:

- salaries, including holiday and sickness pay and superannuation
- stationery
- postage
- telephone and telegrams
- travelling
- office equipment and repairs
- office furniture
- insurance
- heating and lighting
- building maintenance costs including cleaning
- rent and rates
- depreciation of office equipment and furniture
- depreciation of buildings
- miscellaneous expenses

The budget shows expenditure for which someone – a manager, supervisor or chief clerk – should be responsible. The money resource is an extra to all the other resources that are needed to carry out an activity. As a control mechanism, budgets have often proved inadequate because of the tendency to look at last year's budget, consider the current rate of inflation and then add x per cent. This is obviously unsatisfactory and unlikely to institute the right degree of cost-consciousness. Methods that have been applied in budget preparation which tend to introduce some cost-control discipline are:

1   Budget committees   A number of managers are assembled to agree budgets. There is danger that they will have too little time and experience to determine whether a budget is realistic or not.

2   Budget breakdown   Each budget is broken down into its component parts. For example, the staff in a department are listed by name and their current and future salaries quoted, along with their job duties. This method gives reasonable clues on how money is being spent.

3   Budget validation   This is a fairly complicated method of ensuring that the department being budgeted is carrying out such activities so that the money being requested is apparently being spent realistically. Various techniques are used to test the degree of 'realism'.

4   Value administration   A relationship is established between the activity being budgeted and the output from it. In effect this is challenging the worth of the activity to the organisation.

One or a combination of these budget-evaluation methods should be established, otherwise it is likely that money will be wasted.

20.4   Budgetary control

A comparison should be made regularly (at least once a month) between the budget and the actual amount of money spent. Budgets should cover specific time periods and over these periods the amount actually spent should equal the budget. Managers, even in times of considerable inflation, should ensure that they do not overspend. All contengencies that were likely to affect the budget should have been considered before it was finalised.

Regular comparison between actual and budgeted results should be fostered, so that performance can be judged and, if necessary, corrected by action programmes which detail actions that need to be taken to eliminate the variance.

20.5   Absorption of administrative costs

Many manufacturing organisations have adopted systems which 'absorb' adminstrative costs in their pricing/costing methods. This is done by allocating part of the cost on a predetermined basis to each operating unit. The argument for doing this is that only by adding administrative costs to production costs will operating managers be aware of the amount of profit they must make. Without adding such costs, it is thought that operating staff will not try as hard as they should.

Many operating managers resent the arbitary imposition of administrative costs and often suggest that they should be allowed to bear only that administrative cost which they approve. This procedure could have doubtful merit to say the least, but establishing the relationship between the administrative cost being absorbed and the service given would be useful. Operating units, by having the relationships explained to them, should then be able to influence the degree and quality of service offered.

A questionnaire covering the value of administrative services is prepared in some companies. However, with the centre/periphery hostility which often exists, a reasonable response may not be forthcoming.

20.6   Further reading

1   R.M.S. Wilson, *Cost Control Handbook,* Gower (Second edition, 1981).
2   A.H. Taylor and M.A. Pocock, *Handbook of Financial Planning,* Gower (1981).
3   L.D. Huck Jr, *A Practical Guide to Budgetary and Management Control Systems,* Lexington (1980).
4   J. Batty, *Management Standard Costing,* Macmillan, (1970).
5   *Budgetary Control for the Small Company,* BIM (1972).

Twenty-one

Cost Justification of Administration

21.1 Introduction

It is too easy for non-administration people to say that an administrative service is too costly or the clerical functions in an organisation take up far too much of the available money. 'Overhead' is an emotive word, much given to generating abuse. However, determining whether administration is worthwhile is not as easy to justify as the production or despatch functions. This chapter sets out how it might be done.

21.2 Value administration

Value analysis and value engineering have long been applied successfully in production and engineering activities to reduce the value of components, products and materials being used. Ten 'tests for value' have been designed which serve as a checklist to evaluate material and product worth.

Value administration has been devised for the same purpose and hopefully answers the question: 'Are we getting value for the administration costs being incurred?'.

21.3 Analysis required

To ensure that the requisite analysis is possible, the following four types of data are needed.

21.3.1 Functional costs

A function can occur in many different departments and its cost be incurred as part of numerous major systems, e.g. typing could take place in each and every department in an organisation. The total cost needs to be known. For example:

Department	Number	Cost, £
Accounting	3	13,500
Production control	5	15,000
Factory offices	4	14,000
Despatch office	2	12,600
Purchasing department		
Sales general	5	17,500
Sales order processing	7	19,200
Research and development	5	17,200
General sectional	6	110,000
Typing department	8	111,000
Personnel	2	13,000
	47	343,000

Set out like this, the result is often startling, sufficiently so to warrant a major investigation into the function with the object of eliminating or reducing the typing burden. With the kind of spread and cost indicated a special typing pool with centralised dictation might be justified; word processors might be another alternative.

Other functions which proliferate and need centralisation and reduction might be:

- photocopying
- data processing of all kinds
- customer contacts
- handling orders

21.3.2 Departmental cost and value

Departments such as purchasing or accounts tend to grow despite good clerical work control. It is important in value administration that the reason for each department's existence is established as an output. In the case of the purchasing department, placing orders is obviously important while in accounts several outputs may have to be listed such as preparing the balance sheet, producing monitoring information or invoices. The value of the orders or invoices has some relevance, but not too much – it is often as time-consuming to invoice for £10 as for £1,000. Purchase orders are slightly different in that a major contract for £50,000 obviously needs more thought and work than an order for nuts and bolts for £25.

A result of the analysis proposed is shown in Figure 21.1. The departments or functions are listed as well as their budgeted cost. An efficiency measurement has been determined for each department – usually the output from whatever activity is carried on. Some qualification is then quoted as this will tend to determine how valid the measurement is likely to be. Finally a cost per activity is quoted. In the case of accounting this can be the cost per invoice, cost per entry in ledgers, cost per entry in the trial balance, etc.

This analysis facilitates an assessment of the functional or departmental value, and whether money being spent is getting appropriate value. Often it is instructive to look at, say, cost of purchase orders placed over the last three to five years and compare these figures with the rate at which salaries generally have riseri. This comparison will often show where functions or departments have been gaining or losing efficiency.

However, a word of warning is needed – it may be possible for an administrative function to have, apparently, a low value per £1 spent on it, yet still be a vital component in achieving corporate objectives.

21.3.3   Systems evaluation

Like departments and functions, systems also need to be analysed and their value compared with their cost. This is a more difficult activity, directed towards ensuring that systems are designed appropriately and are achieving their objectives. To do this analysis, knowledge of the system and what it is intended to do is required, e.g. in a material-control system the following main elements may be covered:

- Preproduction planning – essentially matching capacity with forecast both short and long term.
- Materials management – stock control of finished goods, raw materials and work-in-progress; material utilisation; quality control.
- Plant loading – matching customers' demand to plant/machine capacity.
- Order scheduling – either master scheduling or job scheduling is usual.
- Production control – including progress-chasing.
- Control of internal transport.
- Despatch scheduling – control of warehousing and all despatch facilities.
- Incentives.
- Performance control – usually linked with a standard costing and budgetary-control system.
- Information and data collection of all kinds.
- Tool control (usually small tools) and plant inventory.
- Design of manufacturing particulars.

The objectives required to be achieved by the system might include:

- Acting as a bridge between marketing and production management to ensure customer service and production resource utilisation, in accordance with the corporate plan.
- Coordinating the use of all corporate production resources to ensure their optimum use, so minimising production costs.
- Balancing the cost of inventory and production order processing against the customer service levels which gain planned levels of sales revenue. The considerations to be taken into account are:

Function	Annual cost, £	Efficiency measurement	General evaluation	Means of assessing value
Accounting	153,000	1 Number of invoices handled 2 Entries made in ledgers	Time and accuracy of accounts, plus conformity to company and tax law must be included in any evaluation	1 Cost per invoice 2 Cost per entry in ledgers 3 Cost per entry on trial balance
Management accounting	127,000	1 Ledger entries 2 Operating statements 3 Costing profit and loss statement 4 Costs	This is an important function, which has to be viewed against the value to line management of the information produced	Cost per ledger entry statement, etc., produced
Purchasing	145,000	1 Number of orders placed 2 Orders received on time 3 Value for money of orders received	Purchasing is a particularly difficult function to validate, as a prime analysis must include whether the orders placed with the supplier will give the best terms for goods of the requisite quality	£ per order placed
Typing department	132,000	Lines of type produced	Types of letters, statements or reports will help determine lines of type produced. The necessity of the typing being done needs to be checked	£ per line of print
Credit control	114,000	1 Number of bad debts 2 Number of day's debts outstanding	The effectiveness of the function must be judged	1 £ per bad debt 2 £ per day of debt outstanding
Office cleaning	117,600	1 Sq. metres of floor space cleaned 2 Cleanliness	The degree of cleanliness will be of prime importance. This will often need a subjective appraisal of the office after cleaning	£ per sq. metre of office space cleaned
Computer department	167,000	1 Machine utilisation	Valuation of the data produced may be more important than machine utilisation. Comparison with service bureau will be	1 £1 per running hour of the machine 2 Costs per tabulation produced

Department	Cost (£)	Measures	Comments	Units
...	...	3 Welfare, etc.	...vices by personnel should be considered and evaluated – industrial relations, welfare, training, etc.	2 £ per industrial relations activity / 3 £ per welfare activity
Organisation and methods	116,200	Savings made	Savings may not be the only evaluation media. Much O&M work may not have quantifiable results	£ spent per savings made
Post room	16,300	Post handled	Daily fluctuations in post handled may be important and may affect value judgements	£ per 10 letters handled
Production planning and control	169,200	1 Orders processed / 2 Effect on factory cost	The overall performance and value will depend upon the impact made on production costs. This may be difficult to determine	1 £ per order handled / 2 £ per effect on factory cost
Stock control	117,600	1 Service levels / 2 Stock levels / 3 Profit/Stock levels	Stock levels have to be 'traded off' against service given. The department should be judged on how effectively it does this	£ per £1 of stock controlled
Sales order processing	162,000	1 Orders processed / 2 Orders processed on time	A variety of efficiency measurements need to be evolved – orders supplied completed, service given, orders processed within a standard time, etc.	£ per orders processed
Sales administration	115,000	Service given to the sales force	The valuation of a services function should always be the service which it gives to line personnel. The ratio of admin./salesmen is important	£ per sales force personnel
Reprographic services	119,000	1 Throughput of the unit / 2 Utilisation of equipment	A comparison with external reprographic services is possible and should be used to judge internal unit's performance	£ per order processed

Figure 21.1 *Departmental cost and value*

- least-cost production
- maximum machine runs
- highest possible material utilisation
- production within a normal week
- maximum output
- flexibility of output
- tool efficiency and control
- least-cost inventories and work-in-progress

The cost of carrying out the various systems elements is given in Figure 21.2. The result of the systems cost can be set out, therefore, in total and by each element in the system.

Often a system will need to be evaluated for labour as well as machine cost and for how long the total process takes. An example of a sales order-processing system is given in Figure 21.3. It takes 25 days to process an order from receipt to invoice. The function costs £474 in labour and £75 in machine cost. The cost of order processing has to be set against the number of orders processed, but 25 days seems a long time to complete the total activity and it is likely that more money spent on weekly machine cost would reduce the cycle time.

21.3.4 Mandatory and discretionary activities

A further analysis needs to be made between those activities that are vital to the organisation and those that can, if necessary, be dropped. The cost of each should be determined. Vital activities include sales order processing, invoicing, and preparing the balance sheet. 'Optional' activities might include publicity and publicity material preparation, much of the typing which is done, some audit routines and control information preparation of all kinds.

Systems element	Personnel involved	Cost
		£
1 Pre-production planning	1	6,600
2 Materials management	4	30,200
3 Plant loading	7	46,200
4 Order scheduling	3	18,000
5 Production control	7	47,000
6 Information and data collection	2	8,600
7 Typing	5	15,000
8 Tool control	1	6,200
9 Making particulars	1	6,200
TOTAL	31	184,000

Figure 21.2 *System cost production planning and control*

	TIME/COST TABLE		
System *Order processing*		Date: *10 Nov 1982*	
Day	System	Labour cost weekly	*Machine cost weekly
1	Check customer's order	£30	
	Translate and check stock	£51	
	Type order master	£45	£18
2	Send acknowledgment	£24	£6
	Run off despatch set	£30	£12
	Make out works documents	£24	£9
3	Record material out of stock	£42	£6
	Filing	£30	—
4-15	Load building and programme issuing	£75	£12
4-22	Progressing	£75	—
5-25	Issue of invoice	£60	£12
	TOTAL COST	£486	£75
	*Includes stationery cost		

Figure 21.3   *Time/cost table*

Once an appropriate division is made, the value of the discretionary activities needs to be determined, starting by asking the question: 'What would be the worst result if the activity was discontinued?'.

21.4   Cost justification

The total amount of data collected should prompt the following questions:

- Does it appear that we are getting value for money for the costs being incurred?
- Are the functions that have been analysed helping to achieve corporate objectives?
- Is it possible to measure each function to indicate the value being obtained?

- Do we always search for alternatives that can be used to compare with internal value/cost measurements?
- Do we challenge budgets for each function when they are submitted? If so how do we do this?
- Have we an appropriate budget-validation system which establishes a logical challenge mechanism for every budget submitted?

In profit-making organisations, every £1 spent on administration should be related to the potential amount of profit earned. For example, spending money on O&M personnel should be seen as an alternative to the need for more stock or more clerks and typists.

21.5   Instituting the programme

Introducing a value administration programme starts with the analysis set out earlier in this chapter. However, the whole activity is very much business-orientated. A team with, say, the chief accountant, senior administration manager, chief personnel officer and perhaps a systems analyst, would best be fitted to carry out the valuation administration programme.

Each function should be analysed in the way suggested and the results listed so that a speedy comparison can be made between the value being obtained in each function. The team should be aware of the business situation of the organisation and, in the light of this and the analysis, the feasibility of insisting on greater value for money in the activities where too little value is being obtained.

It may be possible to derive standards of value to help judge whether current achievements are good enough. Indeed the organisation's situation may dictate that certain standards are met. It may be best to approach value administration as this example suggests:

- A budget of £1.5m will be established for administration for the next year. Personnel of the value administration team will establish appropriate value standards for each administrative function and help ensure that they are met.
- Immediate and high redundancies are obviously not an attractive proposition, and a gradual move to a high-value administrative position is required.
- Control systems, based on the value standards, need to be put in train.
- Training of administrative supervisors is required so as to meet the targets.
- A slow change in personnel with movements from one function to another should be planned.
- The value administration team should meet regularly, perhaps once a month, and discuss progress and results.

Twenty-two

Objectives for Administrative Personnel and Performance Appraisal

22.1 Introduction

Perhaps of all the advice that an office administration manager might consider, the best by far is that everyone including himself should have one or more objectives to achieve. Without objectives people tend not to know what is expected of them. The conscientious might work hard to no avail. Those not so conscientious will probably not work hard at all. Objectives provide direction and the means to measure progress. Their importance cannot be overestimated.

Any attempt to introduce objective setting will nearly always unearth unclear and ambiguous job descriptions. Job descriptions of a type may exist, but nearly inevitably they will have to be rewritten. Responsibilities will be blurred, special company arrangements may have been made that impinge on resource control, bringing numerous constraints that inhibit objective establishment.

One of the first activities in applying objectives, therefore, will be to appraise job descriptions so that appropriate objectives can be established at each managerial level. It will be necessary to indicate the degree of responsibility for:

- Decision-making – plans and company development, specific functions and operations.
- Certain personnel, their functions and operations.
- Equipment – machinery, buildings, stocks and money.
- Any other responsibilities, either in full or shared (if it is not possible to avoid sharing).
- The constraints imposed on decision-making and the limitations implicit in carrying out the functions.

22.2 Setting objectives

Setting objectives should revolve around two factors:

- The level at which specific objectives need to be established.
- The type of objectives which are to be agreed.

Objective-setting is a hierarchical activity. At each level in the organisation, decisions concerning policy, strategy, tactics and day-to-day operations are made. It is essential that such hierarchical differences are made clear and that managers low in the organisation are not asked to make policy decisions.

The type of objective is extremely important. As far as possible they should be either very explicit or quantified, e.g. the cost accountant's major objective might be to report on the financial state of the organisation within eight working days of the end of the previous month to ensure that board members are aware of:

- current profit and trends
- current velocity of working capital
- variances from standard of all kinds
- contribution earned by major product lines

Only occasionally should less definite objectives be set, e.g. to develop a personnel strategy that reduces absenteeism and labour turnover. A more satisfactory way of saying this might be: absenteeism to be reduced by 25 per cent; labour turnover to be reduced by 20 per cent.

22.3 Key results

Most managers tend to work hard at whatever crosses their desks. Some plan their day, most accept what occurs, whether this is a committee meeting, some clerical trivia, or planning an activity that could gain or lose several million pounds.

While much of the 'management by objectives' activity can be brushed off as 'doing what we always do', recognition of key results is not a natural phenomenon. In every job, there are key factors or activities which, if done well, will have a major impact on the success of the job as a whole. Recognition of, and concentration upon, these will inevitably lead to better job performance, than if every element in a manager's job is assumed to have the same comparative importance.

Usually there is a large discrepancy between key results and the time spent on them. Most trivial jobs seem to gain most attention. Key results such as planning production so as to achieve 85 per cent machine activity, 87 per cent labour utilisation, 95 per cent customer service, should inevitably be firmly followed, rather than, say, appearing on a canteen committee, or handling some return that a clerk should complete.

All supervisors and managers should have targets of some kind. However, how many, for what period of time, how easily they can be achieved, how precise they should be, will all be debatable.

There seems little merit in setting objectives which do not stretch people to some extent. Asking a subordinate to suggest an objective often, surprisingly, produces one that is more ambitious than any which might have been imposed on him.

A supervisor's objectives should always be established before those of subordinates. Too many objectives or targets will only produce diffuse effort and diffuse results.

22.4   Action plans

Another recommendation in objective-setting is to complete action plans or programmes. Achieving agreed objectives or gaining lost ones will probably always be easier if an action programme is made listing the actions needed to gain an objective, the resources to be used, the time to be taken and the personnel involved. It will monitor progress in achieving the objective, highlight when corrective action is required and whose responsibility it is to carry it out.

22.5   Performance appraisal

It is, perhaps, curious that performance appraisal, even when carried out, tends to be haphazard and often proves unsatisfactory for both appraiser and the appraised. Appraisals are difficult from human, organisational and performance points of view. It is difficult, for example, to be highly critical of a subordinate on only one day of the year – when he is appraised. Why have faults that are discussed then not been brought up and corrected earlier in the year? Why should an unsatisfactory performance wait until it is discussed formally? Why should the appraisal be unbiased? A manager must surely feel that he must support his own staff. A poor appraisal, he may think, will reflect badly on him, not his subordinates.

Appraisals, therefore, should be handled very carefully. Most people should already be aware of their performance – if their objectives have been set out appropriately and monitored. This should be the key to the appraisal. Its nature should be to look forward not back. 'How can we do better?', should be the key question.

Performance reviews often try to cover too much ground. They are used for merit rises, training, promotion and succession planning, reviews of corporate strategy, etc. A clear understanding of the purpose of the review is needed.

Scales may be used for measuring performance. Giving a mark from 1 to 10 or A to G is often used. Ranking is another method which is applied. Forced choice reporting has also been in vogue.

It is important that a performance review is made and that action of some kind follows from it. It is no use suggesting that a junior manager is board material and then doing nothing either to train him or give him better experience before promoting him. Performance reviewing can easily run into disrepute and fail in its most important aspect of ensuring that the organisation as a whole improves in consequence.

This checklist sets out the questions usually to be answered by an appraisal:

- What has the line manager achieved?
- How far has he failed to achieve his objectives?
- What reasons for failure can be given?
- Are these reasons under the manager's control?
- What can be done to correct out-of-line performance: in the short term; in the long term; for the reasons quoted?
- List the personal factors that have inhibited the manager from achieving his objectives.
- On the basis of current performance, does the manager deserve: promotion; demotion; training in depth – quote subjects; a merit increase of some kind?
- Has the manager's performance been discussed with him?
- If so what was his general attitude towards his performance appraisal?

22.6   Further reading

1 B.H. Walley, *Profit Planning Handbook,* Business Books (1978).
2 J.W. Humble, *Management by Objectives,* Gower (1975).
3 R.G. Greenwood and R.F. Barton, 'Management by objectives revisited', *Academy of Management Review, (USA),* (April 1981).
4 C. Cooper Jones, *Business Planning and Forecasting,* Business Books (1974).
5 S.V. Bishop, *Business Planning and Control,* Institute of Chartered Accountants (1966).
6 C.R. MacDonald, *MbO Can Work – how to manage by contract,* McGraw-Hill (1982).

Part Four

Improving the Productivity of the Office

Twenty-three

The Office as a System and Management Information Systems

23.1 Introduction

There are two possible definitions of 'system' which can be of use to the office manager. The first is 'a complex grouping of human beings and machines joined together to achieve a goal or goals'. The second is 'a series of connecting clerical activities which perform a required service either as an end in itself, such as order processing, or in the production of information for management to plan and control the business'. The former is a human activity system, the latter usually a paperwork or computer-based system.

Figure 23.1 shows the company or human activity system. It suggests that the company or organisation carries on some activity. For a manufacturing organisation the activity will be production of some kind. For a distribution company it will be distribution. For a commercial concern, whatever the commercial function is.

The company system shows that there are inputs to the system. These will be such things as capital, technology, materials, management. Individuals will put in their time, effort, skill and attitudes.

Output can be divided again between company and individual requirements. Company outputs will be profit, cash flow or perhaps survival. Individual outputs will be job security, high pay, interesting jobs. Where there are shareholders they will require dividends, growth and security for their investment.

It will be seen that the system is 'open', i.e. it interacts with its environment, technology, government and trade unions, the economy and the social and cultural mores of the country, and hopefully adapts to meet environmental change. For the office manager, thinking in such broad systems terms can be extremely useful.

a   Defining the system helps to define its boundaries, what influences it has and so in consequence what response needs to be made.

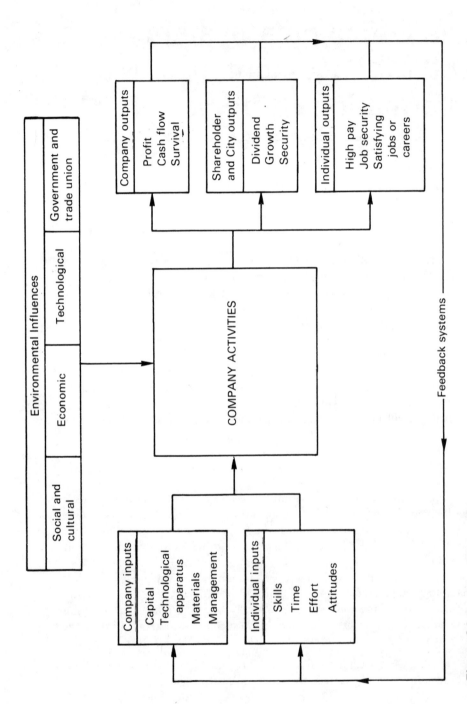

Figure 23.1 *The company system*

b It aids clarification of the system's objectives and why there are clashes between individuals and the organisation and what can be done to prevent them.

It should motivate thinking as to why the total system is not as efficient as it could be. It might also help to indicate that the system is not really under the control of management at all. This will provide analysis for a review of authority, responsibility and power and who has them. It is possible, therefore, that organisational restructuring might follow from a review of the human activity system.

23.2   Information systems

To analyse why the human activity system is not as efficient as it could be or why there is a dichotomy between responsibility and power will need knowledge of how the broad system works. For example, being aware of the relationship between input to the system and the output from it seems vital. Whether objectives are being achieved might be easy to determine for the company but less so for individuals. How is job satisfaction to be measured for example? It may be important for management to know this fact.

The boundaries of the human activity system lie firmly in the national and perhaps international environments. How the organisation has reacted, is reacting and has to react in the future could be vital in ensuring the success of the total system.

All these factors point to the need to design information systems that monitor the human activity system. The possibility must be faced that there may be a need for individual or worker information systems as well as management information systems.

The 'organisation as a system' approach suggests that paperwork systems should be concerned with three factors as well as the environment:

- resources and their use
- work organisation
- motivation and payment systems

23.2.1   *Resources and their uses*

The organisation will use many resources:

- money
- material
- people
- technology

Money will be converted into the means to carry on the business:

- machinery
- buildings

- power
- transport
- stocks of various kinds – raw materials, work-in-progress and finished goods

People can be divided into types – clerk and manager, specialist and non-specialist, skilled and unskilled. 'Resources' in the human activity system are input into the system in order to achieve an end-result or objective.

Adjusting a resource – adding or subtracting from it – could make a measureable difference to company objectives. Management information systems, therefore, need to be based on 'input/output' relationships as follows:

Area	Resources	Output
Company resources:		
1 Total company	All resources Net worth People/skills	Profit Sales revenue Added value Market share
2 Production	Fixed capital Machinery Labour direct and indirect Working capital Raw materials Components Power Packaging Ancillary services	Production Added value Productivity
Individual resources:		
	Material Maintenance costs Electricity	Material yield Machine efficiency Machine uilisation
3 Stocks	Finished goods	Stock/service Sales revenue Cash flow
4 Marketing	Sales force Depots Finished goods stock	Sales revenue Profit Contribution Market share

Area	Resources	Output
	Delivery/ transport service Sales promotion Merchandising	
5 Administration	People Office equipment Office space and local environment	Orders processed Purchase orders placed Secretarial services given Credit controlled Accounts prepared Production planned Invoices raised
6 Transport	Lorry fleet Drivers Maintenance Running costs Depreciation	Lorry miles covered/ tons of products delivered

23.2.2   Systems design

Systems design should take account of the need to measure resources, both in total and marginally, by a limiting factor analysis. This considers the following:

- One resource may be restricted in some way and its potential influence on profit or output should be known.
- Contribution costing and associated analysis.
- Cost/profit/volume relationships.
- Fixed-capacity budgeting.
- Backward interaction.
- Zero budgeting.

As suggested, all resource systems should be designed to operate on the input/output principle. Input of resources to an activity is carefully measured and then compared with the output. The input is measured and controlled so that adjustments that achieve the most favourable relationship between inputs and outputs can be made.

23.2.3   Work organisation

Systems associated with work organisations should measure the organisation's effectiveness in achieving company objectives. Systems should be established so that the activity of a particular work organisation can be planned and monitored. The activity can then be compared with objectives achieved – or not achieved. Such systems will also be on an 'input/output' basis. Indications of the effect of the environment on the organisation will also be necessary.

23.2.4   *Motivation and wage payment systems*

Recognising why people work and what might make them work harder and more effectively is a topic which should engage the mind of any office manager. People are a key resource in any human activity system and the various means of motivating them should be carefully monitored.

Morale, discontent or dissatisfaction should also be measured as this is a major element in the feedback between the 'input of people' and whether their personal objectives are being achieved in a manner satisfactory to them.

Morale might be judged in a number of ways:

- Labour turnover – though some people will stay in a company through sheer inertia, and there may be personal reasons for leaving a job, a high turnover is generally indicative of low morale.
- Absenteeism and poor time-keeping.
- The number of accidents.
- Failure to cooperate with management.
- Inferior or low-quality output.
- Bad housekeeping.
- Failure to use social and other facilities provided by the company.
- Lack of discipline.

Another factor to be measured is fatigue – if alleviating activities are undertaken the effect of these should be known.

23.3   The design of information systems

It is likely then, that anyone who has been asked to look at or redesign management information systems should start by considering the business needs of the organisation. Considering the organisation as a human activity system will certainly help in this respect. The design process might follow these lines once the system as a whole has been drawn:

1   Establish the objectives of the total business and the various sub-businesses, departments or functions within the business.
2   Establish the needs for information – by measuring the relationship between resource inputs and outputs for example. Determine what resources are used.
3   Establish what needs to be 'measured, planned, controlled and motivated'. Define the units of measurement. Define the purpose of the information.
4   Determine the hierarchy within the management structure and relate authorities, responsibilities and power with resources used and objectives

to be achieved. Designate appropriate control information for each hierarchical level.

5 List areas, functions, or departments that will supply and receive information.

6 Determine the frequency of the information – daily, weekly, monthly, randomly, etc. The information should be produced in time for a significant response to be made to it – if necessary.

7 Suggest file structures and processing activity for the information. Suggest data processing means for producing the required information.

8 Determine how much it costs or will cost to produce information and what, if anything, will be gained by its use. The potential benefits should far outweigh the cost of producing information.

9 As far as possible, systems should be simple and exception-reporting be the rule rather than the exception.

23.4 Further reading

1 E.I. Cleland and W.R. King, *Management – a systems approach,* McGraw-Hill (1972).

2 G.M. Jenkins, 'The systems approach', *Journal of Systems Engineering* (1969).

3 F.E. Kast and J.E. Rosenzweig, *Organisation and Management – a systems approach,* McGraw-Hill (1970).

4 B.C.J. Lievegoed, *The Developing Organisation,* Tavistock (1973).

5 R.N. Anthony, 'Planning and control systems', *Harvard Business Review* (1965).

6 A.E. Mills, *The Dynamics of Management Control Systems,* Business Books (1968).

7 T.J. Bentley, *Making Information Systems Work,* MacMillan (1981).

8 H.C. Lucas, *Information Systems Concept for Management,* McGraw-Hill (Second edition, 1982).

9 A. Parkin, *Systems Management,* Arnold (1980).

10 A. Parkin, *Systems Analysis,* Arnold (1980).

Twenty-four

Analysing Functional Efficiency

24.1 Introduction

As well as a general diagnosis of the total administration activity, individual functions need to be analysed on these lines:

a   The reason for their existence – what purpose do they serve and do they appear to give value for money?

b   Can costs be reduced in any way? Details of how this might be done need to be established for each function.

c   The development of the function, perhaps organisational or through data processing.

The first analysis should determine whether the function has a role and, if so, whether it is being done appropriately. The second analysis should determine whether the function can be carried out more cheaply than at present. The third analysis should indicate whether there are any ways in which the function might be developed to make it more effective.

Once these analyses have been carried out they should be unified to present a coherent picture of the function and provide the basis for its improvement.

Because of its fairly universal application, the purchasing function, plus stock control, have been chosen as an example of the application of this analytical approach.

24.2 Purchasing function

24.2.1 Reasons for existence and main functions

Purchasing is the obtaining of raw materials, tools and equipment, machine and service supplies which help to ensure that the company operates successfully. Diagnosis of the purchasing function should help to ensure that:

■   All supplies are bought as cheaply as possible.

- The quality of items should be such that inspection and quality control are minimised.
- Purchases are bought to a prescribed delivery date and goods are delivered accordingly.
- Quality inspections are made so that few, if any, substandard purchases have to be rejected.
- Purchasing research is organised so that all possible sources of supplies are regularly contacted, and that purchases are made only from suppliers that can deliver at the lowest price for the quantities, quality, delivery date, etc., required.
- Economic quantities are bought when necessary.
- Long-term contracts are established when these are deemed essential.
- Standardisation and variety-reduction is in force wherever possible.
- Quotations are obtained wherever necessary, except for very low-priced purchases.
- Tests of the market are taken at all times.
- Suitable stock-recording and control systems are in operation for raw materials, components, etc.
- Relative cost advantages of buying out as opposed to making internally are known.
- Specific terms of purchase are always quoted on orders.
- All paperwork systems associated with purchases, quotations, order progressing, inspection and quality control, return of empties, etc., is simplified and efficient.
- Tests on purchasing efficiency are carried out.

24.2.2   Cost reduction

1   Purchasing research   There are two ways in which to reduce material costs:

- By improving material utilisation.
- By purchasing at less cost.

Purchasing research is a process whereby all possible suppliers are regularly contacted, so that company purchases are made at the lowest possible cost consistent with quality and delivery required. A systematic search of all alternative sources of supply, with the possibility of using alternative materials, is made. What the material or article should cost might be calculated by the company's technical personnel. Is all this being done?

2   Supplier evaluation   If it is essential to carry out R&D in purchasing and also to ensure that the activities listed at the start of this section are carried out appropriately, two checklists are essential. Their application would ensure, very largely, that purchasing control is being pursued. The two checklists refer to:

- supplier evaluation
- buying activity evaluation

Every supplier used should undergo the following evaluation:

a   Has the supplier any edge in price or discounts and how do his prices compare with other suppliers?
  - more
  - less
  - same
  - if more or less, by how much
b   Has the supplier's quality always been appropriate? What has been rejected – how much, how many times?
c   Does the supplier always keep to promised deliveries? If not, by how much have deliveries been delayed? Is this consistent or rare?
d   Is communication with the supplier always good and response accurate? Is the supplier always obliging?
e   Does the supplier always help in emergencies, e.g. when supplies are needed urgently?
f   Are labour problems (strikes, etc.) rare at the supplier's works?
g   Is invoicing always carried out correctly?
h   Are the company buying terms always accepted without question?
i   Are rejected quantities always replaced as soon as possible?
j   Are all technical questions dealt with efficiently? Are the supplier's technical personnel of a high calibre?
k   Is the packaging used by the supplier always good?
l   Are credits and other financial considerations always handled expeditiously?

3 *Buying activity evaluation*

1   Does the buyer always know what he is buying? Is he technically competent to discuss his purchases with both the supplier and departments ordering the purchase?
2   Are a sufficient number of potential suppliers contacted and quotations gained?
3   Are orders over £X,000 always agreed by the chief buyer?
4   Are suppliers asked for a cost breakdown of purchases?
5   Does the buyer understand fully the discounts, price breaks, economic order quantity situations, which apply?
6   Would it be advisable for the buyer to gain some cost analysis information from company sources?
7   Is the company's legal department always asked to comment where necessary, particularly on contracts of major importance?
8   Has a make/buy decision been made after due calculation?
9   Are buyers always aware of the supplier's past performance when placing orders?

10   Will any development carried out by the supplier be charged to the company? If so will the buyer be aware of this when a replenishment is ordered?
11   What special handling problems exist in the following?
● quality
● inspection
● despatch
● transport
● packaging, etc.
12   Do buyers cooperate well with:
● warehousing and delivery personnel
● stores and stock personnel
● quality control staff
● engineering departments
● all ordering departments
or are buyers trained to do activities listed?

4 Purchasing budgets and financial control   It is important that the purchasing department conforms to strict budgetary control practice. Monthly, annual and, perhaps, project purchase budgets need to be established. Possibly these should be broken down by departments requesting purchases. Cost centres may also be a useful means of allocating purchase control. Monthly additions of purchases need to be made and the value allocated to departmental and cost-centre budgets accordingly.

One important analysis that ought to be carried out to help budgeting is products classification. Coding of products and raw materials should help to assess budget requirements and budgetary control. A significant coding system will often help this procedure, i.e. one that indicates the product's type, quality, size, use, etc.

To help in the budgetary control procedure, a purchase requisition vetting procedure is essential. Unless some validation of purchases is carried out, it is likely that budgets will be overspent. It is in this activity that a purchasing department's technical know-how, knowledge of standardisation and variety reduction, value analysis, etc., will be at a premium. Everything requisitioned should be challenged.

5 Purchasing policy   To optimise purchase costs and inventory holdings, various purchasing methods should be tried:

a   Long-term buying policies   These should be based on statistical analysis of past demand.
b   Inflation buying   Frequently the rate of inflation or an imminent price rise indicates that a purchase should be made despite the fact that there is no immediate use for it.
c   Seasonal trends   Seasonality in price, delivery, and availability will dictate seasonal purchasing.

d Commodity futures Raw materials and commodities generally often have violently fluctuating prices. Buying futures or forward commitments should be considered.

e Other purchase methods include:
- purchases for specific periods in the future
- marketing purchasing
- group purchase of small items
- schedule purchasing

6 Purchase orders Purchase orders should state simply and clearly what is required. The following should be shown:

- All details in recognised national or international terminology which are acceptable in the trade.
- Tolerances for all items.
- Brand or trade names where applicable.
- The catalogue number, if buying from a supplier's catalogue.
- Specifications (which should be sent to the supplier when necessary) should show physical characteristics, chemical analysis and/or other technical/analytical constraints.
- A blueprint, or sample, if necessary.
- The use of the purchase which will help to identify the item being bought.
- Packaging may be important and should be quoted.
- Arrangements for inspection, where this has to take place on the supplier's premises, for example in the case of steel-making.

7 Purchase control Various data should be produced to determine the effectiveness of purchasing:

- Net purchases as a percentage of the sales value of products.
- Price reductions/discounts obtained/total orders placed.
- Late deliveries as a percentage of total deliveries.
- Value of material lost due to bad purchasing.
- Purchasing department cost per number of orders placed.
- Value of stock holding/value of production.

24.2.3 Development of the function

If other organisations have developed the purchasing function along certain lines it would be useful to test these developments against the in-house organisation and determine whether these might be applicable:

1 Materials management A more useful way of looking at purchasing is to link it with all other functions, which should ensure that materials management is effective. Figure 24.2 illustrates this method. Figure 24.1 shows the linking and integration which may be required.

Does it seem likely that the introduction of the concept of materials

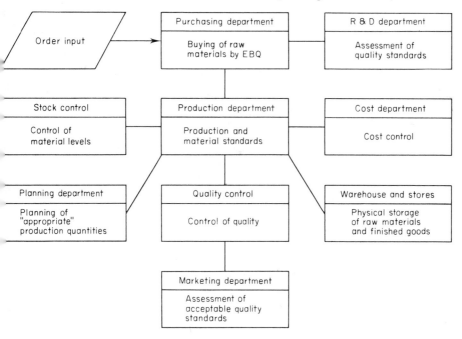

Figure 24.1 *Materials management: integration*

management would help to improve the efficiency of the purchasing function?

2 Computer use   Computers have been used in all the following processes. Is there a need to develop in the same way?

- purchasing ledger
- supplier/order file
- stock control of finished goods
- raw material stock files

3 Stock control   Do we carry out the following stock recording, either on the computer, by hand or other means?

a   Company's reference number (part number) for an item.
b   Supplier's reference number for the item.
c   Parts of which the item is a subassembly.
d   Parts which may be substituted for the item.
e   Units of measure for the item.
f   Units of measure of stock issued.
g   Cost of stock – FIFO, LIFO:
  - average or standard cost
  - system should take account of problems of invoice delays – pricing stock received which has not been invoiced
h   Selling price including market segmentation discounts, etc.

Activity analysis	Purchasing	Marketing	Quality control	Production department	Cost office	Stock control
1 Stock levels	1 Buying procedures					1 Stock control – demand forecasting
2 Material utilisation	2 Buying procedures			2 Use of an MU system with feedback	2 Design and control of appropriate system	
3 Use of EBQs	3 Buying procedures					2 Stock control mechanism
4 Least cost purchasing	4 Purchasing control (supplies research)					
5 Material standards		5 Competition in the market place	5 Quality control standards		5 Embodied in cost control systems	
6 Scrap control				6 Scrap control as part of production process	6 Cost control systems	
7 Value analysis		7 Competition in the market place		7 R&D and production		
8 Minimum work in progress				8 Production planning and control system		

Figure 24.2 *Materials management*

i   Units and value for stock at depots, export, future allocations and in total.

j   Transactions:

- receipts from suppliers – supplier code, part number, quantity, price, order number, date when order was placed, promised and received, and difference between each
- warehouse/depot, depot/warehouse, and depot/depot – part number, quantity, from, to, date, etc., for each
- company to supplier – supplier code, part number, quantity, price, order number, date when order was placed, promised and received, and difference between each
- sales and returned sales – customer number, part number, price quantity, date from, to, and order number for each
- stock adjustments – stocktaking, scrap/breakages and others
- bulk order record code number/depot/quantity/value date
- back orders (deliveries) records
- forward orders (with date) records

k   Visual records for management information.

l   Time scale – delay in updating computer records.

m   Measurement of accuracy or degrees of error permissable.

n   Appropriate explosion breakdown.

Stock control within a materials management function would obviously be much extended and a much wider view of its efficiency and effectiveness would be needed. The emphasis would change from bought-in items, such as raw materials, to made items if the purchasing function is within a manufacturing organisation.

4 Inventory assessment by value   It is axiomatic to allocate most resources to those items contributing most profit to the firm. Factors to be considered should be:

- A breakdown of the inventory by item contribution to turnover/profit, in ascending or descending importance.
- To ensure allocation of resources to the most important stock items.
- Control and re-evaluation of all references on a continual basis.

5 Financial contraints   The following financial details concerning stock should be available:

- Cost of each item.
- FIFO, LIFO, average or standard cost, whichever is appropriate.
- Selling prices including discounts.
- Cost price value of stock held by:
  - products
  - product range
  - turnover category
  - total

- Stock profitability by:
  - product
  - product range
  - turnover category
  - depot
  - company
  - gross margin/turnover
- Stock should be categorised by turnover and profit achieved and number of items to be shown in each category.
- Value of stock, shown by safety stock carried to cover variations in both sales demand and lead times.
- Marginal and average total cost of holding stock by depot.

6 Warehousing constraints   Warehousing considerations are an essential element in a stock control system. The effect of the following constraints should be included in the inventory control system:

- Necessity of regional warehousing.
- Siting/location of warehouses.
- Usable floor space and cubic capacity.
- General materials handling and physical environment.
- Transportation and overall distribution including packaging.
- Warehouse control procedures.

7 Marketing constraints   The system should be able to take cognisance of the following contraints:

- Service levels by:
  - product group
  - product
  - geographical location
  - market segment

  Standard service-level groups will probably be most useful, i.e. 99, 97, 95 per cent, etc. It should be possible to calculate the effect of changing service levels on total inventory.
- It must be possible for factors derived from market planning and market research to be included in the stock requirements calculation:
  - planned increases in sales, including effects of promotional activities
  - trends
  - seasonability
  - competitive response
- The system must recognise splash demand which must not be treated as a normal part of demand pattern.
- Analysis to aid marketing activities, which must be of positive use in setting, achieving and budgeting marketing objectives.

8 Audit routine

- Perpetual inventory. Regular physical stock check. Comparison at regular intervals between recorded and actual stock and investigation to discover causes.
- Audit reports on the following:
  - variances
  - causes
  - dead stock
  - write-off stock
  - stock adjustments

9 Forecasting A stock control system must have some means of forecasting future demands on the stock held or required. Attention to the following factors is essential:

- Environment and expected market growth.
- Expected market share and effect of promotional activities.
- Analysis of past sales demand patterns.
- A tracking system and error analysis used to monitor forecast systems.
- Re-order points
- Frequency of forecast required for stability in recalculating reorder requirements.
- Service level considerations to estimate safety stock requirements.
- Lead times and their variability to the existence of production constraints.
- Desired accuracy of forecasts – must be better than any other available system.
- Forecast must be based, where appropriate, on explosion breakdown of parts.

10 Interaction of stock control system with other systems The stock control suite must be compatible with the following EDP systems in the company:

- Sales analysis and sales statistics.
- Sales ledger
  - customer type
  - customer value/profitability
  - customer discount structure
- Purchase ledger:
  - supplier
  - supplier value
  - supplier pricing structure
- Invoicing and statement production, credit notes, credit control.
- Cost control – budgets and expenditure data for standard/actual performance comparison.
- Any data-based system which the company builds up including the use of interrogation packages.

24.3   Conclusion

Any audit of functional efficiency sets out to answer three questions:

- How are we doing?
- Could we do better?
- How can we do better?

This chapter has shown how a purchasing function might be audited to determine its functional efficiency. The skills of local personnel, management services, outside consultants or other sources can be used to determine the questions which might be asked of any function in an organisation. My book *Efficiency Auditing* (see below) aims to provide this kind of guidance.

24.4   Further reading

1   B.H. Walley, *Efficiency Auditing,* Macmillan (1974).
2   *British Institute of Management Checklists* (Regularly updated).
3   W.C. Shaw and G.J. Day, *The Businessman's Complete Checklist,* Business Books (1978).
4   K.F. Jackson, *The Art of Solving Problems,* Heinemann (1976).

Twenty-five

The Use of Management Services and Other Efficiency Specialists

25.1 Introduction

In the 1970s many hybrid departments linking organisations and methods, clerical systems study, systems analysis, computer programming and data processing operations and even, in some cases, work study, were created under the title of 'management services'. This is a curious name. All sorts of departments such as 'personnel' or 'economists' also give a service to management, but have never received a sobriquet such as 'management services'.

In many organisations, computers and management services now take up to 3 per cent of the total budget, yet their relevance in the fight for organisational survival appears to have declined somewhat from those heady days when operations research was going to solve all problems, computers would do all data processing cheaply, quickly and accurately, and line managers would get all the information they needed at the press of a key on a VDU.

There has been increasing scepticism about the value of the role of a management services department. The staff of such departments have often lacked humility; they have frequently failed to communicate appropriately and the solutions to problems they have produced have often been unworkable in practice. Many computers, though seemingly indispensible, are certainly not paying their way and the people in the computer department occasionally appear to speak a language peculiarly their own.

This is not to say that management services departments are not vital in improving the efficiency of any organisation. They are. If the organisation of the department is right, if people in the department have behavioural as well as technical skills, if the ethos of the company is right and line managers are keen to ensure that profitable change is carried out, then management services can be a dynamic, highly profitable means of improving organisational effectiveness.

25.2 The role of management services

A specialist by definition is a person who devotes himself to a particular branch of a profession or science, etc. It may be inferred, therefore, that management services personnel are specialists in management. This is not often the case. By training, aptitude and career, a member of a management services department will usually be a specialist in a series of management techniques (perhaps computer-orientated) with enhanced analytical ability. They will not be generalists, as most line managers have to be, and many will not have the basic business knowledge that is essential for senior line managers.

Their role should mostly be advisory but it is possible, perhaps on some occasions vitally necessary, that MS personnel will take executive authority for an activity.

There is a good case to be made for MS departments to provide auxiliary line management ready to step into a line manager's position when a crisis occurs only to relinquish it when it is over. It is possible, therefore, for a management services department to have three roles:

- *The extra resource* Line managers are very often quite capable of carrying out some element of change themselves, but lack the time to do it. On these occasions they will need reliable, competent individuals capable of working with the manager and his departmental staff as a team to bring about the desired change. The management services people act as an extra resource. They are seconded to work partly in a line capacity for what may be a comparatively short period.
- *The problem-solving role* The second role which management services people are likely to be called upon to carry out is to solve problems. Their skill in problem-solving should support line managers who could lack such expertise.
- *The policeman role* Perhaps the least satisfactory role that management services is likely to be asked to perform is that of performance monitoring or policeman. Audits of line manager activities are occasionally called for.

These three roles are often interlinked and the business consultant/systems analyst who set out to design a computer-based stock control system often has to perform all three roles. The skills required could differ for each role. The extra resource could demand line manager-orientated personnel who believe in the profit motive and are capable of line management. The problem-solver will obviously need to be skilled in problem-solving techniques and perhaps would be more intellectual by nature. The policeman, on the other hand, needs to be audit-orientated with a professionalism perhaps based in accountancy.

25.3 Organisation of a management services department

It is perhaps a pity that many management services departments appear, from experience, to have become totally computer-based. Most systems design is orientated towards using the computer. The role of organisation and methods and business consultancy is subordinate to computer systems analysis.

This is an undesirable, even retrograde, development. There are many business problems that will never be solved by using the computer – the wide range of behavioural problems, for example. Simple manual systems are often easier to implement and occasionally give considerably more reward for effort than computer-based ones. Management services is not 'computer system services'. The organisation of the department should reflect this view.

It might be useful to list the various factors that have helped to determine the organisation of MS departments.

1 *The company and company style.*
2 *The scope given to the department*   What it includes: organisation and methods; work study; operational research; EDP; business systems study; training of various kinds; job analysis; monitoring company performance; etc.
3 *The importance given to each function*   For example, is EDP paramount? Has O&M been abandoned in favour of OR? Is OR considered to be so important that it is established as a separate function divorced from other productivity services?
4 *The client relationship*   Is the department to operate as an entity on its own, perhaps on a consultancy basis where all services have to be paid for? If so, an appropriate structure will be one which is basically a 'consultancy organisation' established to sell its services. Conversely, it is possible that the department will be used to provide productivity technique knowledge and experience within a project team situation.
5 *Status awarded to the department*   This will largely determine the number and calibre of the members of the department. This in time will help to formulate departmental relationships, numbers of senior and junior members, etc.
6 *The job description given to members of the department*   In one company the definition of systems analyst will differ totally from another organisation. This may have little to do with the overall function of the department but everything to do with how the department is organised internally.

There are other, probably more important, functional factors. For example, the problem of centralisation *versus* decentralisation is greater than most companies realise. The benefits of a centralised unit are:

a It is more likely that a greater breadth of vision, the interplay of ideas and the generation of new thinking will take pace if the members of the department encourage brain-storming and creative thinking. Several one- or two-man units operating on the periphery of the company may establish good client/MS personnel relationships, but have no opportunity to generate new ideas by intellectual combat with fellow practitioners.

b   Pay-off usually goes with scale. The optimum use of resources will often be enhanced when a match can be made between the demand for MS personnel and total personnel available.

c   A large unit should have a discipline that fosters the project team idea that makes use of all the MS talent available, not just the techniques that one or two personnel can provide.

d   A large unit will also provide the basis for a career structure which small peripheral units are unable to give. This should lead to greater stability, decreased tension and improved morale.

e   Training, especially gaining on-the-job skills, should be enhanced by the interdisciplinary facilities available in the department. This in turn should promote more highly trained personnel.

A centralised organisation, therefore, has considerable advantages over small peripheral units. They, in turn, however, may be able to establish client/specialist relationships which help to ensure that good assignments regularly come their way and that they have a large chance of successfully implementing what they propose to the satisfaction of their clients and themselves.

The importance of the behavioural aspect is stressed. Certainly it has been proved that it is often far more important than knowledge of one or more techniques. If peripheral location can help achieve good working relationships between line and staff, then this is a potent reason for having such an organisation.

25.3.1   Types of organisation

Figure 25.1 suggests what has now come to be accepted as the standard MS organisation. It is assumed that there are three distinct areas of activity in the department: computer or EDP; operations research; and organisation and methods. The predominant influence in the organisation is the computer unit and its associated staff.

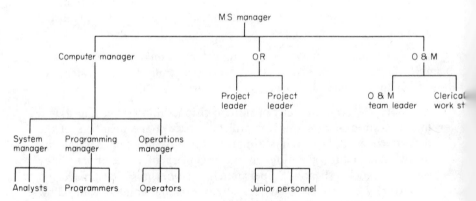

Figure 25.1   *Standard management services organisation*

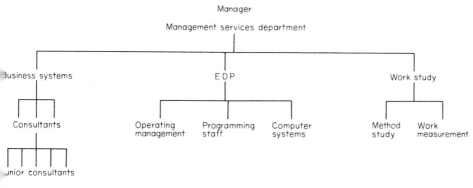

Figure 25.2 *Business-oriented management services organisation*

Having separate OR and O&M sections suggests that techniques will be pushed assiduously. Far better, perhaps, to have a unit similar to the one suggested in Figure 25.2 where the OR and O&M people have combined to form a business consultancy group that can be supported by computer and work study people. This, from practice, seems a much more realistic organisation where the division in specialism is between understanding the business and what systems it needs to measure, plan, control and motivate, etc., and how these systems can be translated so that they can be run by a computer, if necessary.

25.4 Assignments and plans

Assignments normally arise from three sources:

- Problems which arise suddenly in the organisation.
- A desire – perhaps long term – to improve company profitability, such as reducing stock, or improving delivery service.
- Conceptual thinking of some kind.

25.4.1 Problem or 'fire brigade' assignments

This is the worst type of assignment that a management services department can be offered. A crisis can blow up at any time, even in the best planned organisations. Environments can change rapidly, but for every assignment to be of a crisis nature is to impose fundamental constraints on the efficiency of management services. Consider the situation where every assigment comes unheralded out of the blue.

- MS personnel will be forced to suffer a feast and famine in workload. Planned utilisation of scarce technical resources is impossible.
- Matching MS resources and requirements will be impossible. Expertise and planned opportunities to use it will be non-existent.

- Inevitably skilled personnel will have to carry out unskilled activities. Talent of the highest quality will often have to be squandered on fairly profitless ventures.
- Consequently, recruiting and retaining personnel will be difficult. Frustration and overwork will ensure a ready turnover of personnel.

Yet many MS departments have long accepted this role, content to sit quietly for considerable periods in exchange for brief moments of intense activity, mainly because senior management feel this is how an MS department should be run. An 'always on call' situation is implicit in the department's establishment.

25.4.2   Attempts to improve company profit performance

These assignments often result from the organisation coming under pressure to improve profits or reduce costs. Occasionally a 'fire brigade' philosophy will ensue, with all the shortcomings listed in the previous section, but more often a planned approach will be made and thinking should be more contemplative than crisis-dominated.

The most desirable situation will be motivated by using profit planning or corporate strategy techniques. It is hoped that such management methods will ensure that key results will be recognised and MS personnel utilised first on the major areas of profit improvement. This would be an obvious advance on fire brigade operations and it should be possible to plan MS activities to match expertise to company requirements.

Yet a line manager harassed to make a cost-reduction plan may not know how MS personnel could help him. He may not be aware of the full range of techniques that he could usefully have deployed on his behalf. He may be under such pressure that his judgement of the aid required will be warped. His timescale may be inadequate; he may underrate how long term the required improvement may have to be.

25.4.3   Conceptual thinking

The line manager who actively asks for MS personnel to help him in some aspect of conceptual thinking is rare. When such an opportunity does occur it is usually in line with a desire by MS personnel to have a research and development role. It helps such personnel to practise unique skills; techniques and systems thinking can be advanced.

In an environment that is normally sceptical, if not vaguely hostile, MS personnel can be forgiven for welcoming such opportunities to work with dedicated line managers. The trouble is that they may become too dedicated, absorbing MS personnel's time out of proportion to the importance of the assignment.

25.4.4   Management services plans

Why make a management services plan? To any member of an MS department suffering from a feast and famine in workload, the answer is obvious. Any plan which sets out to optimise the use of departmental resources must start with the question of what resources are needed. What comes first, the tools to carry out a job or the job itself? This is a difficult problem not easily answered. It depends to a large extent upon the organisation for which the plan is being made. For example:

1   Company A has many obvious weaknesses, line managers are reasonably cooperative with staff functions and the likelihood of many future profitable assignments is great. In these circumstances it seems justifiable to recruit specialists in anticipation of an enhanced workload for the department.
2   Company B has few obvious weaknesses even though line managers are cooperative and inclined to utilise service personnel to help them. Here the department should be built up slowly so that there is a gradual expansion of workload. It will be inevitable that, initially, departmental recruits will be under-utilised, even when recruited slowly.
3   Company C has many weaknesses, but line managers are uncooperative and not inclined to use specialists. Recruitment to the department should be extremely slow. Potential assignments might be in excess of available personnel to carry them out.
4   Company D, despite a need for help, has an agressively independent line management that does not anticipate using staff functions at all. Until attitudes change it seems undesirable to recruit.

25.5   Charging for the use of management services and the computer

Often, one of the most crucial factors in the use of management services personnel is whether the using departments are asked to pay for the services offered. Conditions vary from one company to another. In some organisations no payment is made. In others the transfer of cash is regarded as a 'wooden dollar transaction' and of no particular importance. In some units where budgets are tight a charge is regarded as a serious and unwanted increase in what the local manager can spend.

Many organisations charge-out the use of the computer on a usage basis. Others spread it over all revenue-earning departments, charging users and non-users alike. It is difficult to determine which method gives least offence. The second tends to promote a feeling that, if a charge is levied, then some use of the services should be made.

It is possible that the use of management services and computers can be hindered by a charging system. But if the skills of a management services department are not used when they are obviously needed, because they need to be paid for, then the charging system is wrong.

However, from experience, if line managers consider that management services are worth using they will pay for them. If they have no faith in the service being offered they will not use it even though it is free.

25.6   The use of outside consultants

Even with a considerable managerial services staff, it is still occasionally worthwhile to use outside consultants. Where few, if any, managerial services personnel are employed using outside consultants may be the only way in which major profitable change can take place. In either situation there are rules that might be applied in considering whether professional consultants should be used.

a   A prime use may be when a new technique, skill or knowledge is required in which members of the organisation are deficient. On these occasions it seems important that key personnel are seconded to work with the consultants so that there is every chance that a strong residue of skills and experience will be left once the consultants depart.

b   There are situations where an outsider's analytical ability is an advantage. These occasions should be rare as they indicate that internal personnel lack such ability, which should be corrected as quickly as possible through training.

c   A more usual occasion for using outside consultants is when all internal staff are already fully committed to line or service projects and it is essential that extra technically competent staff are obtained. Extra work-study staff may be called in (a growing trend) or systems designers and programmers may be required. Normally the extra resource will be in a discipline where outside help can be easily assimilated.

d   Outside consultants are often used as alternatives to the creation of internal managerial services functions. If such aid is only spasmodic, the economies may be justified. If it is not, then one or more managerial services departments will be financially preferable, as they will retain knowledge inside the organisation.

e   There could be an earthquake or discontinuity situation. For example, occasionally when a new chief executive is appointed he will want to totally reshape his organisation. His subordinate managers may not be psychologically attuned or skilled enough to fully aid the reorganisation. Outside consultants can provide help and experience to create the discontinuity required.

There are equally a number of good reasons why outside consultants should not be used:

1   Cost is an obvious drawback. To introduce a major management information system may cost, at 1982 rates, in excess of £200,000. Employing two good management accountants for, say, eight years, would cost as much.

2 Experience needed by internal personnel could be another reason. Most organisations have personnel capable of wrestling with and finding solutions for major problems. Calling in consultants when anything other than a simple systems amendment is required denies local staff the chance of gaining experience that might prove invaluable in the future.

3 Using outside consultants will not guarantee that proposals will be acceptable and implemented. Using consultants often prevents line managers from playing the leading role in creating change. Many times, their influence is minimal. The speed at which consultants have to operate could preclude a soft behavioural approach.

4 For some organisations the use of consultants is vital shock therapy. In others their intrusion is resented and their recommendations, no matter how good, will be automatically frustrated. The effective use of consultants and managerial services personnel depends largely on organisation and organisational style – if this is not conducive to change, then the task is difficult, if not impossible.

5 Calibre and experience of consultants may be suspect. Consulting organisations occasionally have difficulties in recruiting good people. The characteristic for which a consultant is employed – experience – may be missing. Someone has to be a guinea pig for the implementation of a new technique or the gaining of requisite skills.

Consultancy organisations are not usually keen to talk either of their successes or failures, except in a general and overall way. It would be useful to know what impact they have had compared with the many millions of pounds spent on them.

6 Anyone contemplating the use of professional consultancy units should appreciate why they are needed. This is not as facile as it sounds. As many consultants will admit, their terms of reference, like icebergs, only show a fraction of the total assignment. Rarely, it seems, are the real reasons why consultants are called in given. Precise terms of reference for the assignment are necessary. There should be an assurance that the consultants' activities will not creep into other areas, so prolonging the assignment. A precise cost-benefit analysis should be considered both at the beginning and the end of the assignment.

25.7 Further reading

1 R. Dick Larkham, *Profit Improvement Techniques,* Gower (1973).
2 B.H. Walley, *Management Services Handbook,* Business Books (1973).
3 J.D. Marver, *Consultants Can Help,* Lexington (1980).
4 N. Harris, 'Research in education – the management services function', *Management Services* (July 1971).
5 *Management Services in Large Companies,* BIM (1963).
6 B. Mills, *Management Services in the Boardroom,* MCB (Management Decision) Ltd (1973).

7   F. Davidson, *Management Consultants,* Nelson (1972).
8   B.H. Walley, 'The changing role of management services', *Management in Action* (February 1974).
9   N.Harris 'Management services in the UK', *Management Services* (December 1979).
10 R.G. Harrison, 'Management services practitioners as internal consultants', *ibid.* (December 1981).
11 C.S. Deverell, *Business Administration and Management,* Gee (1973).
12 D. Whitmore, *Work Study and Related Management Services,* Heinemann (1977).

Twenty-six

Techniques to Improve Office Efficiency

26.1 Introduction

In many ways, the whole of this book is dedicated to improving office efficiency. What this chapter suggests is that there are various procedures or techniques of which anyone interested in improving office efficiency should be aware. They are not difficult and can largely be self-taught. Despite the advent of word processors, computers, data transmission links and threats of the paperless office and fully automated office procedures, there is still plenty that can be done by using plain common sense and basic techniques, like work simplification.

26.2 Work simplification

Perhaps the technique that an office manager should find most useful is work simplification. The definition will provide an indication of the scope and type of technique it is. Work simplification is a method of simplifying work and reducing costs by recording and analysing one or a series of operations, and then, by applying a questioning technique and a certain amount of common sense, evolving simpler methods.

The first operation, as with methods study, is to find out what is going on. To do this, it is necessary to know:

- What is going on at present.
- How long this now takes to perform.

Daily log sheets filled in by the personnel involved in the exercise will solve both of these problems. Each participant should be asked to complete an 'activity log sheet' (see Figure 26.1), dated and headed with the name of the department and section undergoing the simplification, followed by the person's name and job title. Work performed is then recorded under the following headings:

- Job duty – e.g. order translation, material allocation, filing, etc.

			Date	
Name H Rogan			**Section /department** Production planning and control	

Activity	Job category	Number of documents processed	Time taken	Interruptions
1 Program detailing	1	1	4hr	Discussion with works personnel 1½hr
2 Filing	2	54	½hr	
3 Control meeting	1	-	½hr	

This sheet should be completed daily and given to supervisor

Figure 26.1   *Daily log sheet*

- Job category, i.e.
  - repetitive jobs – entering an item on a stock record card, etc.
  - conditional – activities that occur when certain conditions apply – reordering a product once a reorder point has been reached, etc.
  - general queries arising from the job duty
  - special jobs occurring at regular intervals
  - supervisory or advice-giving activities
- Number of items processed.
- Time taken in minutes.
- Interruptions - telephone calls, general discussions, etc.

The sheets are usually completed daily and handed to supervisors who, from their knowledge of the job, can check that they have been completed with accuracy and in sufficient detail.

Once the sheets are completed, there is a variety of collation, compilation and general analysis that has to be carried out. In a clerical operation it might work like this:

a   The easiest and perhaps most effective record of what is happening is a document flow chart. Copies of all documents used are collected, specimen entries made and then the documents are set out to form a wall chart showing how the system operates. This is often very instructive, especially when everyone concerned can view it at a glance.

b   The methods study process of charting all operations with symbols should not be ignored, as this too will show weaknesses in the system.

c   Various consolidations of job activity will be needed. Function analysis should be tried, for example. This should collect together all operations of the same type, filing, recording, etc., and should lead to suggestions that

ction Sales order processing		Week ending									
		Names									
	Total	D HAMMOND	G HANKIN	T FORSYTH	A ADAMS	D DEAR	P GAWTHROP	S SMITH	T COOPER	S WARREN	V DIXON
Order translation	18	6	6	6	6	0	0	0	0	0	0
Credit checking	18	0	0	0	0	6	4	2	2	2	2
Order pricing and coding	63	10	10	10	6	6	7	7	7	0	0
Customer contact	138	24	24	24	24	12	10	6	8	4	2
Total	380	38	38	38	38	38	38	38	38	38	38

ure 26.2 *Work distribution sheet*

such operations might be done at the same time, so leading to cost-reduction.

d   A work distribution chart similar to the one shown in Figure 26.2 is also useful in this field. These show – under various functional headings such as order translation, material allocation, filing, etc. – the number of man hours each individual spends on them. This activity highlights duplication and shows which activities can be combined or eliminated. It also pinpoints where highly paid individuals are doing simple, routine jobs.

e   Movement diagrams are also extremely useful in indicating excess movement and activities carried out in obviously wrong locations. Journey times should be calculated and total non-productive time assessed. Lessening movement is an important element in reducing the complexities of activities.

All this analysis should lead to the consolidation of the following information:

■   What work is done?
   ● by definition
   ● by category
   ● by time
   ● by person
■   Where is it done?
   ● location
   ● time
   ● travel distance between activities
■   What activities are productive? Time spent on each.

- What activities are non-productive?
  Time also spent on each.
- The following should be highlighted:
  - duplication of effort
  - effort not commensurate with reward
  - the purpose of documents
  - indications where work can be simplified

This latter part should be helped by a checklist which the line manager completes as follows:

- Is the organisation correct? Use organisational theory and general precepts for this challenge.
- Is the workload equalised between personnel of the same grade?
- Is it obvious that every same-grade operation is necessary?
- What idle time has been found?
- Are too many clerks doing the same job?
- Can work be reorganised so that senior personnel do only work for which their seniority fits them?
- Is more than one record-checking operation or analysis being carried out for the same transactions?
- Can workflow be improved by cutting down transfer and movement time?
- What duplication of effort is obvious?
- Can handwriting take the place of typewriting?
- Does each operative fully understand what he is doing?
- Can peak periods be overcome in some way?
- Is all equipment useful, in good repair and appropriate to the function it is designed to carry out?
- Could more equipment be used with benefit?
- Are operatives well trained?
- Is interchangeability practised frequently?
- Can standard forms (especially letters) be used more, so that clerical effort can be reduced?

There are five key words in carrying out work-simplification analysis: elimination, combination, reduction, rearrangement, simplification.

Elimination is obviously the most important. If something can be eliminated then the long search for improvement in an operation is not required. Elimination should be attempted before simplicication or any other of the proposed activities:

- Is the operation necessary?
- Why is it carried out?
- What benefit accrues from it?
- Is it a duplication?
- Can any of the associated contingency operations or general interruptions be eliminated?

- What does each part of the operation contribute?
- How many of the filing movements, inspections, etc., can be eliminated?
- Can any forms be eliminated?

Combination often results from the answers to the questions which begin – where? when? who? Functional analysis often suggests where operations can be combined:

- Can any of the operations be combined?
- Who should do the job?
- Where is the best place for the total function to be carried out?
- When should the operation be performed?
- Are the right people now carrying out the function?

Reduction should be taken into account when looking at the size of reports or documents generally. Reductions in time are important and these should be looked for diligently:

- Can any part of the system be shortened or speeded up?
- If so, how?
- Why are so many copies of documents produced?
- Can these be reduced?
- Can the size of documents be reduced?
- Can filing and recording be reduced by using copies of documents stored away in order?

Rearrangement Improvements in a system can also stem from the questions which begin – where? when? who?

- What rearrangement can be carried out in function, location and job duties so as to improve document flow?
- When should work be done?
- Where should work be done – in what location?
- Who should do what work?
- What is the best sequence of operations?
- Can work be rescheduled so that bottlenecks are avoided?
- Can work be issued so that each clerk has a regular work pattern and output to achieve?
- When is the best time to carry out the operations?
- Can an operation be simplified by moving it out of its current sequence?

Simplification When all the foregoing analysis has been carried out, operations can often be simplified, so simplification should be used as a final challenge to current methods of operating practice:

- What appears to be complex in the activity being performed?
- Is it possible to eliminate any non-routine work?
- Is it possible to simplify any operations? How?

- Do operatives find difficulty in any part of the jobs they perform? Why?
- What parts of the system are obviously wasteful in manpower and other resources?
- Is too much time spent in discussions and interruptions that could be eliminated? If so, how can the job be simplified to enable such elimination to take place?

A useful example of the technique in operation can be seen from the following example in a sales order processing system.

Office	Function	Staff	Time
Sales order processing	Order receipt translation recording	2	Day 1
Accounts	Credit control check	1	Day 1
Sales order processing	Order typed and sets run off	2	Day 2
Production planning and control	Delivery promises inserted (stock records searched)	1	Day 3
Sales order processing	Order set completed and issued. Acknowledgement sent to customer	1	Day 4
Production planning and control	Stock records again searched to confirm if ex stock or to be made by production. Works order set made out	1	Day 5
Transport	Transport order set made out.	2	Day 7 (if ex stock)
	Vehicles ordered for despatch	1	
Planning department	Mark off production planning records when delivery made	1	Day 8
Sales order processing	Mark off office records, send copy of order to accounts	1	Day 9
Accounts	Make out invoice	1	Day 10

Set out like this, the system shows immediate defects, but to the local personnel each function could appear necessary and the delay in despatch (even from stock) seems reasonable in the circumstances. What happened in practice?

A project team of local line management supported by MS personnel was set up and the system recorded. Document flow charts, procedure charts, movement diagrams and a time analysis schedule similar to the one above was made. Some functional analysis was also carried out. The result of applying work-simplification techniques in this case was one combined office for sales order processing, production planning and control (including stock control) and transport/distribution was established. The system was amended to:

	Time
Order receipt and translation – record made	Day 1
Delivery promise and stock check	Day 1
Order set completed including	Day 1
works and transport documentation	Day 1
Credit control check carried	Day 1
out (1 order copy to accounts)	
Transport arranged	Day 1
Despatch of goods	Day 2
Invoice sent to customer	Day 2

Benefits achieved:

- Reduction in despatch time from 10 to 2 days.
- Reduction in paperwork, filing and record-keeping.
- Reduction of staff by 45 per cent.

Comment   Too much emphasis on the technique and not enough on the behavioural problems it raises will certainly not help a successful application. It is a technique that needs the cooperation of staff at all levels; if, in consequence personnel are likely to be made redundant or asked to take less interesting and perhaps less rewarding jobs, it is not likely that cooperation will be forthcoming.

The benefits from work simplification should not only be in monetary and efficiency gains. If appropriately applied, and staff are totally involved as they should be, then a legacy of friendliness, mutual cooperation, teamwork and improved human relationships should also follow.

However, if work simplification has been applied badly and staff ignored, or the gains ultimately made are taken entirely by management, then the result could be the reverse.

26.3 Methods analysis

In many ways work simplification and methods analysis are similar – they use the same recording and analytical approach. The end-result should be the same – a more efficient activity or activities. Methods study, however, is normally applied by work study or management services people who should be specialists in the technique.

Methods analysis is usually described by six words – choose, record, examine, develop, install, maintain. These are the canons of method study law, long used by most management services personnel.

Choose   This is an indication that a choice is possible (often this is not so). The need to recognise what is important in attempting to improve efficiency is what 'choice' should be about.

Record   Appropriate recording techniques are an essential element in methods analysis. Some practitioners tend to record badly or not at all, which is a crucial mistake. Analysis is impossible without accurate initial data, appropriately recorded.

It is not sufficient to merely record; quantification is perhaps more important still. Recording in the following ways will be necessary:

- Daily log sheets.
- Flow process charting.   A preprinted form similar to the one shown in Figure 26.3 is used to record operations by symbols. A brief description of the operations is also made. Using symbols for inspection, storage, delay, etc., has been practised for a long time – they enable anomalies and weaknesses to be seen quickly. It has been the practice to count the symbols in the original system and then again in a revised version. If there was a significant decrease, the new system was considered to be superior to the old, but this could be misleading as a symbol could be for an indeterminate time. A reduction of 50 per cent in symbols does not necessarily mean a reduction in the total time spent on the system.

Examine   This part of method analysis is often known as critical analysis, 'critical' referring to the detailed questioning which takes place. The use of checklists seems mandatory. As many improvement ideas as possible should be generated and brainstorming is a useful technique by which this can be done.

The essential factor is a disciplined approach, otherwise vital parts of the recorded method will be glossed over. A critical examination sheet similar to the one shown in Figure 26.4 is necessary. Purpose, place, sequence, people performing tasks and resources provided need to be discussed under the headings shown. Alternatives ought to be recorded and those that need to be developed should be stated.

Develop   This, the fourth stage, is usually in the methods analysis procedure. It could equally be called 'finding the best solution' or 'devising a new method'.

There are no set rules or patterns which can be utilised in carrying out the

System or department	Procedure for Order receipt and entry
Sales dept	
Chart No 1	

Ⓒ Clerical operation		☐ Inspecting for quantity operation		Elimination		What? } Is	
Ⓣ Typing operation		◇ Inspecting for quality operation		Combination		{ How? Who? } Could { Why?	
Ⓜ Machine operation		◻ Temporary storage operation					
⇨ Transport operation		▽ Permanent storage operation		Change of sequence		{ Where? When? } Should	

Operation Number	Symbol	Description of operation (or step)	Quantity	Time	Distance (metres)
1	Ⓒ	Accept orders from the mail	41	–	–
2	Ⓒ	Stamp order number on each order	41	0.05	–
3	Ⓒ	Translate into company terminology using translation form	41	1.2	–
4	⇨	Orders/translation sent to typists	41	–	20

Figure 26.3   *Methods analysis: unit document*

inductive leap between examine and develop. The 'solution' is often dependent upon the calibre, experience, and knowledge of the investigator.

Using the techniques quoted in this book is often beneficial but some other guidance may be necessary:

■ Was the problem solved? The original problem should have been solved. If not, why was this impossible? If a partial solution only has been devised the practitioner should explain what conditions and constraints have prevented a total solution.
■ Full cooperation by line management is necessary in devising any new solution. They will need to help install it, so should have had a large say in its development.
■ Time, cost, accuracy and control – these four factors are the kernel of any method or system.

● Time is often the key element. Is there any way in which the time taken to do the job can be reduced? How much time has been cut from the original method?
● Cost   How much cost-reduction has there been? Could more have been done, if so how? Has a time/cost table been made? (In systems study this could be established under the following headings; day, the

Job ____________________ Description of element ____________________

Department ____________________ Reference number ________ Page ____ of ____ Date ___ / ___ /19 ___

The present facts		Alternatives	Selected alternative for development
Purpose – WHAT is achieved ?	IS IT NECESSARY? Yes No If YES – why ?	What ELSE could be done ?	What SHOULD be done ?
Place – WHERE is it done ?	WHY THERE ? Advantages Disadvantages	Where ELSE could it be done ? A D	Where SHOULD it be done ?
Sequence – WHEN is it done ?	WHY THEN ? A D	When ELSE could it be done ? A D	When SHOULD it be done ?
Person – WHO does it ?	WHY THAT PERSON ? A D	Who ELSE could do it ? A D	Who SHOULD do it ?
Means – HOW is it done ?	WHY THAT WAY ? A D	How ELSE could it be done ? A D	How SHOULD it be done ?

NOTES

Figure 26.4 *Methods analysis: critical examination sheet*

time taken to process documentation, the system, labour cost weekly, machine cost weekly.)

- Accuracy   A predetermined accuracy level should be established. Often systems accuracy, etc., is set at a level that is far too high for the functions being performed. Accuracy can be bought at too high a price.
- Control   Is control over the new method effective? Will the proposed savings really be made? Will installation go as planned?
- Environmental and job duty factors   Have all environmental and job duty factors been taken into account? Have all psychological and physiological problems been considered?
- Simulation   Have the new methods or systems been simulated in any way to ensure that they will work successfully once they are introduced?

Install and maintain   Selling the new method is an important factor in achieving success. The basis of the sale should be to appeal to the self-interest of the person buying the new method.

Presentation is nearly as important. A simple, well documented, easily understood solution should be made, though most of the details should have been discussed and, as far as possible, agreed with the line manager concerned during the inspection. Once agreed, installation should be made by a well controlled timetable which fully exploits all available resources.

Training is an essential prerequisite – operatives, managers and supervisors all need to be trained to the degree and depth that will ensure installation success. If necessary, a pilot scheme should be started. If this succeeds, confidence will be gained so that full implementation can proceed.

Control can take many forms – overall cost control, labour control, output control, quality control. The controls should be such that deterioration from a predetermined standard can easily be seen by the manager controlling the personnel operating the new method or system.

Conclusion   Work measurement is an important element in any methods analysis. One of the most powerful reasons why a new system or method should be adopted is because it will save time or labour which can only finally be proved by work measurement.

Methods analysis is a significant tool in the fight for efficiency improvements, but it will never solve problems which are not right for methods solutions. Organisational deficiencies and lack of good management and training often masquerade as methods problems and practitioners can spend many weary man-weeks working on methods solutions only to have the problem remain as formidable as ever.

26.4   Integrated systems and the four-file system

In preceding chapters of this book the supposition has been that a 'system' should be seen in its widest possible context, otherwise a number of subsystems will be designed that will waste time, increase labour and cost and impose a lively climate for mistakes and errors. For example, in a manufacturing unit it has been normal practice to consider the various elements of order handling as a series of separate and occasionally totally independent systems, e.g. order receipt and acknowledgement, stock control, production planning and control, order-chasing, invoicing.

What happens when the system is seen as whole, from order receipt to despatch and invoicing?

The four-file system   At its simplest, it should be possible to operate a manufacturing sales order processing system with four computer files:

1   *The customer order file* which lists customers, their orders (date of receipt, items requested, date of despatch, payment details), discounts, lengths of credit, etc.
2   *The product file* which records all items made, stocked and sold, their standard factory costs, relationships within the product hierarchy, if these exist, alternatives where these are possible, fitments with which the products can be associated.
3   *The stock file* which gives free stock, total stock, stock on order and probably delivery date, back orders, stock cost, A, B or C classifications, economic ordering quantities.
4   *The order file* which records where in the process an order has reached – it enables factory-planning personnel to build up requisite loads which match factory capacity.

Given that these four files can be 'on line' and the appropriate data entry terminal and screen made available to one operator, then it should be possible to:

■ Check order requirements using the product file; verify that the item requested can be sold by the company; give standard factory cost.
■ Put order on customer file; check customer credit rating and pricing/ discount policy; calculate sales price.
■ Check stock file; verify stock availability; make out despatch instructions; raise new stock orders if necessary; put order on 'back order' if no stock is available; allocate stock if other items are to be sent at the same time.
■ Put order on the order file, which accumulates a queue of orders for manufacture; calculate length of queue and add manufacturing lead time; send acknowledgement to customer listing delivery time.

The four files can be operated by a single operator if the daily number of orders handled warrants it. The following actions can be carried out:

■ Sales order raised; acknowledgement made; customer/order credit control carried out; pricing done.
■ Stock records adjusted; stock control carried out.

- Sales ledger entries prepared.
- Invoicing prepared.
- Factory loads prepared.
- Work-in-progress accounting facilitated.
- Order progressing achieved.
- Despatch documents and despatch instructions made.

From the four files, other systems or activities can be carried out: payroll analysis comparing work done with wages paid; sales forecasting; production planning and control; statement preparation; sales analysis.

The advantages of an integrated system, therefore, are many:

- Once written or produced in a form acceptable to electronic or mechanical data processing equipment, the data need not be reproduced.
- Speed of data handling is increased.
- Errors in copying are eliminated once the initial data has been input to the computer; checking is not necessary in subsequent stages.
- Improved reporting and control should follow from a streamlined data flow based on a computer.

26.5 Forms control and design

When organisation and methods (O&M) was first introduced in the late 1950s and early 1960s, a major part of the function was 'forms control'. The most rewarding way to control and eliminate superfluous forms is to examine the associated clerical systems. If a system is eliminated or simplified the associated forms will be correspondingly reduced. Emphasis on systems study and work simplification may be preferred to forms control. However, forms control provides the base of much systems design and should be seen in that light.

26.5.1 Forms control

The reasons for forms control are to:

- Combine and eliminate as many forms as possible; all forms of a like function or usage should be examined to see if they can be combined.
- Reduce the size of forms in use.
- Prevent new forms being introduced indiscriminately.

26.5.2 Forms design

Function A form which only carries out one function should always be suspect. Function is directly related to the system of which the form is part – a systems study would be a prerequisite to introducting a form fulfilling three or four similar functions.

Obtaining information If the new form needs to be designed as part of a systems change, the investigator should be fully aware of all the form's requirements – who will use it and for what purpose, its size, design details and type of paper on which it is to be printed. He should be aware of the systems' background.

The form itself Standard paper sizes should always be used where possible and the forms should fit available filing equipment. The size of the form should be the smallest that will accommodate the information required without looking cramped.

Paper quality should be in keeping with the form's intended use. Even forms for outside correspondence should not bear extravagant embossing or be of superfine quality. Different-coloured paper should be used with discretion, particularly multicoloured sets. Non-standard sizes, carbon interleaved paper, no carbon required, continuous stationery, snap outs and gummed pads should only be used if there is a confirmed economic use for them.

Other considerations which will influence the size and quality of paper are:

- Number of copies required from one initial operation.
- The method to be used to reproduce the form.
- Trim size.
- Width of margins required (for filing purposes).
- Gripper edge for printing.

Paper and paper sizes The A sizes are based on the A0 sheet which is 841 × 1,189 mm; the rest of the standard range is a derivative of the whole:

Designation	Size (mm)
A0	841 × 1,189
A1	594 × 841
A2	420 × 594
A3	297 × 420
A4	210 × 297
A5	148 × 210
A6	105 × 148
A7	74 × 105
A8	53 × 74
A9	37 × 53
A10	27 × 37

Adhering to standard paper sizes will ensure less wastage in cutting and rationalisation in printing. If there is likely to be much erasing, paper which is tougher than normal will be required. Flimsy paper, though cheap, inhibits handling, although it may be needed for 'airweight' purposes. Tougher paper will be needed for documents likely to be in constant use, especially if put into a file for scrutinising purposes.

Design The appearance of a well designed form should proclaim its efficiency. It should look neat, well drawn and purposeful; be easily understood; instructions should be unambiguous and the space provided for answers to questions should be proportionate to the amount of information required. Design must be related to the people who will fill the form in. Special consideration must be given if the public will use the form.

The form's identification, title or description should take up as little space as necessary, yet should clearly indicate the function and identity of the form. Sufficient space should be left between the edge of the sheet and the title (and any other printing) so that words are not concealed when a gripper or binder is used. Company titles should not be used on internal forms. Space for signatures should be provided at the bottom right of the form.

Instructions on filling in the form should be placed as high as possible on it. Serial numbers should be placed at the bottom left edge of the form where they cannot be confused with any other data. Numbering of any kind should be used when absolutely necessary. As much preprinting as possible should be done so that actual clerical recording is minimal. Where a stock quantity will always be in metres or kilogrammes, the unit of measurement should be preprinted.

Spacing between lines of forms on which entries have to be typed should be 4.5 mm for single spacing and 9 mm for double spacing. Where forms need to be handwritten, the space should be in 7 mm units. Sufficient space should be provided for the entry required, but too much should be avoided. Where typing is concerned, space should be provided at the rate of 10 to 12 characters and spaces per 25 mm. Average handwriting is more difficult to judge; 5 to 6 characters per 25 mm is usual.

The thickness of ruled lines should determine:

- The boundary between pieces of data.
- The boundary between parts of the form.
- Areas which need special attention.
- Lines where signatures or data are required.

A design where *ballot boxes* are placed sequentially beneath each other is preferable – the form will be easier to design, neater in appearance and consequently easier to follow and fill in. It will be possible to make use of tabulator stops on a typewriter.

Wherever possible, the form should be designed for a minimum of data or words, e.g. a tick or a cross to indicate the answer to a question is better than yes or no.

Information flow should help to determine the layout of the form. Where data is being recorded sequentially, the boxes or columns should also follow in sequence. The most-used sections of the form should also follow in sequence and be placed together at the top of the form.

Wording should always be 'soft' – 'please' and simple words should be used wherever possible.

Data input forms for data processing need to be clear and easily read, with adequate spacing between lines. Information should be divided between fixed and variable and that to be punched clearly designated. The design of the form should be such that speed and rythm of punching is facilitated. The sequence of information should be the same as that on the punched document. As far as possible, data should be recorded vertically and not horizontally.

26.6   Further reading

1   B.H. Walley, *Management Services Handbook,* Business Books (1973).
2   M.J. Clay, *Work Study in the Office,* Anbar (1977).

Part Five

Office Equipment

Twenty-seven

Office Equipment

27.1 Introduction

For many years the threat and promise of a technological revolution in office equipment has hung over the heads of office managers and their staff. Now the promise is nearly a reality. The silicon chip and a new and more demanding economic climate are forcing the pace. Office working methods and work done are about to undergo profound change.

The 'chip' is largely responsible for a convergence of computing and communicating facilities which have shrunk the cost of data processing and the transport of information to a considerable degree.

However, while much equipment may be available, all the old problems of maximising its use, of designing appropriate systems and establishing suitable work organisations remain. It was too early, in retrospect, to catch computer euphoria. The new equipment may equally give disappointing results if its application is misjudged. What may suit one organisation may be anathema to another. Most companies may benefit more by a step-by-step approach than by a technical earthquake. The talk of a paperless office may be premature – though not without foundation.

27.2 Obtaining equipment

People can be expensive, troublesome and inflationary. Once equipment of some kind has been bought its cost is known (though servicing and maintenance may be a problem) and it does not answer back. Apart from power shortages, it is not likely to go on strike or complain that it is overworked.

On the other hand, people can be flexible and have a definite ability to adapt to changing circumstances. They can think and carry out non-routine tasks with comparative ease. However, in many offices, continual staff problems have led to a strong move towards using machines wherever possible. Computers are being justified on the basis that the workload they carry cannot not be handled in any other way.

This logical approach is occasionally taken to extreme but within reason should be followed wherever possible. Where, then, should office equipment be used?

a   Where it obviously has a return on investment which is appropriate with the organisation. The economic decision must always be the most important one to make.
b   Where obtaining staff to carry out a specific job or function is very difficult or impossible.
c   Where work has to be done extremely accurately.
d   Where work is of a dull or boring nature.
e   Where it will have a significant effect on customer service.
f   Where the work can only be carried out by equipment. This will include information storage and processing, speed and means of communication.

27.3   Renting, leasing or buying office equipment

The alternatives of renting, leasing or buying are governed by fairly complex financial considerations – the methods of acquisition need to be evaluated extremely carefully. There are no easy ways of determining the right course of action.

27.3.1   Renting

Renting will only be an available option if the equipment manufacturer is directly involved. Many small computers are bought through agents, so renting will not normally be available. Potential renters will find that it has a greater cost than leasing or buying. It is useful if equipment is needed for a comparatively short time as rental agreements are usually short term. Beyond three years, it is preferable to lease or buy.

27.3.2   Leasing

Leasing is a tax-efficient form of borrowing to gain the use of valuable resources. Its use should be judged on an after-tax calculation. Most companies or organisations should lease when their marginal tax rates are low or non-existent.

Leasing normally allows the leasing company to claim capital allowances, when the lessor is incapable of doing so. Low or non-existent profit, stock relief, high capital allowances or past payment of advance corporation tax will all promote the payment of marginal tax rates. Leasing should normally be cheaper than borrowing cash or having equipment via a hire purchase agreement, because of the lessor's tax credit position.

Leasing arrangements tend to run from three to seven years with high penalties if the lease is terminated prematurely. There are two types of leasing arrangement. The financial lease charges enough to cover the cost of the equipment, plus interest over its leased life. An operating lease works on the basis that the equipment will have a considerable life (leasing potential) when the leasing period is over, but with rapid technological change this will become less and less attractive.

Leasing does not need an initial capital sum and if the lease payments are equalised throughout the lease period inflation will ensure a real diminishing payment. After a leasing period has been completed, the lessor can usually renew the lease on very favourable terms.

27.3.3 Buying

Buying is normally the user's cheapest option – if the tax situation is right in the first years of purchase. Disadvantages are that a capital sum is required initially and after purchase the user will stand the risk of obsolescence, so denying rapid change to meet new circumstances.

27.4 Office automation – the alternatives

Those who have long used a computer, mainly in batch mode, will perhaps be concerned at the advance of word processors or stand-alone minis and wonder if somehow automation with its advantages is passing them by. It is possible that it is not.

What are the possibilities in the way of equipment, systems, philosophies and viewpoints which need to be considered? The main alternatives are:

1   *Batch use of a computer with a reasonably large mainframe*   As Chapter 28 suggests, there are still many reasons why batch processing is preferable in many systems applications – it is cheaper; the systems are simpler and easier to introduce; mainframe/hardware costs are reducing rapidly. There is a danger, however, that the batching process delays input and occasionally goes wrong. Document for document, it must be quicker to use dedicated punch people than have local input.

2   *Remote job entry*   This has proved extremely popular in many systems. It permits input to the computer to take place in departments where the transactions are generated – thus reducing handling time and cutting out the possibility of mistakes in batching. Local personnel have to be well trained to operate RJE.

3   *On-line data processing*   Prime time is normally used for this process, unlike batch processing which can use any available running time. Processing is interactive, which is very necessary in some transactional arrangements such as booking hotels or airline seats.

4   *Local stand-alone computers with local files*   File storage is usually limited, so processing must be limited to some extent. The local user, however, is in control of the operation and consequently is likely to become computer-orientated and so very active in introducing the new system.

5   *Local distributed processing*   Depending upon the facilities provided, local distributed processing can involve local stand-alone data processors which can carry out data processing but also use the data base provided by a large mainframe.

    Because the cost of processing data is falling faster than communication, local processing has to be favoured over on-line facilities. Distributed processing can provide the advantages of both of them. Like local stand-alone computers, distributed processing should promote local accountability for computer activities. It should shorten development time and be upgraded progressively. In the event of a failure at the centre, local processing should still continue. However, as complexity grows, so does expense. (The central computer will need a dedicated professional team, but gives economies of scale and perhaps a more professional result. Software is often greater and perhaps better.)

6   *Independent word processors*   Like local stand-alone computers, line management will be deeply involved and hence local enthusiasm may be greater than if a central service of some kind was offered.

7   *Linked word processing using local area networks*   The possibility of linking word processors and perhaps stand-alone minicomputers (all joined to a central mainframe) is a major step towards the paperless office and all this implies in communication speed – and cost. Complexity of systems design will be a problem.

    Cost trends may seem to favour putting more and more equipment into the hands of local line personnel but systems design is still a problem and might need superior systems analysis which only a well founded management services unit can provide. The possible future may lie in a combination of independent data processing facilities of word processors and minicomputers linked to each other by a communication network, but with a central mainframe providing a data base.

27.5   The paperless office

Much has been written about the paperless office where all transactions and storage are carried out electronically. How valid is the suggestion? Several companies, particularly banks, have eliminated considerable amounts of paper internally but little has yet been done between companies. What paper does is an important part of the discussion.

Transmission   Paper is light and can easily be transported. Mailing is geared to handle letters rapidly.

Storage   Paper provides a good storage medium. It is not too bulky and does not deteriorate too much.

Data processing is easy and calculations can be made fairly simple. If, however, electronic equipment can become equally convenient, are the days of paper limited? The following comments are important:

- *Transmission*   Facsimile transmission is already possible but it requires that the receiver and sender have compatible electronic apparatus, which will restrict transmission for some time to come.
- *Storing*   Microfilm has long been used as a storage medium but as yet it has made no serious inroads into the use of paper. Data storage of huge quantities of information is already carried out by computer.
- *Data processing*   Again, computers already perform many data-processing tasks which previously have been done by clerks armed only with pencils and paper.

There is no doubt that there either exists now, or will in a few years' time, the means for abandoning paper to a large degree. Yet the most-used device of many computers are not VDUs but printers. People prefer paper, perhaps because it is tactile. Resistance to change will often outwit a technological breakthrough. There will be other aspects – financial and organisational – which will inhibit the rapid elimination of paper. It will be around for a little while yet.

27.6   New office equipment – the human problem restated

Earlier in this book, various comments were made concerning change and how it might be handled. The equipment revolution will only exacerbate any human relations problems that already exist:

a   If offices become capital-intensive, then the same shift patterns may need to emerge as those on the shop floor, if equipment is to be used effectively.

b   The new equipment will make many peripheral activities redundant. The associated people will suffer accordingly if reallocation of tasks and retraining is not possible. Typists, for example, should be reduced in number. Mail services will need to change.

c   Equipment maintenance could become a problem and a separate office equipment maintenance engineer may be needed.

d   Desks and office layouts will change to accommodate a work station with a word processor, VDU and a telephone. Whether the keyboard will be out of date in five years' time needs consideration.

e   Eye strain and stress associated with using VDUs will become more commonplace.

f   Fairly ambitious guidelines for union/management negotiations were laid down by the TUC in *Technology and Employment* (1979).

g   Retraining is far from being a painless process. Workers will find it difficult to switch skills late in life. Greater intellectual effort needed to operate new equipment may not be possible from some staff.

h   Unionisation is likely to grow as the challenge of new equipment and its potential influence on employment prospects is recognised more and more. Militancy among white-collar groups may become far more prevalent.

27.7   Office automation – the union viewpoint

A clerical union such as APEX or NALGO will have members in high and lowly paid jobs, spread throughout the country. A uniform response to office automation may come from the general secretary or union executive, but frequently individual office response will vary. Office managers may have to tackle their local problems, realising in some way that they are unique. These facets are important:

1   Unions are concerned about jobs (and so members!), pay and health – perhaps in that order.
2   Jobs – if unions are member-hungry, then even the office managers' old standby of natural wastage may not be acceptable, though it may be the best available.
3   In any situation where change is possible, the sooner the unions are told the better – decisions about future staffing levels and who does what are very important.
4   The use of VDUs and local health and safety has received much union attention – scotching rumours with fact is important.
5   Work content and related rewards will be an obvious part of consultation; restricting use of new equipment until 'pay aspirations' have been met is fairly normal practice.
6   What happens to displaced people will perhaps be the most sensitive discussion point. If people are not made redundant, the equipment may never justify itself – it is better to know this before an acquisition is made.
7   Who gets new jobs will be debated at length; seniority rather than suitability will be stressed – wrongfully – by most office managers.
8   Productivity bonuses based on key strokes have been resisted by some unions.
9   Not all unions are against office automation as such. In 1978, APEX published *Office Technology – the trade union response,* which covered the possibilities of 'new technology agreements' with management – a step in the right direction.

27.8   Office automation – gains and losses

The two preceding sections suggest that the gains from office automation may not be so great as anticipated. Why is this? Some of the reasons not previously mentioned will include:

a   Office work often needs a high degree of mental skill, which is difficult to reproduce electronically.
b   Typists – the people usually displaced by word processors – are not the most costly nor the most numerous staff members; this distinction lies

with managers and supervisors. Hence, reducing the number of typists and improving the productivity of the remainder may not result in significant cost-savings.

c Electronic equipment, especially VDUs, may be technically sound, but not ergonomically suitable for good operating. Stable screen images, flexibility in operating practice, good keying and control are all necessary.

d Work stations could be badly designed with inadequate working surfaces; the work station should not be cramped or set out so as to constrain the operator in any way.

e The vocabulary used with electronic equipment, such as word processors, may not meet normal business standards; computer jargon could be used which could inhibit the good use of the equipment.

f A potential limitation on data communication will be public networks; substantial investment will be needed but may not be forthcoming.

There may, however, be gains other than staff savings:

1 Boring, repetitive jobs may gradually disappear; enhanced skills may be needed to work new machines. There should, in consequence, be less job alienation.

2 Accuracy of reports may improve along with the layout; work quality should also be enhanced.

3 Speed of retyping and script changing should improve considerably.

27.9 The way in

Planning the move to office automation has many advantages over 'just letting it happen'. Incompatibility, technological shortcomings, under-utilisation of equipment, are all factors that could emerge from an unplanned march into word processors or other forms of office automation. The human relations problems are far too grave to allow an *ad hoc* approach to succeed.

27.10 Further reading

1 *Computer Technology and Employment,* AUEW/TASS Conference Proceeding (January 1979).

2 H.F. Farrow, *Computerisation Guidelines,* NCC (1979).

3 G.L. Simons, *Introducing Microprocessors,* NCC (1979).

4 S.G. Prime, *Introducing the Electronic Office,* NCC (1979).

5 Peddar Associates, *How Close is the Office of the Future?,* Gower (1981).

6 Hamish Donaldson, 'Trends in office automation', *The British Journal of Administrative Management* (April 1981).

7 I. Borovits and S. Neumann, *Computer Systems Performance Evaluation,* Lexington (1979).

8 R. Morris, *Computer Basics for Managers – a practical guide to profitable computing,* Business Books (1980).

9 *Computer Manpower in the 80s,* HMSO (1980).

10   M. Laver, *Introducing Computers,* HMSO (1976).
11   T.F. Fry, *Computer Appreciation,* Butterworth (1981).
12   C.J. Sippl and F. Dahl, *Computer Power for the Small Business,* Prentice Hall (1981).
13   E.H. Mandani and B.R. Gaines, *Computing Skills and the User Interface,* Academic Press (1981).

Twenty-eight

Computers – Large and Small

28.1 Introduction

The office equipment revolution is having a considerable influence on the battle between large and small computers and so the whole pattern of use of computer equipment. Electronic data processing was once expensive; now by any standards it is extremely cheap. What are the possibilities of and reasons for using either a small or a large computer configuration?

28.2 The basic axioms

How computer developments are planned and introduced and what systems should be computerised have been well recorded on numerous occasions. To restate the basic axioms might be considered superfluous but they do add considerably to the debate about data processing and the equipment needed. The axioms are generally considered to be:

1 Computer or management services staff should not dominate systems development. Line managers or supervisors, perhaps even clerks, should direct agreed development and largely be responsible for the systems that are actually introduced. This infers that line personnel have both the time and expertise necessary to carry out the computer systems development. This is rarely so.

2 The computer should be used to help decision-making in key activities in the company – stock control, production scheduling, performance monitoring, etc. There are still many people who consider that a computer should be used wherever it can be justified economically. This assumes that the choice of application is not limited in any way and development resources are available to take up every opportunity which is financially sound. Normally neither of these two factors will apply completely – or at least not in the short term.

3   Many of the problems associated with the remoteness of large central processing units can be solved by using distributive processing. Local line management is given a facility to carry out its own data processing. So as many 'hands on' activities as possible should be built up. Line personnel, through terminal use and simple programming (such as the application of BASIC) should become part of the operating of the computer, so reversing their traditional role of outsiders demanding a service.

The 'hands on' approach will ensure that most of the systems so developed will be on-line. This ignores the probability that the most economically efficient systems design and, consequently, hardware use may still only be achieved through 'large sytems' with an appropriate data base and perhaps mainly operated in batch mode.

4   Hardware costs as a ratio to other computer costs have been reduced considerably in the last decade. It pays to get computer systems introduced quickly even if this does utilise hardware inefficiently. However, when a major enhancement to the computer is necessary the true economics of this approach become a little clearer.

5   If large systems are contemplated, then there has to be a major investment in data base design and associated management. The systems should be interrelated so that the best use is made of the computer, so gaining the highest return on development and hardware costs.

Data bases and large management systems need computer systems people of considerable skill, who are often difficult to recruit and equally difficult to retain once recruited. The large systems often become ends in themselves, dominating all systems development even when they have run out of economic or any other justification – that is until some brave person decides to abandon the whole project.

These axioms suggest that there are still major pitfalls which need to be considered if computers of any size are to be deployed effectively. The cost/value relationship and ease of application is changing constantly and what appears to be right one year could be wrong the next.

28.3   Organisation and the large computer

A perennial problem associated with large computers has been who has control over them within a company. Initially most computers and computer people were controlled by chief accountants or financial directors. There was a fairly predictable result and computers were mostly employed on accounting systems – payroll, sales ledger or invoicing.

Some management services departments thought they were luckier to respond to the chief executive or managing director but unfortunately the results were usually no better than having a link with the finance function. The potential lack of bias in choosing systems for a large computer application needed to be supported by a chief executive who had the time and the expertise required for the successful management of a department of computer people and the knowledge to see that the computer hardware was used effectively. This was very rare.

Where the large computer fits into the overall organisation, who controls it, who generates the development plan and who guides its day-to-day activities seems to have a greater influence on achieving effective computer use than whether the management services or computer people have every last technical skill in systems development, programming, or computer operating. Without any effective organisational framework for their ability they could be practising their skills for little purpose.

It seems essential, then, that the organisational relationship between the computer and its staff is one where computer use can be directly related to the rest of the functions with which it is linked. For example, when accounting systems were the main application for the computer it was probably right that computer people responded to the head of the accounting function. However, when the key systems applications change to, say, stock control, factory planning, or performance monitoring, it seems right that organisationally the computer becomes more closely linked with operational planning activities. In this way the computer specialists become part of the development team. The difference between line and staff becomes blurred as each person works within the same function and strives for the same objectives.

28.4 Large versus small computers

Much has been written about the battle between large and small systems and the preceeding two sections have served to highlight some of the problems. By any count many large computers have not been successful. Computer installations have become bogged down in their own inefficiencies, a prey to overbuying or leasing of equipment, often surrounded by devoted systems analysts and programmers who lack a fundamental knowledge of the real business world. The reasons why computers have failed to live up to their glittering promise are many and need to be carefully considered by anyone who either has, or thinks he requires, one.

Some specialists suggest that within this decade the terms large/central/mini/small computers will become meaningless and drop out of use. Currently they mostly do mean something. They indicate not just the size, cost and power of equipment, but the way in which it is used and perhaps the uses to which it can – or should – be put. The case for either can be summed up as follows:

a   The trend in data processing is towards shared resource systems. Memory and printers are still comparatively expensive pieces of equipment. Local work stations may need data capture and microprocessor facilities, but it would be advantageous from a cost viewpoint to have a central mainframe data store with an information despatch and retrieval index.

b It is likely that information stores will grow to an enormous degree. It is equally likely that the massive stores needed will be on hierarchical disk storage because of the associated economies.

c A trend obvious in many companies with large mainframe computers is the growing number of small computers (linked to the central computer), used solely by local line management. This method of distributed computing allows local computing facilities to managers who can then design their own systems. This in turn should motivate the use of data processing. Information should be totally relevant and access to it speedy. The consequences of systems failure will be limited.

d Central processors are ideal for processing large quantities of data on a batch basis. This type of data processing may be alien to the requirements of many line managers.

e Companies often change their organisational structure and so their data processing and information retrieval needs. Flexibility is likely to be best with small local systems.

f Local data processing is based on the philosophy that the line manager user is the centre of the data processing universe, not the computer system team and their large mainframe. The emphasis is different.

g Local data processing, however, could lead to an inefficient use of resources, if computer expertise does not match up to achieving a reasonable equipment utilisation. Centralisation provides corporate control and monitoring not always possible with local processing. Cost-savings, by avoiding duplication and software proliferation, are probable.

h The central data processing systems unit still has the major proportion of technical skills and their under-use or misuse could provide a poor return for the overall money spent on data processing.

i A compromise between the use of a central mainframe and local data processing is to divide systems between large-scale batch processing on a mainframe and provide minis for local on-line processing. These latter machines should normally be utilised for 'one-off processing'.

28.5 The computer

28.5.1 Hardware

Hardware is the physical equipment and comprises the following:

The central processor The central processor has three major divisions. The control unit – which houses the executive programme which controls the interaction of processor and peripherals; the arithmetic unit which carries out the calculations needed; an internal storage unit which is normally called core or main store. The core store is one of the vital measurements in determining the size of the computer. Usually it is constructed in modular form and can be expanded by the addition of another module. Depending upon the computer supplier, core store is measured by bytes, characters or words.

Access and cycle processing time are the two measurements used to determine the speed of the central processor which is expressed in microseconds (thousandths) or nanoseconds (1,000 millionths). Access time is the time taken to transfer data to or from store. Cycle time is the time taken to carry out an activity between output and reinput of data to store.

Back-up storage   The central processor's· core store is expensive and will usually require back-up storage. Magnetic disks and tapes are normally used for this purpose and often they are considered to be compatible within one configuration. (In some computer systems punched cards are still used as a file media.)

Magnetic disks are either fixed or interchangeable. The storage areas look rather like a normal LP record mounted on a central spindle. Each side of the disk stores data in concentric recording tracks. As the disk revolves a read-write head searches for the data which the computer program requires.

Data input and output devices   Input can be via punched cards, paper tape, encoded magnetic tape, mark sensing, remote job entry, etc. Output is either hard copy via a printer or display information via a VDU or a medium similar to that which input the data, e.g. magnetic tape.

28.5.2   *Software*

It is possible to pay as much for the means of ensuring that a computer works effectively as for the machine itself. The machine – the hardware – is useless without the computer programs which make it go – the software.

It is possible that the choice of available software is more important than choosing hardware. For some equipment independent software suppliers may be more important than the maker of the equipment.

Software can be of three types:

Operating systems   In most computer or data processing configurations, the interaction between the central processor and its peripherals and between · peripherals themselves is highly complex. An operating system is tailored for each machine type to ensure that the total configuration accepts data input, transfers it between peripherals and processor and is finally output so that maximum efficiency is obtained.

Operating systems will control the use of a combination of programs (time-sharing). Error detection of various kinds is also part of the system. Communication also comes into this category. The computer, either through the user's console or VDU, reports on the state of the central processor/peripherals in use, files being interrogated, etc.

In-house or bespoke software   Most users believe that some at least of their data processing transactions are unique in some way, so they insist that they write their own software either by using simple languages such as BASIC or more complicated commercial high-level language such as COBOL, FORTRAN and ALGOL and their derivatives.

Packages   Many commercial applications have a basic similarity no matter what organisations use them. Payroll, stock control, invoicing and sales ledger are applications of this type. Many, if not most, computer suppliers provide programs/software to meet these requirements, which can be amended to some degree to cover the user's specification. These programs or software are called 'packages'.

Programming aids   Some software has been developed so that it can be inserted into the bespoke programs which are being written. These parts of programs are called subroutines and can be used to carry out basic processing, such as sorting.

Where there are several data processing specialists, as in a management services unit, it is likely that computer programming will largely be bespoke. Their job pride will demand it. This situation could be a costly mistake.

The changes occurring in software for data processing are in these areas:

- *Networking architecture systems*   IBM, for example, has developed SNA – a systems network architecture package which connects data terminals and office information exchange. Teletext standards are being developed for the same activity, but of course they are not compatible with the IBM software.
- *Local area networks*   LAN is software which links disparate electronic equipment such as word processors or computers together to permit the shared use of available information. It can be likened to an electronic machine service. This is discussed further in the next chapter.
- *Composition software*   Large company data bases need to be accessed by VDUs and be output on video disk, viewdata or microfiche, instead of the traditional paper tabulation. Composition software is being developed for this purpose.
- *Word processing*   The need for word processors to be able to communicate with each other and the addition of data processing enhances flexibility and so useful word processing software – again this is discussed further in the next chapter.
- *Information retrieval*   Computer specialists have wrestled at length with file design and information retrieval systems, as data bases grow larger and stored information covers more and more functions and activities in the company. Irrespective of how it is stored, these functions need information given to them in a format they can use effectively. Information-retrieval software development is concerned with the means of storing and retrieval of information so that functions receive exactly what they want, when they want it.

28.6   Small computers

According to the British Standards Institute a computer is 'any device capable of automatically accepting data, applying a sequence of processes to the data and supplying the result of those processes'. Confusion about small computers is perhaps increased with the use of the term visual record computer. The proposition that 'most visual record computers would use magnetically striped ledger cards to carry out ledger posting and similar activities' might be added to the BSI definition.

What constitutes a minicomputer is perhaps still a matter of debate. The cost/performance of such equipment is not in doubt; it has improved enormously over the last 10 years and the advant of microchip technology has produced something of a breakthrough in small computer costs. Equipment available (which is increasing rapidly) can roughly be divided into two types:

1   Minicomputers   Like their larger brethren, minicomputers are capable of accepting automatic input with full facilities for automatic output. They have the means of processing data under the aegis of an internal program, which can be amended as the user wishes – within reason.

It seems comparatively easy to add peripherals to minicomputers to the extent that there appears to be little or no difference between them and full-size computers. Mostly, data is stored on small disks or magnetic tape. It is this area where technology is being applied currently, to produce some less cumbersome form of storage medium.

Minicomputers may not necessarily be required to be free-standing units carrying out their own systems activities. They are now used on a whole range of operations where linking to a major computer is essential. Process control is an important application. They are also acting as 'intelligent' terminals in data processing networks, perhaps assembling data from remote terminals to pass on to a main central processor.

2   Visual record computers   Information to the machine can be input via a keying process from a typewriter or adding-machine keyboard, fed automatically from punched paper tape or cards or magnetic striped ledger cards. Recent developments suggest that cassette tape input will be used more in the future. Data can be held on magnetic disks or fed in from another computer via a terminal facility.

The computer facility lies in the equipment's ability to carry out required calculations such as invoice calculations, entering further details on ledger cards and updating items such as stock record cards.

The limited speed and memory capacity of the equipment dictates that only fairly simple and routine activities can be carried out. The normal accounting functions of invoicing and ledger posting are good examples of the systems usually tackled.

Statistics can be derived quite simply from these routines. Sales data concerning product sales to specific customers, etc., could be a valuable by-product. The systems each need a set of instructions. The program can be (and usually is) written by the equipment's supplier, so no programming expertise is needed by users. However, though the introduction of such equipment may appear to be simple, usually an organisation's working system will need to be reorganised to achieve maximum benefit.

28.7 Terminals

A terminal, as its name implies, is a piece of electronic equipment at the end of a data transmission cable. The simplest and most usual terminals have been input devices for computer systems or, conversely, the means of retrieving and displaying data. The VDU, which is used to input stock movements and display the balance on a screen, is typical of terminal use. These conventional or dumb terminals have had no local data processing capability.

The next advance in terminal use has been to provide the means for the terminal user to program an activity and provide a local data processing function independent of the mainframe computer that would normally be used.

Whether having such a terminal will enable users to substantially reduce the paper they use or, indeed, eliminate paper altogether is still being debated.

28.8 Why computers fail

Some of the reasons why computers fail are easy to suggest:

a   The wrong equipment was specified.
b   Various pieces of software associated with the computer have not worked.
c   Computer techniques have not been well enough understood or applied appropriately.
d   Computer staff have been poorly trained and inadequately motivated.
e   Systems applications have been chosen badly and applied indifferently.
f   Line management has abdicated its responsibility to lead and control the systems development.
g   The pychology of introducing a computer has not been understood.

28.9 Choice of equipment

Obviously the machine must do what it is supposed to do. So a checklist for evaluation purposes might be:

- Does the configuration do the jobs required?
- What apparent spare capacity is there?
- What is marginal in the configuration in terms of capacity?
- How much is the next enhancement?
- How long is it likely to be before an enhancement is required?

Consider:

- Ease of installation.
- Packages available – proved and running.
- Ease of operating the configuration.
- First cost of the configuration.
- Possible subsequent cost.
- Delivery, maintenance and second-shift costs.
- How easy is it to expand?
- Minimum core store to carry out the systems designated including operating systems, program areas, overlay area and data area.

As well as the hardware, the evaluation ought to include all the customer support services given by the computer supplier – training, systems and programming support, and general help in getting the machine operational, including planning the installation, for example:

- What other machines are there of a similar type in the area, which could be used for back-up facilities?
- Space and general environmental considerations.
- Service bureau assistance for program testing.

Software

- Languages: assembly; high-level, e.g. COBOL.
- Operating system – how good is it?
- Housekeeping and utility routines.
- Linkage and integration of systems.

Systems loading and timing An exact assessment of the full capacity of the proposed system for each main application is necessary. Timing should distinguish between productive and set-up time. The amount allowed for contingencies should be stated. Summaries of daily, weekly and monthly times should be required.

Economics of the computer A configuration best able to carry out the applications required over the next four to five years should be chosen. Quotations should give:

- purchase price
- retail price
- rental price
- lease price plus any other terms the computer supplier might operate

The number of shifts planned will help to determine costs, so the timing of proposed systems applications is important. The cost of the configuration should be broken down as follows:

- computer equipment

- data preparation equipment
- options
- supplies – cards, disks, tapes, etc.
- air conditioning
- power supply
- delivery costs
- maintenance costs
- shift premium
- program testing time if this is not free
- cost per hour of service bureau facilities
- cost of training

Reliability   Statements on down-time for individual pieces of equipment in the configuration should be called for.

Contractual terms   A copy of the proposed contract should be carefully studied before it is signed. Copies of blank contract forms should always be called for when hardware requirements are being discussed.

These are the main items that should be considered when the computer configuration is discussed. More important, what the computer must do must be specified – basically, this means what the computer will be asked to do. A computer is a piece of equipment of more and no less importance than a new production machine of some kind. Its relationship to profit should be exactly the same. The worst view taken about computers is that they are an 'act of faith'. Somehow, so it is stated, a computer will be a catalyst for vast improvements in company efficiency. How wrong that view can be. By themselves computers tend not to motivate action of any kind. Managers will not use them if they have been left unaware of the machine's potential and, more important, of changes in management methods that will improve profit, and which the computer can aid.

28.10   Developing computer applications

28.10.1   The development plan

Recognition of key systems or activities is the essential precursor to establishing a systems development plan. This should largely be the responsibility of local line management, though some guidance is obviously needed from systems personnel. Once key systems have been defined or an overall strategy for functional development determined, a feasible plan can be made.

The plan must obviously match the available development resources, both in numbers and skills, but it should be established so that it is 'manageable'. This factor nearly inevitably leads to a modular approach being taken. For example, in any 'order fulfilment activity' in a manufacturing organisation there will be the following processes or systems:

- order processing
- stock control
- forward loading
- factory scheduling
- work-in-progress monitoring
- order progress monitoring

Each is dependent on the other for inputs and outputs and the same data bases are needed. The linking aspect is very strong, but it is probable that once the linkage has been examined and the appropriate data bases set up, each module can be developed as a single system.

Systems development is often lengthy and occasionally could go out of close control. A good rule to consider is that all systems development should provide some tangible result within six months. The objective should be very clear and success or failure measured carefully.

28.10.2 User specification

It seems essential that users set out systems requirements themselves. It is possible that these need only be a series of strategic or practical objectives, but in special cases a major length system specification is required, e.g. in fairly technical systems such as management accounting.

In the past the business specification has been used for the same purpose, but this too has usually been written by systems analysts and not line personnel – a mistake.

28.10.3 Computer systems specifications

The user specifications should be translated into a computer system specification by a systems analyst where consideration of the following is needed:

- data collection and analysis
- design of output requirements
- design of input requirements
- file content design
- program specification writing
- program and systems evaluation
- general systems maintenance

Between program specification writing and program and systems evaluations, the programmers will code or program the systems specification. The systems analyst may not always be in sole charge of the latter two items and may share responsibility for them with a programmer. The systems analyst will be mainly concerned with:

- Finding out about a system and collecting data about it.
- Designing the formats which will ensure that the computer provides suitable outputs.
- Writing a specification from which it will be possible for a programmer to code instructions for the computer operation.

Normally various standard formats will be used by the systems analyst. Standardisation should improve communication between the EDP department and potential and actual users of data processing services; improve communication within the data processing department itself; and tend to improve the efficiency of data processing personnel.

The following charts and formats may also be necessary:

- Organisation charts.
- Activity charts
- Systems recording reports using words and symbols.
- Input design documentation – punching documents, paper-tape record specifications, etc.
- Output document specification sheets.
- File record specification sheets.
- Systems function diagram (computer).
- System flowchart (computer).
- Computer flowchart.
- Program function flowchart.
- Decision-control sheets.
- System-test schedules.

The normal method of recording systems procedures, whether manual or computer, is by symbol. Unfortunately these are not standardised and IBM symbols tend to differ slightly from those of ICL. The definition of each symbol also varies with the user. Personal preference plays a large part in establishing the symbol representation.

28.10.4   Input design

The systems analyst will be concerned with:

- The means of inputting data – RJE, batch, etc.
- The documents needed for input purposes.
- How the documents will arrive at the data processing department if batch processing is used.
- How the document is to be input into the computer; to do this a form of input must be chosen – punched cards, punched paper tape, magnetic tape encoder, etc; the input will need to be designed.
- Input will then have to be verified as being correct and a suitable method for doing this will have to be devised.

- Sorting data may then be necessary, e.g. it will be important for input to be in the same order as data contained on file.
- A control procedure which helps to ensure that all input documents are processed when required.

The main method of data validation will be the computer program, and usually a 'data vet' is specified with great care by the systems analyst. The data type must be verified, then each item of information is examined and checked. 'Check digits' are often introduced for verification purposes.

Data preparation control is another essential control element. For example, a check to determine whether all data has been received must be made, ensuring that none has been lost in transit. Sequential numbering of documents may be necessary. Batching of incoming documents is usually practised and batch totals made where possible.

28.10.5   Design of outputs

Outputs provide users with their main contact with the computer. The design of output documentation is thus very important. Well designed output documentation will substantially aid the selling of computer services – again if batch processing is used.

A line printer is the normal medium for producing output, though other equipment is sometimes used such as xeronic printers, graph plotters and VDUs, if on-line processing is needed.

28.10.6   File design

The systems analyst has usually to choose between reference and dynamic files. The major purpose of a dynamic file is to record events, e.g. a stock file recording the current stock position is a dynamic file; a file listing product prices is a reference file.

File design is important. It can considerably influence the running time or operational cycle time of the computer, as well as the complexity of the programming required. Computer files can be stored on either magnetic tape or disks and occasionally on paper tape or magnetic card.

The systems analyst should design computer files so as to take account of the speed of data required and the volume of data to be handled. The design of the file will be a compromise between the constraints of the file medium and the data to be stored. The more important elements to be considered will be:

- Fixed variable-length records; fixed lengths waste space but facilitate programming.
- Possibilities of adding or deleting items.
- Speed at which interrogation is possible – or desired.
- Location procedures – most file items have a key field or identification number; the relationship of key fields is known as the 'file organisation';

serial and random methods are used; serially organised files are usually held on punched cards or magnetic tape.

28.10.7   Systems design

The systems analyst will be faced with many problems in linking input and output and file design. He should determine the processing and computational aspects of the system which are needed.

The systems flowcharts will show the relationship of the computer with the documents required to provide input to the computer. The computer flowchart will record the run number of the systems element, a narrative description of the run and a symbolic representation of the activity being performed. The program function chart is a support record for the program specification and should ensure that the program and sequencing of activities are coded appropriately.

The systems analyst should be aware of all the systems design facilities which he can utilise, including:

- *Multiprogramming* The computer may be capable of multiaccess, allowing numerous users to access the computer at the same time. This quite costly facility needs to be exploited by the systems analyst as fully as possible.
- *Single, double or multi-entry systems*   These will determine whether the systems analyst can apply a matching procedure for data input or must have single entry. File design will largely determine the sequence of data input and appropriate sort programmes may be needed to ensure that optimum run times are achieved.

Computer suppliers' own software should be well known and the operating system used to a maximum. Off line sorting is usually essential if maximum use of the central processor is to be achieved.

28.11   Conclusion

Computer technology is advancing at a breathtaking pace, but perhaps too much is concentrated on the equipment itself and its efficiency, and not enough on human problems and actually getting local personnel deeply involved in computing. Until the use of a computer is considered to be just as commonplace as a pen and paper, computer use will be stultified in some way. User involvement in computer systems design and equipment use is essential.

28.12   Further reading

1   *Thesaurus of Computing Terms,* NCC (1976).
2   S.J. Waters, *Systems Specifications,* NCC (1979).
3   B. Lee (Editor), *Introducing Systems Analysis and Design,* (2 volumes) NCC (1978).

4   D.H. McKeone, *Small Computers for Business and Industry,* Gower (1979).
5   Peddar Associates, *The Continuing Role of the Large Computer,* Gower (1981).
6   O.H. Bray, *Distributed Management Systems,* Lexington (1981).
7   R. Green, *Using Minicomputers and Microprocessors,* NCC (1978).
8   P.C. Sanderson, *Management Information Systems and the Computer,* Pan (1975).
9   F.F. Coury (Editor), *A Practical Guide to Minicomputer Applications,* IEEE Press (1972).
10 H. Brunner, *Introduction to Microprocessors,* Prentice Hall (1981).
11 V. Lines and Boeing Computer Services, *Minicomputer Systems,* Prentice Hall (1980).
12 R.H. Eckhouse and L. Robert Morris, *Minicomputer Systems,* Prentice Hall (1979).

Twenty-nine

Word Processors and Associated Data Transmission Equipment

29.1 Technical considerations of word processors

It is likely that before the end of the 1980s, there will be around 10 million word processors in use throughout the world. The price of word processors has fallen since their inception and is likely to fall further in real terms as their components become cheaper and simpler.

A word processor is designed to juggle words like a calculator manipulates figures. It can store words, lines of type, reports of all kinds and retrieve them in order or sequence designated by the operator. The major sub-units of a word processor are:

1 A keyboard Normally this is like the keyboard of any standard typewriter, but with the addition of various control keys that activate the machine to carry out certain duties.

2 A processor This comprises silicon chips and a microprocessing unit which houses the instructions or programs that control the machine and enable it to carry out prescribed functions. These are the equivalent to operating software in a computer.

3 Storage facilities The most common storage media for word processors and small computers is diskette or floppy disk. They are used for storing text and the operating programs. Access times for data retrieval can be up to a second, but within a word processor activity this is no hardship. They are very inexpensive (only £8 to £10 at 1982 prices). The standard floppy disk has a diameter of 178 mm and will hold up to 300,000 characters depending upon whether it is soft-sectored or hard-sectored. Soft-sectoring is a process where data format is controlled by the operating system while hard-sectoring is where text selection is partially carried out by electromechanical means. If the diskette holds the operating program, storage can be reduced to approximately 200,000 characters.

Cassettes and magnetic cards are also used for storage purposes. A cassette may hold up to 225,000 characters – about 90 pages of A4 typing.

Security can be a major headache with word processor storage facilities. Security copies of magnetic card are possible and where a word processor has two-station cassette operation, a similar process can be carried out. Many floppy disk machines are single drive and copying is not possible, though 'write protection' routines embodied in the software will prevent inadvertent changes taking place.

4   A printer or VDU or both   The printer is the means for achieving a 'hard copy' of the completed and revised typescript. The VDU can be used to help to edit the stored information. More and more word processors appear to have a VDU attached to them.

The printer can either be part of the word processor or located some distance away and linked to the word processor by a 'local area network'. The printer in these circumstances could serve more than one word processor or, indeed, another type of data processor altogether. As an alternative to a VDU, some word processors have a 'thin window', a slot in the machine where the string of words being manipulated can be seen.

Another alternative in word-processing equipment is between stand-alone machines and those which have one or more shared facilities. Sharing a printer has already been suggested. Another shared resource is a memory or data base, which can be accessed by several word processors in order to provide the texts which need to be manipulated and changed in some way. Such shared resource networks with large data processing capacity could prove more economical to many medium-sized companies than a stand-alone facility. The small stand-alone word processor will have only a minimum capacity to carry out data processing with perhaps 64 Kbytes of storage. For most active word processing, where a mixture of reports, letters, quotations, specifications, or product or job records are held, this amount of storage will be too small and a move to the next step – 120K – will be necessary.

It is clear therefore, that word processors are almost small computers and the difference in some situations is very small.

5   General equipment   Conventional machines should have most of the following facilities – check before purchasing or leasing:

- full text-editing facilities
- paragraph selection
- automatic page numbering
- information retrieval
- sorting and merging facilities
- decimal alignment
- proportional spacing
- page display
- highlighting of amendments

- user programmable
- communication facility

29.2   Use of word processors

In the 1960s and 1970s, various automatic typing machines were put onto the market. None really made the grade as a means of improving secretarial performance. Secretaries mostly do not type – activity studies have proved that approximately 90 per cent of a secretary's time is spent on work other than typing. A word processor, therefore, may not improve productivity significantly. The automatic typewriter of the 1960s proved that the use of standard letters and phrases and the editing of reports already on file is a process which has to be carefully learned.

Despite this view, the word processor has tended to replace electro-mechanical mechanisms with electronic devices. This phase seems to be coming to an end. The main advantages of using a word processor are:

a   Letter/report automation   Once a letter or report has been typed, it can be stored and standard lines or whole letters retrieved and used in new reports and correspondence.
b   Error correction   Correction of mistakes is simplified to one or more key strokes, the final version being indistinguishable from an original.
c   Text editing which can be carried out simply, by deleting or adding words or lines of print.
d   Filing   The files allow considerable data to be stored and used over and over again.

29.3   Word processors – the choice

1   The choice seems truly bewildering and there is a strong possibility of over-specifying and so adding considerably to the cost. Any consideration of choice should start by analysing work which the machine will be expected to perform:
    - number of documents/letters/reports and class and quality required
    - number of lines per document/letter/report
    - number of copies
    - errors
    - number of retypings
2   The cost of equipment should be determined and whether it will be able to perform the duties required – text editing, filing/data storage, etc. The facilities offered must match requirements. Costs may look different according to whether equipment is leased, rented, or purchased.
    Other costs need to be determined before a decision is made:

    - Salary costs including all-in costs such as pension contributions, national health, etc., maintenance of machinery, floor space occupied, paper cost.

3   Service required from the machine should be assessed – document turnround could be important.
4   What will machine utilisation be?
5   How much data needs to be transmitted to other users? Should the word processors stand alone or be linked with a local area network to other similar equipment or even a central computer?
6   Does the machine need to be compatible with other equipment either currently in use or likely to be brought in?

After completing an analysis of this type an equipment specification can be written. Some machines are better at text editing than others; some are good at data storage and retrieval. Perhaps the machine should be considered from these points of view: tasks required; back-up maintenance service; ease of operation; cost of equipment; perhaps in that order.

29.4   Training to use word processors

Training can be of several types:

a   One-to-one at the location of the word processor – this assumes that a 'training one' is available.
b   Programme learning (as computer training) which allows the operator to proceed at an individual pace.
c   Some suppliers offer free training, others charge up to £50 a day.

However, face-to-face discussion about problems is always important, which makes self-teaching slightly suspect. Five full days' training seems enough for an average operator, after which some operating fluency should be expected.

Whilst word processors are not as complicated as even a small computer, there are still complications. However, the machine itself can help. The following features will improve the machine's usage:

- good screen visibility should be ensured
- the cursor must be firm and visible at ail times, but not too big
- there should only be one execute key for all commands
- mnemonics will help to eliminate mistakes and establish the system
- displayed text should mirror print-out completely in line length, etc.
- warning should be displayed when errors are made

29.5   Local area networks (LAN) and word processing

LAN is a software development which links numerous, perhaps dissimilar, pieces of office equipment, such as word processors, computers, printers, so that sharing of information is possible. The comparison of local area networks with an electronic mailing service is apt.

The cost of intelligent work stations based on word processors is falling fairly constantly, but the related costs of printers, disk storage units, etc., remains high. LAN will permit work station users to access centralised facilities such as file stores and communication devices. LANs offer low error rates and high speed, mainly through the technique of packet switching – when a message is chopped into equal-length portions or packages.

Systems such as 'Ethernet', which has been developed by Xerox, use ordinary coaxial cable as the means of joining various work stations together. Work stations are joined physically to the cable and receive messages or information destined for them. Such networks do not need a central controller and are able to transmit 10 million bits (equal to 300 double-sided A4 sheets) per second.

Broad-band techniques making use of the kind of coaxial cable used in television relay systems can be used to run a series of Ethernet-type applications.

Another contender for local network devlopment is 'ring technology', one commercial application being 'Polynet'. The ring is based on the principle that empty data slots will constantly be circulating in a network and can be filled by transmitting stations. When the data passes a receiving station they are attracted to it and data is copied or used and the slot emptied.

The final frontier in LANs is voice and text/data transmission handled on the same network. Some systems using computerised digital PBX are being developed and could be in use within the next two to three years.

29.6   Voice transmission

Perhaps this is one of the few real problems left in introducing the paperless office. It would be valuable if a separate internal telephone system could be replaced by a combined text and voice transmission system. Digital private branch exchanges seem to provide this facility. 'Digitisation' of the voice is carried out at the handset and, by using a LAN, it may be possible to have code and format conversion thus allowing a variety of input and output devices to communicate with each other.

29.7   Electronic mailing

The technology now exists to transmit messages – say from one word processor to another. The text of a message can be set up on one machine and then sent to another, where it can either be screened immediately or held on file until called for by the receiver.

The technology of 'facsimile' is used for this purpose. This method accepts a typed page, scans it and then converts it to a digital form. The digital coded message is transmitted to a decoder held by the receiver, which converts the digital message back into a typed script.

Equipment presently available suggests that all local messages are likely to be transmitted more economically by facsimile than by any other means. However, once longer distances are involved telex and letter post become cheaper.

Telex is a form of 'electronic mailing' which has been in use for a long time, but it has no graphics, a slow printer and often poor print.

Communicating word processors have a comparatively high cost with no graphics. There are no international standards. They are, however, compatible with other office equipment. Digital facsimile will provide graphics and text transmission facilities at high speed, but it cannot take direct key input.

29.8   Further reading

1   A series on word processing in *Management Services Journal* (1980).
2   Pedder Associates, *Word Processing – current usage and future trends,* Gower (1981).
3   'Dictation and word processing', *Which Word Processor?* (September 1981).
4   H.T. Chambers, *Making the Most of Word Processing,* Business Books (1982).

Thirty

Other Office Equipment

30.1 Introduction

Computers and word processors are by no means the only important equipment required in an office. The following equipment has not been mentioned previously and is important enough to be considered as a near-essential requirement. Like computers and word processors, all office equipment is undergoing rapid technological change and consequently only the main details are given.

30.2 Copying

Plain-paper copiers, especially those based on the electrostatic principle, have practically taken over the copying business. PPCs are easy to use and produce excellent quality reproductions. The use of electronics ensures that there are fewer moving parts and so consequently the possibility of breakdowns has been erased. Paper jams, the bane of copiers, should be reduced. Most available machines are efficient, in fact, often too efficient, as they tend to be misused or abused. Preventing extraneous copies being made will always be a problem for the office manager.

Some machines are better for small-volume runs than others. Some are basically 'systems machines', with all that this implies. The choice of copier should depend upon:

- Copying requirements:
  - size of documents
  - whether reductions are required
  - speed
  - number of copies per day/week/month (there may be peak demands)
  - systems copying
- Back-up facilities, speed of repairs.
- Will the machine stand some misuse? How robust is it?

- Cost per copy, first year and subsequent years, including service and maintenance costs.
- Are supplies of toners, paper and spare parts adequate? What is their price?
- What technology is used?
- Is the machine to be liquid or dry; heat or cold-pressure fusing? Are microprocessors used? Advantages and disadvantages will emerge depending upon the technology.

There is still something to be said for the simplest and most reliable machine. Automatic input of originals, on-line sorters, monitors of the machine's condition, might only be useful and worth the cost in some instances. The replacement of moving parts by integrated circuits has helped to sophisticate machines and also reduce their cost.

30.2.1   Coated-paper copiers

In this type of copier the paper used has a photoconductive surface – a coating of zinc oxide. A toner transfers the image of the document needing copying onto the coated paper and a light source delineates the image of the original.

30.2.2   Plain-paper copies

The generic term for plain-paper copiers might be 'transfer electrostatics', not the more common 'xerography'. Many machines no longer use the photoconductive drum which is common in xerography.

30.2.3   Wet process or liquid toner transfer (LTT)

A photoconductive surface is provided inside the machine by either a belt or a drum. An indirect imaging process is used. A charge is applied to the selenium- or cadmium-coated belt or drum and the image or document to be copied is exposed by means of an optical system. The charge fired at the drum or belt is only retained where the image has been.

Toner particles charged with reverse polarity are then attracted to the image. Transfer to paper is then carried out by charging the paper so that it attracts the toner and thus the image. The image being transferred is then fixed either by heat or pressure, or both.

The toner is of considerable importance since it is the means by which the latent image becomes visible and permanent.

This type of process was first marketed in the mid-1970s and can give up to 20 copies per minute. Its advantages are that the equipment tends to be simpler than the dry process and thus less expensive. Disadvantages are the comparatively poor reproduction of dense or solid blue areas. Hydrocarbons are used in the process and these are expensive and occasionally difficult to obtain.

30.2.4 Dry processes

The basic image making is the same with both wet and dry processes, but in the dry process the toner is transferred to the photoconductive belt or drum by a magnetisable iron powder developer. The toner sticks to this by means of a tribo-electric charge. As the drum or belt revolves, paper passes between it and a transfer corona and the image is finally deposited on the copy paper by attraction of toner. The image is fixed by heat.

The dry process gives good quality results on plain paper. The process is well proven, but it needs a more complicated machine which is liable to break down more frequently. It also needs complex toner replenishment and vacuum cleaning. It is more expensive than the LTT method.

30.2.5 Developments in copying equipment

- 'Mono-compartment copiers', which mix together toner and developers, producing low-cost machine use. They tend to give a poorer quality reproduction than more complicated equipment.
- Cold-pressure image fusing – the machine is subject to less stress without heat, and should be more reliable.
- Copiers can be fitted with microchips to eliminate potential electromechanical failures. Diagnosis of internal machine problems is another application, e.g. paper jams.

30.2.6 Comment

Unfortunately, copying requirements tend to grow, and it seems appropriate to get a machine that is designed to cope with more than the current requirements. Over-utilised copiers tend to break down more often than ones in normal use. A 'good buy' is a machine that does just more than will be asked of it.

30.3 Printing

The benefits of internal printing might not only be economic – quality might be improved; urgent jobs tend to occur at most inconvenient times, and it might be faster; it will probably provide a more secure service, free from security leaks.

The possibility of in-company printing should be analysed, as follows:

1 Current printing services

- Do these seem to be uneconomic for the service given? Are quotations from many suppliers called for? Could batch sizes be increased so that a better economic situation is produced?
- What paper is bought from suppliers? Could this be reduced either in quantity or quality?

- What service is offered? Could this be improved with pressure?
- What is the average cost per order?
- What is the cost of placing one order?

2 *Equipment*   What equipment would be wanted?

- type
- cost
- depreciation
- maintenance (service contract)
- manning levels
- speed
- potential utilisation

3 *Staffing*

- What staff would be required?
- What special skills are needed?
- Can personnel with such skills be obtained or trained?
- Do proposed staffing levels cover the following?
  - peak loads
  - sickness and absenteeism
  - holidays
  - training

4 *Accommodation*

- Where can the print room be conveniently housed?
- Has the floor loading been checked?
- From a service point of view, is the accommodation suitable?
- Suitable shelving and working surfaces are needed as well as a good dust-free environment; fire risks should be taken into account.

30.3.1   *Installation of in-house printing*

In-house printing tends to be abused more than out-of-company printing and more rigorous control over orders and usage may be necessary.

A good manager who is well versed in modern printing techniques is required. His management skills might need, however, to outweigh his technical ability – but he needs both.

A straightforward printing of comparatively short runs needs a unit very different from one where very high quality printing, say with half-tone prints of photographs, is required. Forms control may have to be slotted into the overall printing requirements – the two may be firmly linked together.

Some control over quality and quantity of output and paper waste is required. Appropriate systems are needed which will plan and control output and cost the result on a continuous basis.

Most of the main printing machine suppliers provide training programmes as part of their sales service. These should be used where appropriate.

The learning curve effect will apply in printing as much as in any other activity. It will take from six months to a year for an operator to become totally proficient with platemaking, offset litho printing, etc.

30.3.2 Equipment

A choice will have to be made between small and large systems printing machines. The choice will depend upon:

- cost
- ease of use
- ease of changing over from one job to another
- length of run
- quality of printing
- speed at which completed prints are required
- whether prints or photographs are required
- convenience and cost per copy will usually be the deciding factor

The most likely requirement will be an offset duplicator. This could be a small table-top machine with a photocopier which can be used to make 'masters'. A more sophisticated machine that will print in colour or be automated to some degree will be the next step. Offset is economic where more than 25 copies are needed, otherwise plain-paper copying is preferable.

30.3.3 Phototypesetting

Anyone who requires high-quality printing such as sales catalogues or annual reports needs phototypesetting equipment.

Some suppliers have combined the function of word processing and phototypesetting on one machine using a standard keyboard, plus a screen. The recording medium is floppy disk.

30.3.4 Platemaking

Plates were the conventional means by which professional printers set up their requirements on a duplicator – normally 'offset'. They were usually metal. Today paper plates are mainly used for short-run work. These direct-image plates can be prepared by an electric typewriter.

Electrostatic equipment is normally used for platemaking in medium-sized printing departments. An electrostatic master will give up to 2,000 copies and cost 8–10p per plate.

Consistently high-quality copies can be produced by the diffusion transfer process of platemaking, where a contact frame and processing unit is used. Quality can be effected by changes in light or the strength of the developing liquid.

Where high-quality enlargements are needed a camera is essential which can cost up to £4,000 at current prices. The camera can make half-tones from continuous tone originals and reduce originals, if necessary.

30.3.5   Other equipment

To complete the print room equipment it may be necessary to supply some or all of the following, if a professional service is to be offered:

- binders
- paper cutters and trimmers
- staplers
- folding/perforators
- numberers
- collators

30.4   Dictation equipment

Dictation equipment can either be personal or centralised. Both systems have advantages and disadvantages, but both are superior in terms of cost and time to non-dictation situations.

Advantages

- Typists can be fully utilised and controlled; work measurement is possible.
- Fewer typists are needed.
- Highly paid shorthand typists are not required.
- There is increased flexibility and service for letter writers who can dictate at any time without having to wait for a shorthand typist to be available.
- Shorthand typists are not tied to the hours worked by the person dictating the letters.

Cost advantages will vary from company to company, but those which have installed centralised dictating have found that they only need upto half the number of typists as previously. Equipment costs have usually been recovered within 18-24 months.

Disadvantages

- Dictators may speak indistinctly. The typist has to refer back to the user to ascertain that she has heard correctly.
- Lack of flexibility. Where one secretary looks after one or two managers she quickly picks up their idiosyncracies, and can perform clerical or other duties if the occasion arises. Centralised dictation removes this kind of flexibility.
- Some users dictate their letters only after writing them out in longhand, which wastes time and defeats the object.
- Typists suffer from transcribing strain, with a resultant lack of accuracy.

- Typists have difficulty in setting out a letter as they do not know its length when the dictation starts.
- The lack of personal contact between typist and letter-writer is not conducive to establishing communications and good human relationships.

Most of these disadvantages can be overcome by good training in the correct use of the equipment. Suitable courses should be organised when dictation units are introduced. Two-way communications between the dictator and the typists is possible on some systems and these should be investigated when considering the communications/human relations problem.

Centralised dictation   Two main systems are in use:

- *The bank system* which provides a central console of recording units from which completed recording media are taken by the typing pool supervisor and distributed equitably among her staff. This is the cheapest form of centralised dictation but it suffers from a lack of personal contact between dictator and typists. Any typists may type the dictator's letter, no specialisation being possible.

- *The tandem system* provides twin recording units on the audio typist's desk. While one unit is being used for transcription the other is taking further dictation. Though more expensive in total, this system permits a retention of secretarial service by allowing verbal communication between the dictator and the typist. A panel under the control of the supervisor measures workload coming into the department, but the equitable spread of work is not so easy as in the bank method.

Word processing and dictation   The possibility of dictating to a word processing work station is becoming increasingly popular. This combines the advantages of both sets of equipment. The word processor should provide the operator with a facility to set out the letter or report, correct grammar if necessary and ensure a visually satisfying result.

30.5   Micrographics

Microfilming is the process of reducing original documents onto photographic film, usually one-fifth or smaller than the original. Reductions of 1/22,500 have been attempted.

The major advantage of microfilming is the filing and storage space savings which result. It is estimated that up to 90 per cent savings can be made. The second advantage lies in the security which it can confer, if a system is properly established. A well guarded retrieval system needs to be introduced when security can – nearly – be absolute.

The most widely used method of producing microfilm is not by using film itself, but microfiche, and perhaps up to 70 per cent of microfilming uses this method. Microfiche is French for file index card.

One of the most important developments in microfilming is in it use as computer output (COM). This system will produce computer print output 15 times faster than normal 'hard copy'. Not only does this enhance the capacity of the computer but gives space economies and faster retrieval.

Microfiche are single sheets of film that can contain 60 pages at a reduction of 1/24 or 208 pages at 1/42. Development is now aimed at producing 270 pages at a reduction of 1/24.

Microfiche provides users with good direct access facilities and is ideal when relatively small amounts of information are being distributed to many points. However, access and control of a very large centrally controlled file would be very difficult. Microfilm would be more suitable for this application. There are indexing problems and systems are available which allow information to be accessed on microfilm more swiftly than on microfiche.

30.6 Further reading

1   R.E. Hanson, *The Manager's Guide to Copying and Duplicating,* McGraw-Hill (1980).
2   F.C. Crix, *Reprographic Management Handbook,* Business Books (Second edition, 1979).
3   H.T. Chambers, *The Management of Small Offset Print Departments,* Business Books (Second edition, 1979).

Index